A M D O

NGHAI

YELLOW R.

E T

Nagchuka

KHAM

YANGTZE R.

KYI CHU R.

Lhasa

TSANGPO R.

Shigatse

Tsetang

Gyantse

CHUMBI VALLEY

Phari

Yatung

BHUTAN

BRAHMAPUTRA

A S S A M

Gangtok

Kalimpong

MEKONG R.

SALWEEN R.

PAKISTAN

Calcutta

B U R M A

BAY OF BENGAL

The Silent War in Tibet

OTHER BOOKS BY LOWELL THOMAS, Jr.

Out of This World
Our Flight to Adventure
(WITH TAY THOMAS—MRS. LOWELL THOMAS, JR.)

The Silent War
in Tibet

BY

LOWELL THOMAS, JR.

Garden City, New York
DOUBLEDAY & COMPANY, INC.
1959

Library of Congress Catalog Card Number 59-12648
Copyright © 1959 by Lowell Thomas, Jr.
All Rights Reserved
Printed in the United States of America
First Edition

Contents

Contents

Across these endless grass-green plains,
   Along this faint and stone-strewn path,
Amid these peaks that stab the sky,
   Astride my iron-hooféd horse,
I ride to meet my enemy.

The storms rage fierce around my head,
   The hail like bullets pelting me;
The snow-drifts roil in white-hot rage,
   Like mighty waves engulfing me—
I laugh and rush into the fight.

My parents, wife and children are
   Forgotten in the thrill of war;
My vengeance is my refuge now.
   No man can stand before my rage;
No foe deny me victory.

—Tibetan War Song

CHAPTER I

Our Day of Warning

If the valley is reached by a high pass,
Only the best friends or worst enemies are visitors.
—TIBETAN PROVERB

O N A bright September day in 1949 a caravan plodded through the Western Gate of Lhasa and came to a halt. Directly above the muleteers and their mules and yaks towered the Potala, the winter palace of the Dalai Lama, an architectural miracle rising story on story to meet its golden roof tops glistening in the sunlight. From the foot of the Potala the suburbs of Tibet's capital city, and then Lhasa proper, stretched away in a maze of streets and alleys. Homes, shops, temples, and public buildings jostled one another, typically Tibetan structures with their rectangular shapes, sharp corners, and glassless windows from which hung a riot of banners and prayer flags.

It was festival time, and noisy, colorful crowds thronged the streets. Dressed in long robes, elaborate headpieces, and ornate sandals, the lords and ladies of Lhasa bustled about their business or their pleasure, contrasting with the less richly-clad commoners and even more with the dusty muleteers in rough clothing and rugged boots. Far beyond the city, standing around it like sentinels on guard, the mighty snow-capped peaks of Tibet's mountains cut the sky line in a jagged arc.

My father gazed about for a moment and then said quietly, "There just aren't any words for it." I don't remember what I answered. I *do* remember that I was awed by the spectacle. The trappings of the Western world had fallen away. There were no automobiles on the unpaved streets, no bicycles, no pushcarts. The eye took in the scene without discovering telephone lines, fire hydrants, sewers, or the machinery so indispensable to municipal life in the West. Staring at the Potala, lifting my gaze to the mountains behind it in the distance, I felt in the middle of a strange fantasy. It would have seemed ordinary enough had Wagner's Valkyries suddenly appeared in the sky above the Potala.

Yet I knew this was no grand opera, no Ring of the Nibelungen. This was Tibet in mid-twentieth century, a nation of our time and facing some of our problems. Before my father and I began our journey to Lhasa we were aware that the mysterious Hermit Kingdom on the Roof of the World had already begun to react nervously to the tensions of international power politics.

That, in fact, was the reason why we were allowed to visit Lhasa. Tibet has been traditionally one of the hardest countries to get into, for the Tibetans grew devoutly attached to their way of life and never encouraged foreigners to bring them alien ideas or hostile ideologies. Their land was for centuries Forbidden Tibet. As Graham Sandberg wrote fifty years ago: "Those, who from the outer world have gained entrance to Tibet and made real journeys in the country, still form a select and notable body of men." That judgment remained true until about ten years ago.

With the permission of the Dalai Lama, we left Gangtok in Sikkim, at the foothills of the Himalayas, early in August. We had hired a caravan of donkeys, mules, and yaks, for nothing else could get us over the massive mountain barrier separating Tibet from Hindustan. We were convoyed by the best muleteers available, and it was their skill and knowledge of the terrain, plus their familiarity with ornery yak psychology, that saw us through. For a month we rode our Himalayan steeds, getting off to walk when the going became too steep or dangerous.

We followed the age-old trade route between India and Tibet, the high, narrow, winding track used for centuries by caravans moving north with tea and cloth, south with wool, musk, and yak tails. Our first day out from Gangtok took us into the thick bamboo forests that cluster along the lower slopes of the Himalayas. As usual it was raining (this part of Sikkim gets 250 inches a year), and the bamboo stalks were shrouded in a ghostly pall as we passed through with mule bells jangling and muleteers shouting commands. To add to our discomfort, leeches were everywhere, attacking us from the sodden clumps of grass underfoot, dropping on our heads from the boughs above. We were constantly being bitten and then hurriedly knocking the repulsive vampires off until we mounted high enough into the mountains to be out of their reach.

Up and up we went, day after day. The bamboo forests vanished behind us. We passed miles of dazzling flowers, including a particular species of yellow daisy that gave off a heady aroma and made your head throb when you were exposed to too many of them. Too far up for flowers, we found moss and then little vegetation of any kind. Our pack animals carried us deep into Himalaya passes, where sheer rock walls on one side of the route were matched on the other by a sheer drop of a thousand feet. Riding through from Sikkim to Tibet is just about the most hairraising trip in the world.

You cross the Sikkim-Tibet frontier before you realize it. We found no government officials and no customs, none of the artificial barriers that impede travel almost everywhere else. We simply rode beneath a yak-hair rope from which fluttered hundreds of prayer flags, and we were in the Land of the Lamas. Baring our heads and bowing in Tibetan fashion, we shouted loudly to frighten off the evil spirits of the place, pelted stones at them (thus adding our bit to the immense pile of rocks thrown by countless previous travelers), and continued on through the Himalayan divide and down toward the Tibetan plateau.

Soon we hit the Chumbi Valley, a deep depression in the midst of the most titanic mountain chain on earth. Here vegetation and animal life reappeared in luxuriant profusion. We saw dozens of varieties of trees, hundreds of varieties of flowers. Monkeys, rabbits, weasels, and rats scurried into the underbrush at our approach. Brilliantly colored birds screamed at us. We were in a naturalist's paradise, but unfortunately time pressed and we could not stop for a second look at the flora and fauna of the Chumbi Valley.

We were headed for the town of Yatung, our first important stop in Tibet. Yatung has always been a major link in the trade route, the place where men and pack animals could rest and freshen up. Our main purpose there was to hire a new caravan since our Sikkimese had to turn around at Yatung and go back. While we were gathering Tibetan muleteers and fresh pack animals, officials from the Dalai Lama arrived to welcome us to their country and to present us with our passports. Now we could rest easy. Lhasa was open to us, if only we could get there.

From Yatung our route lay through Phari and Gyantse, towns with little to recommend them to the tourist trade, but invaluable to strangers who could halt for the night and buy supplies. Now we were on the upgrade again. We pushed our way onto the Tibetan plateau, at more than fifteen thousand feet, to meet frigid piercing winds blowing between peaks rising another mile or two into the sky. Doggedly we struggled along the harsh terrain. We passed beneath walls of forbidding hilltop forts; past sturdy and hospitable monasteries; past Tibetan farmers plowing with yaks and wooden sticks tipped with iron, just as their ancestors had plowed from time immemorial.

The last day of our journey took us past the great Drepung Monastery, the largest in the world, housing ten thousand monks, and across the Kyi Chu River on one of the few steel bridges in Tibet. Then with a thrill of excitement, amid the clop-clopping of mules, the jangling of bells and the shouting of men, we entered the Western Gate to find our dream realized. We were in Lhasa.

"There just aren't any words for it." My father was right. But at that moment we had no chance to do more than glance around. Our first job was to get our things stowed away. The villa of our host was roomy and clean, the windows covered with cheesecloth instead of glass. Of course there was no plumbing, but our host soon produced a tin bathtub. He also brought us a supply of eggs, mutton, and barley, and we felt that we were living in comparative luxury, Lhasa-style.

Established in our villa, we set about seeing the city and talking with ministers and other Tibetans. The summer festival was on when we arrived. Thus the crowds were especially large and animated. We were invited to attend the festival, an invitation we lost no time in accepting. We tagged along to Norbulingka, summer palace of the Dalai Lama, where we mingled with the throng —a couple of Americans among a few thousand Tibetans. We saw the holy leader of Tibet surrounded by his closest advisers. We watched, enthralled, while Tibetan actors in spectacular costumes played out an old Buddhist drama. We ate yak cheese for lunch, supplementing it with a concoction of rice and raisins, coarse barley bread, and thick tea flavored with lumps of yak butter. We saw the Tibetan Army parade in British uniforms of World War I vintage to the squeal of bagpipes! When we went to bed that night we felt tired, dazzled, and thankful for the chain of circumstances that made possible such an experience.

During the next few days we spent a lot of time sight-seeing in the Holy City. One of the pleasantest aspects of Lhasa was the absence of flies, which do not survive easily at that altitude. The most fascinating part of Lhasa was the bazaar, where everything from flashlights to soap could be purchased, provided the buyer could pay the rather steep prices.

The real spectacle in Lhasa, however, is the Potala. You cannot be in the city for a moment without feeling the perpetual presence of the Dalai Lama's winter palace. You see the golden domes while you are still miles away, and when you enter the city gates you do what everybody does—you look first at the Potala, up at its white walls, its red upper stories, its multitude of windows. From then on the Potala dominates your attention as long as you stay; it is the last of Lhasa you see behind you as you leave.

It stands atop Red Hill on the outskirts of the city. What strikes you most about the spectacle is the perfect union of the Potala and its setting, for until you get close it is very difficult to tell exactly where the hill ends and the building begins. "The Potala," wrote Spencer Chapman, "gives the impression not of having been built by man but of having grown there, so perfectly does it fit in with its surroundings." The illusion is accentuated by the inward slope of the walls, which seem to be an extension of the hill tapering toward its summit. But no hilltop ever gleamed with pure gold!

The Potala is nine hundred feet high from street level at the base of its hill. That makes it two thirds the height of the Empire State Building! Its length is also about nine hundred feet and, its width is somewhat less if the massive staircases extending in front down the side of the hill are not included. Most of the walls are whitewashed, but they are colored crimson in the upper central stories where the chapels are located. The windows enhance the natural appearance of the building by being wider at the bottom than at the top.

Our host escorted us through the Potala up innumerable stairs to the roof. Many rooms, of course, were closed to us, but we saw enough to realize that there were more than a thousand of them. We passed the apartments of the Dalai Lama and through those belonging to government officials, monks, and servants. The storerooms, kitchens, treasuries, chapels were pointed out to us. We were told that in the basement were the dreaded dungeons where the worst convicts served their time. As we followed our guide we were accompanied by the sonorous sounds of Lamaist worship—the chanting of monks, the sacred music of cymbals and horns, the whir of prayer wheels. As the echoes reverberated through the gloomy corridors, I could not suppress a feeling of awe.

At the top of the Potala we found the tombs of the Dalai Lamas, decorated with jewels and gold, furnished with priceless works of art donated by the faithful over the centuries. It is the golden domes of these tombs that catch your eye outside. From the chapel roofs all of Lhasa and the surrounding district lie spread out before you. There is the titan of rivers, the Tsangpo, which flows for a thousand miles across Tibet and then turns south through the Himalayas to flow across Bengal as the Brahmaputra. In the distance stand the great monasteries of Drepung and Sera. Directly across the way, on the other side of the city, the Medical College occupies Iron Hill. We later visited the Medical College and found the students taking courses in spells and incantations, the staple of the healing art in Tibet from remote times, although the sorcerers did develop a certain rude knowledge of how to use herbs in treating the sick.

The Potala is one of the world's most illustrious monuments to religious faith. Built in the seventeenth century, it was constructed entirely of stone, every block of which had to be carted laboriously from the quarry to Red Hill. The people of Tibet did the work with the assistance of their tireless beasts of burden and sanctified their toil by offering it to the living gods of their religion, the Dalai Lamas. Their belief was as strong as ever when we were there, and we saw pious worshipers performing the traditional pilgrimage around the Potala, a hike of five miles. The Potala is Tibet's chief witness to the place of Lamaist Buddhism in the life of the nation.

Our reception by the Fourteenth Dalai Lama took place amid all the pageantry of historic tradition. Two splendidly attired nobles arrived at our villa to escort us to Norbulingka. Our party rode horses and mules, and we cantered off at a good pace for our rendezvous with the Living God of Lamaist Buddhism.

At Norbulingka we dismounted in the courtyard to the eerie wailing of Tibetan horns blown by monks on the roof. One monk struck a golden gong, and as the sound reverberated through the courtyard the morning reception began. We took our places in a long line of Tibetans waiting for a blessing from the head of their religion. The line moved rapidly through the audience chamber. We ourselves held up the proceedings as much as anyone since, although we had been carefully briefed about what to do, the reception of visitors from so far away was not something the Tibetans would hurry past.

As we moved up before the Dalai Lama, I saw a fifteen-year-old youth sitting bareheaded on a high throne, dressed in the red robe of a lama, surrounded by all the pomp and circumstance of his office. I noticed in particular the extreme intelligence of his gaze as he smiled and permitted us to advance to the foot of his throne.

Following the Tibetan custom, my father held a ceremonial white scarf in his outstretched hands. On the scarf were placed symbolic objects (such as a book representing speech) which the Dalai Lama took one by one, after which he accepted the scarf. Then my father stepped closer, bowed, and received the benediction which the Dalai Lama bestowed by touching my father's head. The Lord of Lamaism ended by presenting his visitor with a red scarf.

I followed my father through the ritual. Then we were escorted to cushions in the back from which we could watch the rest of the ceremony. The reverence of the Tibetans was almost tangible. They shuffled through the audience chamber with bowed heads and eyes on the floor, not daring to look up. Most of the people received the blessing from a tassel on the end of a rod, for the actual touch of the Dalai Lama was reserved for dignitaries and distinguished visitors.

When the last Tibetan had filed through, we were served bowls of rice, but only for ceremonial purposes. We took one taste of rice and one sip of tea, and that was all. The Dalai Lama did not touch his tea until it had been tasted as a precaution, a custom that goes far back in Tibetan history to the time when assassination attempts were not unknown. Our Lhasa guide went down on his knees before the throne, produced a wooden bowl from his robe, allowed a little of the Dalai Lama's tea to be poured into it, and downed the tea at one gulp. Then the sacred figure on the throne performed the rice-and-tea ritual.

With this over, the reception was at an end.

There are hundreds of monasteries scattered through the provinces testifying just as eloquently to the virility of the creed. The extraordinary number of monks is explained by the fact that around a quarter of the male population enters the priesthood.

Among the monasteries we visited was the largest, Drepung, perched on a mountain a few miles from Lhasa. We rode up the trail to the impressive buildings of whitewashed stone trimmed in red and topped by golden turrets. We were met by two strapping monks, the proctors, whose business it was to maintain order among the ten thousand inhabitants of Drepung. Following the proctors up stairs and ladders, we arrived at the central hall. There the head abbot welcomed us. We had tea with him and his assistant abbots. We talked with them through an interpreter about the Buddhist version of the world situation. With great courtesy the head abbot ordered his proctors to show us around the monastery, after which we rode back to Lhasa, carrying with us a clearer idea of the vitality of religion in Tibet.

But it is not the monks alone who impress the visitor with Tibetan culture. We found the laity just as striking. Their houses often looked poor and bleak to us, but every one, right down to the meanest hovel, boasted its trappings of Lamaist faith—holy emblems, prayer flags, prayer wheels. No Tibetan gets through a single day without reciting the sacred invocation to Lord Buddha: *"Om mani padme hum!"* Hail to the jewel in the lotus!

When my father and I were in Lhasa, the Dalai Lama was only fifteen, still a minor. Thus the actual government of Tibet was carried on in his name by his ministers. At the top of the political hierarchy stood the Regent, Takta, who entertained us at tea after our audience with the Dalai Lama. Takta did not say much about international politics. He left that to his subordinates and concentrated on the place of Buddhism in the world.

The political aspect of the world situation came up immediately when we were received by three members of the Kashag, Tibet's highest ministry. As our Lhasa escort introduced us to the Kashag, we quickly saw that each of these men had one thing on his mind—Chinese Communism and its meaning for their country. The head of the ministry spoke for himself and his colleagues. The conversation had hardly begun when he asked, "Has Communism come to stay in China and will it keep spreading across Asia?" My father responded with the observation that the age-old culture of China might conquer Marxism as it has conquered so many other invasions, both military and ideological.

We would like to have had more time in this wonderful land with its sturdy, industrious, intelligent, religious, friendly people. With real sorrow, therefore, we gathered our muleteers and their pack animals and prepared for the long return journey to India.

Saying good-by to our recently acquired friends, we left Lhasa for the Kyi Chu River, where we boarded primitive skin coracles for a turbulent ride down to Chosul. There we transferred to our mule caravan and started back along the trail across the Tibetan plateau and through the Himalayas.

Our trip in had been child's play compared to getting out. Five days from Lhasa near-disaster struck. As my father was about to mount, his horse suddenly spun around and then bolted. My father was thrown onto the rocks. His leg was broken in several places. This was a most unfortunate thing to have happen far up there on the roof of the world where the air is thin and the cold intense. A man less hardy might have been killed by the pain and shock. At such high altitudes pneumonia usually follows, and without proper drugs you die in a matter of hours. We quickly did what we could to ease his suffering, wrapping him in a sleeping bag and carrying him on an army cot. Miraculously there was an ancient telephone line connecting Ralung and Gyantse, and I was able to put through a frantic call to an Indian Army student doctor at Gyantse. He hurried to Ralung, diagnosed the condition as a severe sprain—he hoped—and put a splint on the patient's leg. Then there was nothing for us to do except try to get my father off the plateau and over the Himalayas before the Tibetan winter descended on us.

For three unforgettable days we pushed on toward Gyantse with my father on a stretcher. As if the agony were not enough, fever and fainting spells began to afflict him. At Gyantse we fixed up a sedan chair and hired Tibetans to carry him in it for the rest of the way. He gritted his teeth; we kept grinding forward over the Tibetan plateau and made our way to Yatung, where we had the overwhelming joy of meeting a rescue party.

Over the final Himalayan pass and down to the plains of India where my father and I boarded a plane for America. Landing in New York, the patient was rushed to a hospital. There an eminent surgeon found, instead of a sprain, that his hip was broken in eight places, and they had to operate, and from October to June he was on crutches.

When we returned to New York I felt compelled to publish a record of what the Tibetans had said to us of their hopes and fears, above all with reference to the already-menacing gestures of Red China. That was how my book *Out of This World* came to be written. My father and I never considered our journey to Lhasa as simply an adventure story involving two Americans, even though it was the most exciting thing that ever happened to either of us. Our Tibetan hosts implored us to tell their story to the world. This my father did through his daily taped broadcasts from Tibet. For my part I hope I did not disappoint them with *Out of This World.*

The present book is a sequel, a tragic sequel that I wish I had never had to write. Isolated, with no one to turn to, Tibet fell to the invading armies of Mao Tse-tung, and the fears expressed to us in Lhasa became harsh realities. What has happened since then on the roof of the world is the subject of this book. It is not an adventure story. It is not a pleasant story. But it is a true story. And we of the free world ought to know more about it.

As we rode out of Lhasa on the first leg of our trip home, we knew that the people who had greeted us so hospitably were facing disaster. And disaster did come to Tibet. The first blow fell a year later. Chinese soldiers crossed the border and attacked Tibetan outposts. The campaign—so the propaganda apparatus of Mao Tse-tung said—was to save poor little Tibet from the Western imperialists. The Tibetans resisted. They had no outside help from "imperialists" or from anyone else. They were forced to submit and to sign a humiliating treaty. The Chinese occupied Lhasa. Once conquered, a curtain of silence descended around Tibet. Our only news from the roof of the world came through the raucous Chinese propaganda channels.

Soon, however, rifts appeared in the curtain. Tibetan traders brought news to the Indian terminal of the main Indo-Tibetan trade route. Tibetan refugees, traveling with the caravans, settled in India but kept in touch with relatives and friends at home. Lamaist monasteries in India maintained contact with monasteries in Tibet. Even Chinese propaganda revealed some truth of what was happening in the now truly Forbidden Land. A picture of occupied Tibet began to take form; it emerged complete with the escape of the Dalai Lama in early 1959.

We know that Tibetans fought back against the Communist invasion. We know that Tibetans resisted the occupation from the start and that they continue to resist even now. The struggle has developed into a bitter war. Large-sized units are engaged in almost constant conflict. Entire armies can be lost in the vast and rugged terrain. Battles are waged at heights that make the breath come in tortured gasps. Modern planes and the latest automatic weapons are used, but so are chain mail and broadswords. The action has characteristics of the Crusades, of Napoleon's retreat from Moscow, and of the most up-to-date military operations.

It is a strange war. Victory or defeat have little meaning in it. Territory is occupied and retaken, but the consequences have little strategic value. Time also seems to have small importance, and presumably the fighting will continue indefinitely. Resistance to oppression is the root of the conflict, but some of the specific issues are almost beyond the comprehension of Westerners.

Finally, it is a silent war, silent in the sense that so little was heard of it outside the remote land in which it is fought. It is the one current example of a violent conflict in no way connected with the "cold war" and the East-West ideological duel. The fighting began in the fall of 1950.

The war is unique, but not the first in Tibet's history. For the last thousand years Tibet has been menaced by the Chinese whenever they felt strong enough to push their authority beyond their borders. When China was disunited and weak, the Tibetans reasserted their independence. Since the disintegration of the

Manchu Dynasty, China's internal strife, British paramountcy throughout the East, and two world wars enabled Tibetans to live free from outside interference.

Liberty to Tibetans is less of a political and more of a cultural concept. Most of all, the Tibetans want to be left alone to practice their own religion. They want the freedom to reject the gadgets—and the frenzy—of modern civilization. They wish to preserve the traditional forms and values of Lamaist Buddhism. Tibetans are self-sufficient in their sparsely settled kingdom, and they ask to be left undisturbed so that they can live as they have lived for centuries amid the harsh natural beauties of their high plateau. Until recently their country was considered the back end of nowhere. Only scholars, explorers, and a few traders knew about it. Now, however, Tibet has acquired the malignant disease of strategic importance.

The key to the strategy is, of course, India. The northern reaches of the Himalayan range are almost impenetrable, but the southern slopes are broken by mountain passes leading to India. Thus the Indians' security requires that they have at least dominating influence over the central region of the Himalayas. Tibet occupies the most vital part of the region. When the British were strong in the Orient and China was weak, British influence prevented other powers from securing a foothold in Tibet.

Today British power in the area is gone. India is militarily weak and preoccupied with internal problems. China has become the dominant military power in Asia. The Chinese intend to subjugate all of Asia, a fact that is only too evident from their armed interference in Korea, Indo-China, and Burma, and from the subversive intervention throughout the area. India and the rest of the subcontinent, however, are the richest prizes in Asia.

The first step of the Chinese toward Asia's richest prizes was to advance China's borders to the Indo-Tibetan frontier. From airfields in Tibet, Chinese bombers would be hardly more than one hour from Delhi. Next Tibet had to be made into a powerful military base from which subversive and ultimately, if necessary, armed action against the subcontinent could be directed. Naturally the military base had to be made secure.

Security of the Tibetan military base required complete subjugation of the local inhabitants. The three million Tibetans could be crushed by force, subverted, and finally, inundated by millions of Chinese settlers. Communist materialism would replace the gentle Buddhist way of life, and the surviving Tibetans would become impoverished, a helpless minority in their own land. In short, the Chinese Communists, in order to operate against India and the rest of the subcontinent, meant to destroy Tibet as a nation, a culture, and a people.

The Chinese followed the customary pattern of Communist domination. They combined blandishment with repression. While outwardly purporting to respect Tibetan religion and institutions, they secretly worked to undermine both. Chinese colonists were brought in and given some of the best land. Leading Tibetans were sent to Peking for indoctrination. Military roads, airfields, and even whole towns were constructed with slave labor. Any opposition to the regime was suppressed, and all Tibetans were subjected to an intense propaganda campaign.

Nevertheless Tibetan resistance grew. Even the Chinese finally had to admit that their hold on the mountain kingdom was not as secure as they had expected. If nothing else, the nature of the resistance proved that the Tibetans hated their conquerors. Despite some collaborators, the overwhelming majority of Tibetans wanted to be rid of the Chinese. The main hope of the Tibetans was that the rest of the world would learn of what they were facing. If the truth were known, they believed moral pressure against Communist China would be so strong that the invaders would be forced to leave. The voice of a few thousand refugees was not loud enough to catch the ear of a world already preoccupied with serious problems. Ultimately, therefore, the Tibetan resistance movement put its hope in the Dalai Lama. If he could communicate with the outside world his authority would command a hearing and his word would be believed. Under these circumstances he might bring about the miracle for which the Tibetans prayed.

The Chinese, however, understood perfectly the danger of the Dalai Lama to their regime. They had no intention of letting him out of their control.

CHAPTER II

Between Two Worlds—a Holy Child

Mirrored in Takpo's magic lake,
I saw myself as I was and shall be;
Both pictures were the same.

—TIBETAN PROVERB

THE young Dalai Lama is regarded by the Tibetans as the fourteenth of the most recent reincarnations of a god named Chenrezi (Avalokitesvara in the Hindu pantheon). This god is a Christ-like figure known as the Lord of Mercy. He is only one of innumerable gods recognized by the Lamaist religion. Today, however, he is the favorite of most Tibetans. Worship of him in his human reincarnation began early in the seventeenth century.

Before that time, of course, Chenrezi was being reincarnated every generation. He existed somewhere in the world since the dawn of history. The people, however, did not know how to recognize him. Nevertheless, characters in Tibetan legends sometimes could be identified as Chenrezi reincarnations by the attributes of power, generosity, and mercy.

The legend that anticipates Darwin's theory and explains the origin of the Tibetan people, for example, mentions a god who probably was Chenrezi. According to the story, a monkey from India once managed to cross the Himalayas and reach the high Tibetan plateau. The monkey fell under the spell of an ogress who kept him in her mountain cave. The unhandsome couple produced simian offspring in large numbers. Soon the population outgrew its food supply. At this point the so-called Compassionate Spirit of the Mountains—probably Chenrezi—took pity on the monkeys and gave them a magic grain. The grain was barley, which is still the Tibetans' staple. The barley was magic because it changed the monkeys into men.

These new humans, however, were as wild and unruly as their forebears. The early history of Tibet, therefore, is unrecorded. As late as the fifth and sixth centuries Chinese chronicles described Tibetans as scattered tribes of ferocious barbarian herdsmen who fought constantly among themselves and were a menace to travelers.

Eventually, however, the tribes were united. This happened in the seventh century A.D. and marks the beginning of Tibetan history. A chieftain named Song-tsen Gam-po from the western district of Ladakh was stronger, more wily and ruthless than the others. He succeeded in forcing obedience from the other chieftains and in welding the tribes into a powerful force.

Song-tsen Gam-po's Tibet immediately became a political force in the Orient. The new ruler soon dominated Nepal, a neighboring mountain kingdom, and he married a Nepalese princess.

This victory made him feel strong enough to challenge the great Chinese empire. Song-tsen Gam-po demanded a Chinese princess as his second wife. He was haughtily refused. The new Tibetan king immediately led his armies eastward. He defeated the Chinese forces and enforced humiliating peace terms on their emperor. The terms included the Chinese princess.

It happened that both the Chinese and Nepalese princesses were devout Buddhists. Between them they converted their warrior husband. With the same zeal he had given to war he now spread the gentle teachings of Lord Buddha among the Tibetans. He brought Buddhist priests from India. The priests devised a written script, based on Sanskrit, so that the scriptures could be translated into the Tibetan language. The priests also helped to convert the tribesmen.

Previously the tribesmen had practiced a shamanistic religion called Bon. It was remarkably similar to the religion of the Alaskan Eskimos and was noted for its demonology and black magic. Buddhism, however, was highly intellectual; in its original form it dispensed with gods and even with an ordained priesthood and taught only a way of life. Such concepts were too difficult for the tribesmen to accept wholly. They began to mix Bon ritual with Buddhist philosophy.

This new religion preserved Tibetan unity. With the death of Song-tsen Gam-po the strong leadership that had held the tribes together was gone. The chieftains might have returned to fighting among themselves until Tibet became once more a land of barbarians. The religion, however, taught peace and harmony. The tribesmen managed to restrain their antisocial impulses.

In the eighth century, a hundred years after the first king's death, the unifying force of religion received further impetus. Padma Sambhava, an Indian missionary, arrived in Tibet. He was a Buddhist, but his teachings were tinged with the Tantric beliefs of North Indian Hinduism. The Tantric Vedas (holy books) taught demonology and ritual which were far more sophisticated and elaborate than Bon practice. The Tibetans accepted the new teachings avidly. Monasteries and temples sprang up throughout the land. The number of priest-monks, or lamas, increased rapidly. Thus the religion that we in the West identify as Lamaism evolved.

Lamaism reached the pinnacle of its success in the thirteenth century when Kublai Khan the Mongol was ruling China. He was the grandson of Genghis Khan, who had conquered most of Asia. The fierce Mongols whom Kublai Khan now led practiced no formal religion. He needed peace to consolidate the empire and to establish his Yuan Dynasty in Peking. He felt that a religion, particularly a pacific one, would quiet his rebellious Mongols and unify his empire. Thus he called in leading representatives of several faiths and listened to their debates. Kublai Khan chose Tibetan Lamaism.

The religion was represented by the Grand Lama of the Sakya Monastery. He was given a jade seal that made him and his successors the consecrators of the emperors of China. This was the beginning of the spiritual-temporal relationship between the two countries.

The relationship is an important point in Tibetan history. It explains the attitude of the Tibetans toward the Chinese. The agreement between Kublai Khan and the Sakya Monastery Grand Lama was freely made. Neither party was in the position of the conquered or conqueror. Thereafter Tibetans considered that their lamas were the spiritual mentors of the Chinese. In return for this function the powerful Chinese nation was to guarantee Tibet's protection. But the Tibetans never considered themselves an integral part of China. If, through weakness, the Chinese could not give the traditional protection, the Tibetans felt free to seek aid and alliances elsewhere.

Ultimately, however, the Chinese thought of Tibet as part of their empire, a vassal state generously permitted limited self-government. This attitude was offensive to the Tibetans, but until 1950 the Chinese were unable to enforce complete subjugation. The Chinese Communists claim a legal right to Tibet and they occupy the entire country. The Tibetans feel that they have been invaded by a foreign power and that the original agreement with Kublai Khan has been violated.

Kublai Khan's agreement also recognized the Sakya Monastery Grand Lama as the ruler of Tibet. This merely formalized a trend that already had become established. The lamas had been slowly usurping political power from the noble chieftains, and now they governed the country. Because power corrupts, the lamas—and thus Lamaism—became corrupted. The deep philosophical roots of Buddhism rotted in the excess of the clergy's temporal power and privilege. A revivalist movement spread and inspired a large following but remained without political power for almost three hundred years, until the eleventh century.

At that time a dynamic reformer emerged from the eastern province of Amdo. His name was Tsong Ka-pa. He led the revivalists to form a new sect. He imposed strict rules of conduct. His followers led an ascetic and devout life. They were celibate. They called their sect Gelupa, or "Virtuous way," but they became popularly identified as the "Yellow Hats" in contrast to the red hats customarily worn by the unreformed sect.

The reformed sect grew quickly, and Tsong Ka-pa founded the

Ganden Lhunpo (monastery) which is still one of Lhasa's "big three." His successor founded the famous Tashi Lhunpo at Shigatse. Tsong Ka-pa's fourth successor, as head of the Yellow Hats, managed to reconvert the Mongols to Lamaism. As a reward for this accomplishment the Mongol ruler Altan Khan gave the Yellow Hat leader the title of Dalai Lama Vajradhara. "Dalai" is a Mongol word meaning "vast as the ocean." The title also was given posthumously to the two previous Yellow Hat leaders; thus the living recipient of the honor became the Third Dalai Lama.

With this honor and recognition the reformed sect gained great prestige. Although the Yellow Hats generally retained their "virtuous way," they acquired wealth and power. Inevitably they came into conflict with the Red Hats. Actual fighting broke out between the two sects. Early in the seventeenth century, during the leadership of the Fifth Dalai Lama, the Mongol prince Gushi Khan entered Tibet. He sided with the Yellow Hats, and the power of the Red Hats was crushed forever. The Fifth Dalai Lama was made the country's sovereign. A son of Gushi Khan held the title "King of Tibet," but he was recognized as being subordinate to the Dalai.

This Fifth Dalai Lama was one of the greatest figures in Tibetan history. He was a man of strong personality and great energy. He planned and set his subjects to work on the Potala, the enormous palace and the Dalai Lama's official residence, which was built on the same hill site as the fort-residence of Tibet's first king. The Fifth also assigned learned monks to the task of setting down a detailed record of the rites and practices of Lamaism. The records compiled by the monks prescribe Tibetan law and custom to this day.

Early in his reign the Fifth conferred the title of "Panchen Rimpoche" (Great Gem of Learning) on his old teacher and gave him a position of spiritual leadership in Western Tibet, with a seat at Tashi Lhunpo near Shigatse. The monks at Tashi Lhunpo had also begun to recognize their grand lamas as reincarnations. The Fifth awarded the same title to his teacher's three predecessors at Tashi, thus making the Panchen the fourth of his line.

After ruling for thirty-five years the Fifth Dalai retired into hermitage, naming a young regent to rule in his stead. The man was a capricious ruler, and when the Dalai Lama died the Regent kept the fact a secret for many years. Thus the Sixth reincarnation, when he was found, was a youth rather than a child. The youth had grown accustomed to worldly pleasures and could not adjust entirely to the proscribed life of a God-King. He spent part of his time in Lhasa's fleshpots. Tibetans ultimately grew tolerant of their Sixth Dalai; they learned to appreciate the songs he wrote and to regard his weakness for wine and women as a test of their faith. Nevertheless the Regent was murdered and the Sixth died in exile. In the resulting confusion rival factions in Tibet supported two potential Dalai Lamas. The country, therefore, was divided and weakened.

Unfortunately this was no time for Tibet to face a test of strength. The Manchu Dynasty in China was expanding its power. The Chinese were in conflict with the Mongols to the north, and they wanted to control Tibet. When Mongols invaded Tibet from Turkestan, the Manchu Emperor sent in his armies. Ultimately the Chinese Emperor, K'ang-hsi, defeated the Mongols. He followed up the victory by establishing two Chinese mandarins at Lhasa. The mandarins had the title of "Amban" and were given wide political power. The Ambans made the choice of which candidate would be the Dalai Lama. They chose the one that was the most popular with the people, but they allowed him ecclesiastical power only. Temporal authority was put into the hands of an old prime minister who really took orders from the Ambans. The Dalai Lama, when he reached his majority, had the prime minister killed and he tried to take over the government. The Chinese sent in troops to back up the authority of the Ambans. This incensed the Tibetans and caused a popular uprising. A whole Chinese army now arrived and crushed Tibetan resistance. Nevertheless, despite garrisons scattered throughout Tibet, the Chinese recognized that they could not hold the country entirely by force. They therefore accepted that the country was autonomous and that the Dalai Lama was the legal ruler.

The Ambans, however, managed to control the country secretly. When the Dalai Lamas were children and the country was under a Tibetan regent, the Ambans intrigued to ensure that the regents would be controlled by them. The Dalai Lamas, then, were simply poisoned before reaching majority. None of the subsequent Dalai Lamas lived beyond eighteen years of age until the Thirteenth Incarnation, who was enthroned in 1880.

The Thirteenth was another remarkable person. Just before reaching his majority, he allied himself with a group of young nobles who had formed a nationalist party. With their help a successful coup removed the Ambans from a position of power. Moreover, the Thirteenth was able to keep the coup a secret from Peking until he had formally attained his majority and had firmly taken over the government. He began to use his power shrewdly and vigorously.

The Chinese in Peking were unable to take counteraction. China was torn by internal disorders. In 1895 the Chinese suffered military defeat from Japan. In 1900 the Western powers defeated China in the Boxer Rebellion and the Manchu Dynasty was tottering. Nevertheless the Chinese still might have taken action against Tibet except for the fact that the British now were the undisputed power in the Orient. The Tibetans had already felt this power and were uneasy about it.

In 1890 the British had made into a protectorate the state of Sikkim, which is in the Himalayas between Tibet and India. They had secured a treaty with China whereby China recognized Britain's authority in the hill state and also accepted the British-demarcated border between Sikkim and Tibet. The Tibetans had not been consulted on this matter; they were offended and refused to recognize the treaty. They spurned subsequent British overtures to establish trade relations.

Having defied the Chinese and spurned the British, the Thirteenth Dalai Lama tended to lean toward the Russians for protection in a world of voracious aggressors. Another reason for this tendency was a Mongolian lama named Dorjieff. He was a Russian by birth and education, but at the age of thirty-five he had retired to a Lhasa monastery where subsequently he became one of the Dalai Lama's teachers. He convinced the Thirteenth that Russia under the Tsar was sympathetic to Buddhism and would make a good ally for Tibet.

The British were inclined to see Russia in a different light. In 1904 they sent another trade commission to Lhasa, this one accompanied by a strong contingent of Indian troops under Colonel Younghusband. The troops inflicted heavy casualties on the brave but badly armed Tibetan Army. As the Younghusband Expedition reached Lhasa, the Dalai Lama fled to Mongolia with Dorjieff. A treaty was negotiated and signed by a trusted representative of the Dalai Lama. The treaty provided for Tibet's recognition of the Sikkim Convention, permitted Britain to establish three trade marts through which India-Tibet commerce could pass, and assured Britain of a "most favored nation" status in Tibet's foreign relations.

The Tibetans were familiar with the practice of the Chinese who often used a thin wedge with which to attempt complete control of the country. Thus they regarded the Lhasa Treaty as such a wedge and assumed that the British would impose themselves increasingly into their affairs. To their surprise, however, when the trade marts were well established, the British forces withdrew.

The withdrawal was not wholly a matter of virtuous restraint on the part of the British. They wanted the profit from what little trade Tibet offered. Mostly, however, the British wanted to establish Tibet as a buffer state. If they occupied Tibet, as they did India, they would be in direct conflict with both China and Russia. With Tibet's trade and with the "most favored nation" status the British could have the advantages of outright annexation without the heavy costs of defending the country. Thus their next move was to negotiate with China and Russia. They conceded that China had "suzerainty" over Tibet and thereby won China's acceptance of the terms they had imposed at Lhasa. This was in 1906, and the agreement was called the Anglo-Chinese Convention. A year later the Anglo-Russian Convention won Russia's

recognition of Britain's "special interest in the maintenance of
the status quo in the external relations of Tibet."

Thus, geopolitically at least, the British had made Tibet into a
buffer state. To the Tibetans, however, their status was much as
it had been before. The Chinese were still trying to dominate
them. When the God-King fled from the Younghusband Expedition, the Chinese had put up proclamations saying that the Dalai
Lama was deposed. The populace had paid no attention to the
posters beyond defacing them with dung. The Tibetan officials
still acted in behalf of the Dalai Lama and referred to him whenever possible. But now the Chinese had another thin wedge
in the vague word "suzerainty" which the Anglo-Chinese Convention had used. They persuaded the Dalai Lama to leave his
exile in Mongolia and to come to Peking. He was humiliated
and was given a title that was meant to demote him slightly. In
short, the Chinese tried to establish precedent to indicate that
their control over Tibet was complete. The Dalai Lama, on the
other hand, made equal efforts to show that his country was
completely autonomous. For example, he sent his emissaries to
call on a number of foreign legations in Peking. When a British
representative returned such a call, the Dalai Lama admitted
having been misinformed about the British intentions in 1903 and
added that he now wished for peace and friendship between
Tibet and Britain.

This admission was more than polite diplomacy. As always, the
Tibetans viewed their relations with China as a spiritual-temporal
arrangement in which subordination of one party to the other
had no place. The fact that for three hundred years the Chinese
had been trying to go beyond the spirit of the arrangement did
not alter the Tibetan viewpoint. China's contribution to the relationship was military protection. The Chinese had failed to uphold
their side of the bargain when they did not prevent the British
Younghusband Expedition from forcing its way into Lhasa. By
this failure the Chinese lost all right to interfere in Tibetan affairs,
and the Dalai Lama would no longer permit China to speak for
his country.

Nevertheless, while he was in Peking the Dalai Lama upheld his part of the China-Tibet bargain. It happened that both the Manchu Dowager Empress and the young Emperor died. The Dalai Lama, fulfilling his traditional role, conducted a service for the deceased. He observed a period of mourning and gave advice to the new Emperor.

The Chinese, however, still refused to accept Tibet's independence. While the Dalai Lama was returning from Peking to Lhasa, a new Chinese administrator for Tibet was appointed and was sent with a large army. The administrator was Chao Erh-feng, commonly known as "Butcher Chao." After years of exile the God-King had been in the Potala for only a few weeks when two thousand of Chao's mounted troops burst into Lhasa. They shot down people in the streets and made for the palace with the intention of capturing the Dalai Lama. The Thirteenth, with some of his ministers, managed to escape with minutes to spare. Despite the pursuing Chinese cavalry and terrifying February blizzards, the Dalai Lama and his party reached India, where the British gave them sanctuary at Kalimpong.

The Chinese now meant to enforce their authority over Tibet once and for all. A proclamation was issued, again deposing the Thirteenth, and the Panchen Lama was asked to become the nominal head of government. The people disdained the proclamation and the Panchen Lama refused the offer. The Chinese began an era of suppression and brutality that was the worst in the Tibetans' long history of suffering.

In Kalimpong the Thirteenth kept in touch with his people. He directed the resistance movement and worked to keep up the morale. He also tried to obtain help from the British. He saw that the Indians, while not politically independent, were free to live their own lives and to follow their own religions. According to Sir Charles Bell, the British representative who maintained close contact with the Thirteenth during these months of the second exile, the Dalai Lama would have welcomed for Tibet a British protectorate such as existed in Sikkim.

Despite genuine sympathy for the Tibetans, however, the

British could not interfere without a full-scale war with China. Even if the British did succeed in driving out the Chinese, the cost of protecting Tibet from further attack would have been prohibitive. Thus the Tibetans had to rely on their own meager resources. They had faith that their God—the Lord of Mercy— would deliver them.

Their faith was justified. In 1911 revolution inflamed China. The Manchu ruler was overthrown and a democratic republican government was established. The unrest spread to the Chinese garrisons in Tibet. The troops mutinied, killed their officers, and spread out to loot among the Tibetan people. The Tibetans seized the opportunity to turn on the occupation force. Army and civilian alike, they took up arms; in a matter of weeks all the Chinese in Tibet were either slaughtered or expelled.

The Thirteenth directed the mopping-up operations from India. He then returned to Lhasa to be welcomed by his wildly jubilant people. Tibet, without help, had won her own freedom.

But even the Chinese Republic did not want to relinquish the mountain kingdom. The Chinese tried a conciliatory approach. The President telegraphed apologies for the excesses of the Chinese troops and said that the Dalai Lama's title would revert to the original wording. The Thirteenth replied that he wanted no title or rank from the Chinese. The spiritual-temporal tie was severed. From now on Tibet would be ruled solely by her Dalai Lama. The Chinese prepared for yet another military expedition to Lhasa.

The British, however, brought pressure against China to prevent the attack. They urged negotiation, and in 1913 representatives from Tibet, China, and Britain met in Simla. The Tibetans wanted nothing less than complete independence. The Chinese wanted the suzerainty that had been mentioned in the Anglo-Chinese Convention of 1906. The British wanted any compromise that would ensure Tibet's position as a buffer state.

The British compromise suggestions at the negotiations resulted in the Inner and Outer zones which many maps show. The Inner Zone, contiguous to Chinese territory, would be under Chinese administration. The Outer Zone would fulfill Britain's need for a buffer state along India's northern borders and would give the Tibetans complete autonomy in a large area which contained Lhasa, most of the country's main centers, and most of the important monasteries. After prolonged negotiations the treaty was initialed by the three representatives. China, however, refused to ratify it. Tibet and Britain then agreed formally to the treaty, and the British began to press for a settlement from China. Unfortunately World War I intervened and pushed the problem into the background. Thus the Chinese never signed the treaty.

Today the Chinese use this fact as the basis of their claim to Tibet; they recognize only the 1906 Convention, which acknowledged their suzerainty over the country.

The British, however, consistently viewed Tibet on the basis of the Simla treaty, thereby giving equal legality to Tibet's autonomy. The Indians, after independence, needed Tibet as a buffer state even more than had the British; thus the government of India consistently regarded Tibet as autonomous. And the Tibetans, of course, never wavered in their insistence upon complete independence from the Chinese.

At the time, however, Tibet's external problems were largely academic; the great powers were too concerned with other grave problems to interfere in the mountain kingdom. Besides World War I there were the Russian Revolution, political unrest in India, more revolution in China, and another attack on China from Japan. The Dalai Lama negotiated a treaty with the Hutukhtu (lama incarnation) of Urga in Outer Mongolia; the two signatories recognized the independence of Tibet and Mongolia and allied themselves in the defense and advancement of Buddhism. Also, no Chinese representative was allowed to set foot in Tibet. Otherwise the Dalai Lama was concerned mainly with internal problems.

He had many internal problems, some of them serious. Because of his two enforced exiles his orthodox subjects considered that he had been defiled. Thus he had to spend many hours daily in prayer and meditation. At the same time he had a staggering load of temporal administrative duties. He had to raise an army. The government needed reorganizing after the years of disruption. Settlement was needed in a conflict with the followers of the Panchen Lama, who was sent into exile in 1924 and remained in China until his death in 1937. The Dalai Lama ruled sternly but wisely until his fifty-seventh year.

In December 1933 the Thirteenth Incarnation passed on. The people were lost. They came in vast numbers to prostrate themselves before the embalmed body and to plead for a quick return in a new incarnation. The normal mourning period was reduced in order that the new Body might be found sooner. In the Dalai Lama's chambers in the Jewel Park Palace his teacup was left out on a low table with a bowl of fresh fruit beside it; this was meant to encourage the new Incarnation.

CHAPTER III

The Search for the Living God

The deeper a gem is buried
The brighter it shines in the light.
—TIBETAN PROVERB

EVERYWHERE in Tibet, in the monasteries and in the altar rooms of huts and tents, at pilgrim shrines and by caravan campfires, fresh prayer flags flew and the people chanted their universal wish. Pilgrimages were made constantly to a holy lake in whose waters meaningful reflections often had been seen. Let the God return!

One clue to the new identity had been seen early. As the body of the Thirteenth had been laid out it had turned miraculously to the east. But the months passed and no new signs were found.

Almost two years went by. One day the Regent was at the holy lake in the Takpo district southeast of Lhasa. In the still water he suddenly saw, as clearly as in a mirror, the reflection of a monastery with a gilded roof and near it on a hill a small house with eaves of an unusual type. He also saw certain letters in the lake. One of these was an "A" which was taken to indicate the district of Amdo to the northeast, the general direction in which the Thirteenth's body had turned.

Search parties immediately set out. More months of fruitless search followed. One of the parties was led by the High Lama Kyetsang Rimpoche. He went far into the northeast Amdo region of Tsinghai, which was a part of Tibet under Chinese administration. Here Tibetan farmers and Muslim nomads lived side by side with Chinese agriculturists in an uneasy interdependence. Finally, south of Sining, the high lama came across a monastery that answered the description of the one pictured in the lake. Near it was a twisting path that led to a small hillock and a house with unusual eaves.

The lama did not go immediately to the house. After making sure that it was the one described from the picture in the lake, he went to the nearby monastery where he disguised himself as a poor beggar-monk. Now he approached the hut and knocked on the door. A woman answered. To the lama's relief she was Tibetan and not Chinese. The woman invited him in to rest himself while she prepared some food. As he was waiting he suddenly heard the happy laugh of a small child. Then a boy of about two years entered. He showed no fear of the stranger in the house. He greeted the monk, but instead of using the dialect of the district he spoke the Lhasan equivalent of "honored sir." The monk leaned down and looked at the boy carefully. "Do you know me?" he asked, also in Lhasan.

The child's smile faded and momentarily tears came to his eyes. "Yes," he said. Then he laughed again and buried his face in the monk's robes. When his mother brought the food the child played nearby while the monk ate. He seemed happy to be in the presence of the kindly old man. When the monk said good-by and prepared to leave, the little boy tried to run after him and had to be held in his mother's arms.

A few days later the monk returned to the hut. Now he was dressed in the robes of a high lama, and he was accompanied by monk officials. The mother stepped back, speechless with awe. The high lama, however, was still a kindly old man, and he asked gently to see the child. The monks took the boy alone to the humble altar room of the hut. Here they placed before the boy objects which had belonged to the Thirteenth Incarnation, along with objects which had not been his possessions. Then the monks watched gravely to see what the child would do. The little boy immediately picked up the simple rosary that had been the Thirteenth's favorite. A murmur of surprise and excitement went through the group of holy men. The child next chose a walking stick that the previous Body had favored. Finally he picked up a rather worn drum that the Thirteenth had used to call his servants. The child paid no attention to the articles that had not belonged to the last Incarnation. Now the monks could no longer hide their eagerness, but they still did not dare to hope. The high lama took the child to him and gently removed his little robe. The body of the true Incarnation bore certain distinguishing marks; under the shoulder blades, for example, were two peculiar growths suggesting the additional pair of arms that Chenrezi was supposed to have, and the ears were large with elongated lobes. The child did have all the distinguishing marks. The monks were jubilant. The Fourteenth Dalai Lama had been found.

Friends who have known members of the Dalai's family well told me the story of his discovery. The family were simple peasants living in poverty. A typical Tibetan peasant in Tsinghai was content to farm his land and, after paying part of his crops to the government for taxes and another part to the local monastery as a religious donation, have enough grain left over to feed his family through the winter. The center of his life was the local monastery, from which he drew the security of familiar authority. Even though the Chinese civil authority changed frequently, and sometimes violently, the monastery community remained constant. Moreover, he felt related to it directly because he usually gave at least one of his sons to it.

The father of the Fourteenth had already given his first son to a monastery. He was typical of the other hard-working, impoverished Tibetan farmers except that he was slightly more ambitious. He wanted to get sufficiently ahead so that he could become a horse trader, the one profession in the area that might offer comparative prosperity. Thus he worked even harder than his neighbors.

He was getting along, but he was not getting ahead. No matter how hard he worked, he never seemed to have more than just enough grain to keep him and his family through the winter. He had five children to feed and another child was on the way. And then misfortune struck. A severe illness completely incapacitated him. He was confined to his pallet and he felt himself getting weaker every day. He told his wife to send another son to the local monastery, and he prepared for the end.

Lying at the point of death, he heard the first cry of his newborn son. A strange peace came over him, and he felt a strong pull of attachment to the child. He rallied his strength and called to his wife. "How did the birth go?" he asked her when she came to him.

"It was painless," she said, smiling. "We have a son. I will bring him to you."

The baby, Lhamo Tondrup, was laid on the pallet by his father's side. Almost immediately the man began to improve. Within a few days he was strong enough to get up. After a week he was able to work again. He left the two sons in the monasteries and lived with his wife and remaining four children.

They noticed almost immediately that the baby was remarkable. He was healthy and grew quickly. He was never fretful or troublesome. He was a happy child, and from the beginning he seemed to be unusually considerate.

Thus when the high lama came, examined the child, and told the parents that their Lhamo was probably the new Incarnation, they were not altogether surprised. At the same time they were incredulous at their own good fortune. At first the great honor had little outward effect on the family. The high lama began the long journey back to Lhasa to report on his findings. He left one of his party at the local monastery to keep an eye on the child, but the family's hard struggle for existence continued as before.

An attempt at secrecy was made, but the whole area was soon alive with rumors. The visit of such a distinguished delegation from Lhasa was an unusual event in itself and caused a great stir of gossip. The fact that one of the Lhasan monks had remained and was watching the family of Lhamo gave people a good idea of what was happening. The father found that his prestige in the community was much higher. Neighbors began dropping in to pay their respects to the child. Before long Tsinghai Tibetans from some distance began coming to the little hut, merely to bask in the presence of the small god. Hospitality demanded that the father give tea and food to these callers, and he was therefore worse off financially than he had been before.

Nevertheless, the father's good fortune increased. His eldest son in the wealthy Kumbum Monastery was also found to be an incarnation. Of course, he was not the incarnation of a great god like Chenrezi; his original predecessor had been a lesser Bodhisattva, that is to say, a human being, probably a monk, who had led a perfect life and had practiced great austerities so that he achieved nirvana. Instead of accepting eternal bliss, however, he had chosen to re-enter the wheel of life in constant reincarnations in order to help others attain perfection. Thus the eldest son was now given high rank and privilege. His monastery sent gifts of food and clothing to the father.

Also, the Lhasan monk who watched over the child would, of course, have provided for the family in any real emergency. The fact was that the authorities had learned from experience to proceed with great caution in deciding on the true Incarnation. Other candidates might still be found with even clearer attributes.

Thus the testing of the child had only just begun. The subsequent examinations, although based on ancient religious ritual, were in effect aptitude and I.Q. tests. They proved beyond doubt that Lhamo was suited for the life of the Dalai Lama and that his intelligence was decidedly above the average. Within a few months the authorities in Lhasa agreed that the new Incarnation had been identified.

But still the news was not released officially. The main reason was fear of the Chinese. As long as the child lived in a Chinese-governed province he was not safe from Chinese intrigue. If Lhamo was declared the Dalai Lama, for example, the Chinese might send him to Lhasa with the guard of an expeditionary force. Or they might capture the child and bring him up as a puppet to their policies. Thus the Lhasan request to the Tsinghai governor was simply that the child should be permitted to go to Lhasa for further tests.

To the chagrin of the Tibetans, however, the Chinese authorities refused permission to take the child away. They gave no reason for the refusal, but eventually they demanded a payment of 100,000 Chinese dollars (about $35,000). The money was raised and the payment was sent—to be followed by further demands, each larger than the last. In the end two and a half years elapsed between the time of the monk-beggar's visit and the departure of the Dalai Lama's caravan.

The caravan which took the child to Lhasa exceeded any dreams of glory that an ambitious father could have. He had hoped to rise above a farmer's grinding poverty; he had dreamed of trading in horses, perhaps even taking a few trade animals as part of a caravan in some distant, prosperous day. Now the richest caravans in the whole area combined to travel together in the entourage of his four-year-old son. Who would set off alone when such an auspicious journey was being undertaken? Tibetan and Muslim alike joined the huge procession which no raider would dare attack. Ten thousand mules and horses were assembled. Thousands of loads of grain, provisions, trade goods, tents, utensils, weapons, and ammunition were packed. No army escort was needed; a bandit would have to be completely insane to attack a force under the protection of a living god. And besides, hundreds of Tsinghai Tibetans, heavily armed, accompanied the procession, ready to defend their little god with their lives.

The little Dalai was accompanied by his parents and his brothers and sisters, including the younger of the boy monks. Only one representative from the Chinese government went along. The High Lama Kyetsang Rimpoche and two hundred Lhasan Tibetans made up the official escort party. Unofficially five hundred Tsinghai Tibetan and Muslim traders made up the bulk of the caravan.

It was a joyous caravan. During the day the holy child was carried in a sedan chair borne by eight men. The men were rotated frequently; always a willing shoulder was not only ready but anxious to take the burden, for the task was a blessing and an honor. In the evenings a tent city was spread out in the plains, a city of glossy black yak hair and blue and white silk. When the animals were tethered and the campfires built, there were singing and dancing, wrestling and other sports, debates and prayers. The journey took five months—exciting, happy months of good camaraderie unmarred by any unpleasant incident.

When the caravan reached Nagchuka, it was met by the "greeting party" from Lhasa. The party was led by a member of the Kashag. He was accompanied by other officials, by a guard of Tibetan troops, and by representatives of the three great monasteries, of the city of Lhasa, and of the Tibetan people. Most of these people were dressed in richly brocaded robes of brightly colored silk so that they made a splash of vivid color in the clear mountain air. A magnificent tent city had been set up outside Nagchuka Fort for the official reception. Spreading out on all sides were the tent suburbs of the unofficial reception; twenty thousand Tibetans had come to welcome back their god.

When the caravan came to a stop, the sedan chair was carried forward and the official reception party advanced to meet it. A hush fell over the great throng. The Kashag member approached the chair, carrying over his outstretched arms an exceptionally long, rich white *kadak* (ceremonial scarf) which he presented to the little Dalai. The child accepted the scarf with grave dignity. Then he turned to his parents. "Mother," he asked, "do you know these people?"

"No, dear. I have never seen them," she replied.

"But I know them," he said. "I know them all."

There was a gasp from the officials who overheard these words. They were so touched that, without exception, they wept. With tears streaming down their faces more than two hundred officials passed by the chair to present *kadak* and other gifts. The child, however, was smiling and happy as he received the gifts and gave each person the blessing as he had been taught to do.

With the official greeting over, the child was taken to a huge tent where a throne had been prepared for him. He was placed gently on the high throne, and now many hundreds more of his nonofficial subjects passed by him to give him gifts and receive his blessing. The little Dalai showed no impatience or fatigue, but after an hour or two he was taken from the throne to his personal tent for a rest. The next day a prolonged audience was held in the throne tent. Every person among the many thousands gathered at Nagchuka wanted the personal blessing of their god. The high lama and the officials were afraid that the child might become overtired. On the third day, therefore, they allowed him to sit on the throne, where the subjects could come and look but not approach for blessings. The people understood and did not object. Everyone seemed filled with great happiness. There were music, dancing, and gaiety everywhere in the encampment. The child loved it all.

On the fourth day the caravan began the last stage of the journey to Lhasa. Now it was swollen to a mighty size and moved across the plains like a river of bright color. After eight days it reached the monastery of Retring, the home monastery of Retring Rimpoche who was acting as the Regent of Tibet until the new Dalai Lama would reach majority. Here the caravan rested again before the final six-day journey to the capital itself.

The procession moved now through a solid mass of people who lined every inch of the roadway. These worshiping subjects prostrated themselves before their returned god. Whenever the child's glance fell on anyone, the lucky recipient burst into tears. Lhasa itself was in a frenzy of joy when the sedan chair entered the city. Hours were required to move the chair through the streets. The Dalai Lama and his family were installed in a group of residences set at different levels; the little god with his seven-year-old brother as a companion had the highest of these houses. Here they rested for a week from the journey. Then they moved to the Norbulingka (Jewel Park) in which was the summer palace, where they stayed for several months.

During these months preparations for the enthronement ceremony were going on. It was a busy time for the child. Twenty lamas were assigned to his personal care. They taught him his part in the elaborate enthronement ritual. He had to be measured and fitted for new clothes. Gradually he saw less and less of his family.

Instead of his mother's anxious eye watching over him at play he was surrounded by seven-foot guards with great curved swords. I can vouch personally that these guards, who came from the eastern district known as Kham, are terrifyingly ferocious in appearance. They were completely gentle with the holy child, however, and he became fast friends with them from the first.

The first week of the new year, a time of joyous celebration in Tibet, was set for the enthronement ceremonies. A week before the young Dalai was installed in the Potala. On the great day he was awakened in the cold dawn. He began an elaborate ritual that had been prescribed in complete detail by the Fifth Incarnation three centuries earlier. First he was taken to a special room for his prayers. Then he was taken to another room to be dressed in the fabulously rich robes worn by Dalai Lamas on state occasions.

At the appointed hour he left his apartments and joined his personal party of two hundred lamas and high officials who would accompany him to the vast throne room. This room was a fifteen-minute walk from his apartments. Every foot of the way was runnered with white silk on which religious symbols were painted in bright colors. Only His Holiness could touch this silk; his personal party walked behind him and along the sides of the corridors.

Preceding him and his followers was the "heralding party." This group included about a hundred lamas and laymen who were given their duty as an honor. They were dressed in ancient robes of great richness. The robes were so well preserved as to appear fresh and new. In addition the robes were decorated with jewels taken from the court treasuries. Each outfit was said to be worth the equivalent of about twenty-five thousand dollars; every item was carefully registered with the government and on these rare state occasions was issued only against a receipt. After the ceremony each item was checked back into the treasury.

The heralding party chanted prayers and played music on traditional instruments. They announced the arrival of the holy child to the throng of five thousand especially chosen guests in the throne room. When the child entered the great hall, everyone rose and stood in utter silence with downcast eyes. The boy walked alone across the hall to the throne and was lifted to its great height. For a moment the assembly remained silent in prayer.

Now the highest lama came forward and addressed himself to the child in a traditional chant known as the "Prayer for the Power of the Golden Throne." The orchestra began to play again, this time a soft background of religious music. In effect the lama prayed to the Incarnation to take the throne and he professed his acceptance of the Dalai Lama's return. The ten-minute chant ended with traditional words of praise and devotion. Afterward everyone in the great hall joined to repeat words of entreaty, acceptance, and praise.

At this point came the climax of the ceremony. The highest Kashag member approached the throne. He first presented the child *kadak,* the traditional scarf. Then he offered a curious golden urn. Inside was a scroll inscribed with holy words, the chop of the Kashag, and the date of the enthronement. The urn was sealed and would never be opened. It symbolized the acceptance of the Dalai Lama by the Kashag and thus by the Tibetan nation. The moment the child took the urn he became officially the Fourteenth Dalai Lama and the spiritual-temporal ruler of his people.

Finally came the hours-long parade of guests before the throne. Each brought a scarf and gifts. Each received a blessing; an important personage was touched on the head by the boy's hand, while a lesser person was merely whisked with the tasseled end of the scepter. An attendant held the arm of the boy and helped him administer the blessings. The child, however, showed remarkable endurance. He remained calm and self-possessed, and apparently he took a deep and serious pleasure in the long ceremony.

Part of the ceremony included receiving gifts and giving blessings to notable foreigners. Conspicuous among these guests was the Chinese special representative. Since Chao and his army had been driven out, no other Chinese official had been allowed to enter Tibet except the special representatives who came to offer condolences on the death of the Thirteenth. Nevertheless, the

Chinese now claimed that the entire enthronement was their show, staged by them to demonstrate their respect for Tibetan people and customs. Their gifts were lavish; they included a personal letter and gift from Chiang Kai-shek, many rolls of rich brocade, and a gold medal. I have talked to several Tibetans who were at the ceremony, however, and not one of them has said that the Chinese representative played a role or received attention in any way different from the other foreign representatives.

The British envoy's position in the ceremony was at least equal to that of the Chinese representative. He too brought rich gifts. These included another gold medal, a signed portrait of the King, some rare books, and a silver model of a sailing ship. In addition, the British gave a few other gifts more suitable to the age of the holy child—a little tricycle, a toy motorboat, and some exquisite imitation birds in a cage.

The child, however, had little time for toys. For several days after the enthronement the Dalai Lama returned to be lifted again to the high throne to receive and to bless countless pilgrims who had converged on Lhasa for this momentous event. Only when the New Year's celebrations were over could the Dalai Lama settle down to "normal" life in his new home, the thousand-roomed Potala.

CHAPTER IV

The Roof of the World

*A man's sins and virtues are like his shadow which,
although not always apparent, follows him everywhere.*
—TIBETAN PROVERB

THE people for whom the Dalai was responsible lived in a
country twice the size of France. Nevertheless the population was
less than three million; great portions of the land were uninhabitable.

More than half of Tibet's area is a vast, desolate plateau called
the Chang Tang. It is surrounded on three sides—to the north,
west, and south—by towering mountains. The plateau floor itself
averages about fifteen thousand feet altitude. The highest point in
the United States, Mt. Whitney, is 14,500 feet. Yet the Chang Tang
is in itself the drainage basin for the surrounding mountains.

The huge basin is a rocky, barren place, dotted with salt lakes.
It is devoid of all but the most stunted scrub growths. It is continually swept by winds which frequently reach gale strength.
Freezing temperatures are common the year around and in winter
may reach 40° below zero. Some life does manage to exist in the
area. Herds of wild horses, antelope, and yak roam the open
spaces. Ducks and geese use the lakes and streams. Human habitation is confined almost entirely to the banks of large lakes in the
southern part of the Chang Tang. Even so, the lake region supports mainly a sparse nomadic population and a few small settlements and monasteries. Some of the lakes are holy and are scenes
of pilgrimage. Trade caravans penetrate the northern reaches of

the plateau to take salt from dried lake beds. Borax is extracted from the southern lake region.

South of the Chang Tang are several ranges of the Himalayan complex. Through the valleys flow the great Tsangpo (the Brahmaputra) and its tributaries. These river valleys average twelve to fourteen thousand feet in elevation, but they can be used for agriculture. Much of the land is irrigated by an ancient canal system. This central Tibetan area contains all the major population centers, including the twelve-thousand-foot-high capital of Lhasa. Here all the trade routes into Tibet converge.

Southwest Tibet is, again, sparsely settled. Four mountain ranges cut across the area at a northwest-southeast angle. The rainfall is meager, and the narrow valleys are too steep and rocky for extensive agriculture. A few peasant villages exist in the Sutlej and Indus valleys, but nomadic shepherds make up most of the population. Nevertheless, during the summer, traders from India and Ladakh (an eastern district of Kashmir) cross the borders and, until the Chinese interfered, some of Tibet's most active market centers were located in this area. It is also a place of pilgrimage for both Buddhists and Hindus. In this part of Tibet, Mt. Kailas, the "Olympus" of Hindu deities, rises sharply to 22,000 feet, and its snows are reflected in the turquoise waters of Lake Manasarowar.

It is from this area or from the south that most Westerners have had their primary contact with Tibet. Thus most of our early accounts of the mountain kingdom describe it as a bleak, barren, and desolate country. Yet parts of Tibet—particularly in the east and southeast—are indescribably beautiful. The valleys are lushly verdant and fertile. In the summer lovely flowers bloom—mile-long fields of wild iris, lilies, anemones, primulas, towering rhododendron trees, acres of dahlias, roses, white gentians, and even edelweiss. Against the rich flower colors the sky is incredibly blue in the thin air and the snow-tipped mountains reflect many-hued lights from the bright sun.

In the beautiful part of Tibet, as in all the country, the people are agricultural workers or nomadic herders. Scholars have tried to establish which came first—the nomad or the peasant. The evidence seems slightly in favor of the nomad as the original Tibetan. He lives in a tent of black yak-hair cloth; the size of the tent varies with his family needs and his economic status. The fireplace in the tent acts as a divider. The men's portion is on the right side. Here the family weapons are stored and such possessions as skins, cloth, saddlery, ropes, and whips. On the women's side, to the left, are the food stores, the equipment for cheese and buttermaking and the looms on which yak hair and wool are woven.

At the back of the tent is the altar. This portion varies greatly according to the wealth of the nomad, but the humblest tent has a shrine with several religious pictures and a burning butter lamp. The shrine of a rich herder may have an impressive portable chapel with images of the Buddha, sacred books, and holy vessels. Outside the tent prayer flags are attached to the support ropes, and in some areas a large pole is planted in front of the tent to fly the holy banners.

Traditionally the herders did not own the flocks of goats, sheep, or yak. The stock usually belonged to a wealthy family for whose ancestors the herder's forefathers also had worked. The labor was performed under several arrangements. One such arrangement was the "increase in flock" principle, under which the herder owed to the proprietor, for example, a set number of lambs for a given number of sheep. Thus the herder eventually could make up a flock of his own out of any increase beyond the agreed-upon figure. If the increase fell short, however, he was obliged to make up the difference.

Another arrangement was based on the products produced by the herd—wool, cheese, butter, or yak hair in specified quantities were turned over to the proprietor. All of these arrangements were time-tested and seemed to work with a minimum of conflict.

In the case of the independent nomads a few families or groups within one family banded together for protection and for co-operation in marketing. It was rare for a large group of nomads to set up camp together. This was because the sparse growth in most grazing grounds would be used up too quickly and many seasonal moves would be required.

To protect themselves from marauders while living in small, isolated groups the nomads trained bloodthirsty mastiffs who attacked any intruder on sight. Visitors to a nomad camp, even though they themselves came from a similar encampment, knew that they would survive only if they galloped in at top speed, whirling weighted ropes or whips in a wide circle to keep the dogs at bay.

The nomad was fond of his semi-isolated life. He made an annual trip to the market where he bartered cheese, butter, cloth, and yak tails for staples of tea and barley and perhaps a few dried vegetables. He had great pride in his firearms and ornaments. If he had a good year he bought colored cloth to decorate the seams of his sheepskin robe, a religious picture for his tent altar, hair ornaments for his women, or a sword with a carved hilt. He was independent and touchy about his honor; he would fight to the death against any interference with his way of life. At the same time he was a jovial fellow, thoroughly generous and hospitable. Above all, he felt superior to the agricultural peasant who was tied to one place, one house, and the narrow sky of a valley.

The peasant was never overworked, for at best the climate allowed no more than one crop a year. The main crop was barley, which grows at altitudes as high as fourteen thousand feet. In the few valleys below eleven thousand feet some wheat was raised and also peas and mustard. Radishes and turnips were the principal vegetables, and both reached enormous size.

The farm implements were primitive, but because the soil was rarely overworked the crop yield was generally fair. Dung, in normal circumstances, was available in sufficient quantities to be used both as fuel and as fertilizer. In many places the fields were irrigated by channels built centuries before. Old records in each *dzong* (county) laid down the rules for the use of irrigation waters, and arguments about priorities rarely made trouble between landowners.

The sowing of seed was done by women. In many localities a priest customarily sowed the first seeds along with a blessing.

Men handled the plow, and a whole peasant family worked together at the harvest.

Crop failures were not unknown, but famine was rare. Grains
could be stored for many years without spoilage. The concentrated
cheeses, which were pressed and dried, could be kept indefinitely;
in fact, cheese was often pressed into cubes, strung into a necklace,
and served as a nutritional ornament. Even meat seldom spoiled
in the high altitudes. Thus, without apparent effort, the country
was always prepared for lean years. Nevertheless, Tibetans did
not take the prospect of crop failure lightly. When the rain was
delayed, or hail or frost threatened, many special prayers were
said. By special government order no building was allowed during
the two months of rain scarcity; a man building a house might
pray for dry weather, and his prayers might offset his neighbors'
prayers for rain.

Tibetan houses, humble or rich, followed a similar pattern and
varied mostly in size. The building material was stone or sun-
dried brick, for no timber was available in most parts of the
country. The houses usually were of two or three stories. The
ground floor served as a stable and usually had a walled courtyard
attached to it. The upper floor was reached by means of a ladder
or a stone stairway. In the less populous areas, where raids were
possible, access to the upper floors was by a removable ladder or
a notched tree trunk which could be pulled up when danger
threatened. The top floor contained the kitchen, bedrooms, and
an altar room. Even the most humble hut had a room set aside
for religious articles, and the poorest peasant owned a few images,
butter lamps, and receptacles for holy water. The altar room also
was used as the "treasury" for any other valuables the family
might possess—festive clothing, women's ornaments, a nest egg
of silver, or a few semi-precious jewels. The flat roof served as
additional living space and work area. Here crops were dried,
grain was winnowed, and fuel was stored. From the roof also
flew prayer flags attached to poles at each corner of the structure.
Finally the roof invariably contained an urn in which incense was
burned to please the gods and to appease evil spirits.

In similar houses—although much larger, cleaner, and more richly stocked with possessions—lived the Tibetan nobles. A nobleman might own a number of houses and estates. Each such family had a home in Lhasa, a few of which had modern equipment. The house, for example, might have glass windows—a rare luxury in Tibet—or even bathroom fixtures which had been carried on a porter's back over the high passes from India. The country houses of the nobility followed the traditional pattern but were often large three-winged structures enclosing a huge court which was walled on the fourth side. The ground floor contained extensive stables and storage rooms. The several upper floors formed spacious living apartments, often richly furnished with brocade-hung walls, thick-rugged floors, and silk-cushioned couches. Such a house often had a number of chapels rather than a single altar room. The best chapel was dedicated to Buddha and to Chenrezi. Another might be devoted to the noble's protective deity. The possessions kept in these chapels could be very rich indeed.

Although a social gap existed between the peasant and the nobles, members of the separate classes were not strangers. When the harvest was in, everyone on the estate joined together to feast, to drink the mild *chang* (barley beer), and to watch a program of theatricals or dancing which the noble arranged to take place in his courtyard. When a nobleman took his family on a picnic—a favorite summer pastime of Tibetans—the servants went along, not merely to serve, but to participate in archery contests, races, games, and singing. Servants' children often studied with the landlord's children under a tutor. Religion made another strong bond between classes. Owner and peasant alike walked carefully to the left of the *mani* wall which guarded the gate to the estate; both sang the same songs of the ancient saints; the protective gods of either might save the estate in time of trouble. The monastery to which the nobleman sent his son might also accept a number of sons from his tenant families.

In exchange for the prerogatives he enjoyed the Tibetan nobleman owed a duty of service to the state. He served in the official capacity to which he was appointed. He received no remuneration for this service, or at best a nominal salary, but the duty could not be refused.

Another, but rather small, class was made up of merchants and traders. The wealthier families in this group lived as sumptuously as the nobles but they did not have the same social position. In Tibet the merchants seemed an especially happy group; perhaps this was because they had a profitable outlet for the innate Tibetan shrewdness and love of trade. The merchants traveled more than other Tibetans and thus had more knowledge of the outside world and were more receptive to modern influences.

The merchant class had too much competition to grow rapidly in numbers or to become powerful. In Tibet business was not the low-caste occupation that it was in most of the Orient. Trade appealed to Tibetans of all levels. Many nobles and officials engaged in it. The government itself had agents who made purchases and supervised official caravans. Even the monasteries did business; both agriculture and trade were important sources of monastery income.

The monasteries encompassed a large segment of Tibet's male population and played a correspondingly important role in Tibetan life. They were socially and politically powerful. Tibet's priesthood was not an isolated group; it was an active part of the society. Every Tibetan family sent one or more sons to a monastery. Occasionally a daughter was sent to a nunnery, but the number of women who devoted themselves to an exclusively religious life was comparatively small. Thus monastery life had a link with every fireside. Many peasants were bound to monastery land; young able-bodied monks often returned home to help with the harvest. Community life centered around the local monastery. The ecclesiastical festivals and music provided color and diversion. The lamas gave comfort and advice to those who sought guidance. They arbitrated disputes and named penances. They block-printed the prayer flags which fluttered from every housetop, and they officiated at the ceremonies which attended birth, marriage, and death.

The Tibetan lamas shared equally with their lay brothers in the nation's administration. The Dalai Lama, as the spiritual-temporal head, governed through an administration in which every important post was held by two officials—one monk and one layman. Thus Tibet had two prime ministers and even two commanders-in-chief of the army.

A four-man cabinet, the Kashag, held administrative responsibility under the Dalai Lama. Three Kashag members, called Shapes, were secular officials, but the fourth was the senior official and a monk. Under this cabinet were two subsidiary groups of four officials each—one clerical and one secular. Four monks had responsibility for appointing and for overseeing all minor monk officials and for supervising the religious affairs of the country. The subsidiary secular group was in charge of all matters of finance and trade. Another official of importance was the Chikyab Kempo, who functioned rather as a lord chamberlain to the Dalai Lama. He also was a high lama, and because of his close association with the Dalai he was a man of considerable influence.

The Tsongdu, sometimes translated as National Assembly, was a large body of officials and monastery representatives convened only by order of the Dalai Lama or the Kashag. It was not an elected body. It was composed of officials of specified rank—heads of government departments, sometimes regional government officials, and appointed representatives from the three great monasteries near Lhasa. Its function was consultative rather than legislative. Issues in the Tsongdu were seldom brought to a vote, for the opinion of senior officials usually was clear and the lesser officials went along with it. The Tsongdu often was bypassed by the Thirteenth Dalai Lama, who found its deliberations time-wasting because he knew his own mind well. During the regencies following his death, however, this group came into its limited own again.

Government in Lhasa was wholly in the hands of the monks for twenty-one days each year. This was during the New Year festival which the Tibetans celebrated with religious fervor and festive vigor. They decorated their houses with religious symbols, chased out the devils with charms and dancing and even with firearms. It was a time of joy, feasting, and high hopes. On the third day of the New Year the monks of the nearby monasteries descended on Lhasa and quite literally took over for the next three weeks. They were housed in huge dormitories, and the normal Lhasa population was lost among the red-robed priests that swarmed the streets. The proctors of Drepung (one of Lhasa's "big three") assumed, by a tradition that went back to the Fifth Dalai Lama, authority for maintaining law and order in the city during the festival of the Great Prayer.

The Great Prayer was for the preservation and protection of Buddhism. During the period six religious services were held each day. Public debates by great Buddhist scholars were a feature of the services.

The most colorful of the festivals that made up the Great Prayer was the display of the butter images, called the Offerings of the Fifteenth (day of the month). Monk artists worked for months to fashion pictures and statues in colored butter. The works showed considerable art and skill. They depicted auspicious designs, symbols, and images in minute detail. Oddly enough, the images were of Hindu deities rather than Tibetan gods. In Lhasa the works were displayed on specially built wooden scaffolds which rose as high as sixty feet along the Barkor, the street which surrounded the square on which the Jokhang, Lhasa's central temple, was located. The outdoor art display was world-famous, and its perishable medium was quite safe in the February cold. When evening came the exhibition was illuminated by thousands of butter lamps. The Dalai Lama and his attendants were invited to circle the Barkor first. Then came the monks and the people—singing, shouting, and praying—to feast their eyes and souls in this enchanted land of Buddhist art. All night the crowds thronged the Barkor, but before dawn the images were dismantled. The leather backings on which the art works had been mounted were saved for another year, but the butter was simply thrown away because the paint had rendered it useless. The beautiful works of art were destroyed to symbolize the fact that all material existence is a passing illusion.

Symbolism was the keynote of the entire festival. The pageantry was on a lavish scale. For several days a mock war was fought between a mounted "army" of Tibetan nobles and officials against the potential enemies of the Buddhist faith. Men and horses alike were dressed in magnificent costumes—ancient armor, helmets, rich saddle robes, and silver-mounted saddlery—and were armed with weapons old and new.

On the final day of the Great Prayer a magnificent procession around the Barkor heralded the advent of the Buddha Maitreya, the next Buddha whom Tibetans call Gyewa Champa or Conquering Love. The image of this messiah was carried at the head of the procession. This was the triumphant climax of the whole festival, and joy was unconfined. After the procession the monks dispersed to their monasteries, but the people spent another few days in celebration; sport was the main attraction, with archery contests, races, wrestling, and other games, accompanied by *chang* and song.

The Lamaist festivals pointed up the mixed origins of the unique religion. Bound to the Wheel of Life in an eternity of births and rebirths, Lamaist Tibetans knew that release could come only through the Three Precious Things: the Buddha, the Doctrine, the Priesthood. This basic belief they held in common with all followers of Buddha. Broadly speaking, a Buddhist had a choice of two basic methods for seeking release. One was almost wholly intellectual; the follower devoted himself to study and meditation until he was able to comprehend truth logically, perceive enlightenment, and thus achieve nirvana. In the other method the follower submitted to priestly instruction, performed religious ritual, and recited magic formula until he, too, had won release.

In addition, a Buddhist had a choice of spiritual objectives for seeking release. In one objective he might strive only for his own escape from the wheel, content to remain through eternity in the bliss of nirvana; any follower of the Hinayana (the Little Vehicle) sought only his own release. A follower of the Mahayana (the Great Vehicle), however, might strive either for his own release or for the release of all living creatures. Generally speaking, the Little Vehicle prescribed little more than a perfect way of life; the Great Vehicle went further by offering magic, priestly ministration, and intervention by semi-divine beings to help the follower attain release. These semi-divine beings, called Bodhisattvas, were humans who had attained the privilege of personal release but chose instead to suffer the wheel of existence in order to help others achieve nirvana. Lamaism was associated with the Great Vehicle. The Lamaist Tibetans generally preferred the method of priestly instruction, religious ritual, and magic formula.

Nevertheless, the Lamaism they practiced was in no way somber. It had its gentle side in its respect for all forms of life, in the millions of fluttering prayer flags which filled the air with sacred words, and especially in its love and veneration for the teachers who devoted their lives to helping others achieve nirvana.

But Lamaism had its awful face as well, a face that was terrifying only to the outsider. To Tibetans the ferocious demon gods were staunch friends and protectors. Evil and sin had to be destroyed. Enemies of the faith had to be kept at bay. Temples had to be guarded from defilement. Each hearth required a spirit to drive away misfortune. And each person needed a demon deity to guard him as he progressed from one life to another in the endless circle. In addition, the demon gods provided color, excitement, drama, and even humor. Traveling musicians sang of their epic battles. Masked dancers in monastery courtyards acted out a vigorous chastisement of devils.

To a traveler in Tibet, however, the most impressive aspect of Lamaism was its tolerance. The people, being one in religion and secure in their faith, had no need to be defensive about it. They were always respectful of the religious practices of others, but proselytism by foreign missionaries was singularly unsuccessful. Moreover, tolerance existed among the various sects of Lamaism as well. Despite the past struggles for political supremacy the Yellow Hats and the Red Hats—and even the Black Hats of the old Bon—now maintained their separate monasteries in peace and harmony. Conformist behavior in religion was not considered a great virtue; each man was traveling a charted course, and his efforts to escape were entirely his own business.

Tibetans were equally tolerant about the social behavior of others, either among themselves or among foreigners. They were not prone to pass judgment on manners or morals, and they seemed remarkably free from the guilt complexes that many religions bred. Because the whole of one's conscious existence was a kind of retribution for sins committed in previous lives, and was at best an opportunity to make an infinitely small step toward better future lives, one felt little need to worry about the mistakes of others. Hatred, greed, and lust (the latter sometimes defined as ignorance) were the three evils which chained one to the Wheel of Life. Without these evils one would have attained escape from life. Hatred, greed, and lust, therefore, were the very meaning of life itself—so why be shocked when you came across them in yourself or in others?

One of the results of this viewpoint was that few sexual taboos existed in Tibet. Although monogamy was prevalent, polyandry and polygamy were also accepted marriage forms. Polygamous marriages were a luxury of the rich, and a man who could afford several wives was respected as clever and successful. Polyandry, as well, had its basis in economics. One girl was often brought into a household to become the wife of several sons. Her offspring were regarded as the children of the oldest son. This system kept the family property from being subdivided among a number of separate households. It also helped to hold down the population in districts where infertile land could support only a limited number of people. No stigma was attached to illegitimate children or to their mothers. All children were welcomed and loved. Families were seldom large, however, because the rigorous winters, the high incidence of disease, and the lack of medical facilities combined to keep the birth rate low and the infant-mortality rate high.

Tibetan women had far more independence than the women in neighboring countries. They mixed freely in social gatherings. They expressed themselves as freely as did the men. They suffered no discrimination as property owners. They could obtain divorces without much difficulty, and divorcees and widows were free to remarry. According to Buddhist teaching, women were considered unable to attain nirvana; they had to be reborn as men in order to gain eventual salvation. This did not seem to dampen their spirits. They might pray for rebirth as men, but meanwhile they made the best of their lot as women—and charming and beautiful women they were.

The Tibetan way of life required help from the priests almost constantly. Priests had their part in the name-giving ceremony of a newborn child. They blessed new houses, the plowed fields, the seeds, the herds, and the flocks. They selected auspicious days for all undertakings. The priests were the medical practitioners, often the moneylenders, and sometimes the arbitrators in a dispute. They were needed so frequently that a wealthy household often had its own priest in residence to give advice, direct ritual, explain omens, determine the auspicious from the inauspicious, lead prayers, and read from the holy books. In some families a son became the household priest. He studied for several years at a monastery and then returned home to be in constant attendance at the family altar.

Lamaism, in short, was a fulfilling religion for the Tibetan people. Every person could find in it the answer to his needs. Every moment that he was free from preoccupation, even the most humble person could communicate with the Divine by repeating endlessly the most sacred words that the human voice could utter, "*Om mani padme hum.*" The more or less literal translation of the words was, "Hail (to the) jewel in the lotus," but the phrase had been made deliberately abstract so that its meaning could be infinite. Thus to the humble Tibetans the words were a mighty *mantra*, a magic formula that offered merit toward eventual perfection. The majority of monks accepted it as a symbolism that they dimly grasped—a hint of the enlightenment they sought and in seeking were set a little apart from and above the mass of struggling humanity. A learned monk found the prayer a goal in itself; the more he learned the more meaning he found in the words. And in the mystic cult among the highest lamas *"Om mani padme hum's"* magic touched upon the study of sonics; through the power of these particular vibrations the lamas perhaps penetrated secrets still closed to our science.

The Tibetans, then, were a people whose religion was their life. The Tibetan might be a high lama, a humble peasant, an arrogant noble, a proud nomad, a shrewd merchant, a brutal bandit, but life without his religion was incomprehensible to him. He lived in a hard country, but he envied no one. The outside world offered nothing he needed or wanted. Safe within his land were the Three Precious Things—the Buddha, the Doctrine, and the Priesthood.

CHAPTER V

The God-King Against the Godless

*When the wheel begins to turn, does the flower
in its path pray to the driver to stop the cart?*
—TIBETAN PROVERB

T HE Tibetans' belief that the Three Precious Things are the
only real possessions worth having explains their reverence for
the Dalai Lama. The Reincarnation of Chenrezi is the divine
representative of Lord Buddha. He is the Protector of the Doctrine.
And he is the great leader of the Priesthood. He therefore might
be called the very soul of his people, and he is at least a living
symbol of their way of life.

The four-year-old boy who began a new life in the Potala in
1939, however, had little understanding of the vast responsibility
he had suddenly acquired. He had to learn slowly and painstak-
ingly his unique place in the Tibetan culture. An unforeseen flaw
in his character or a mistake in the education he received could
render him inadequate for his divine duty; a Dalai Lama who
abused his great power could lead his country into chaos. Thus the
most remarkable aspect of choosing the new Incarnation was not
in the strange and mystic rites that accompanied the process but
in the fact that a truly exceptional child was found and was given
such excellent training for the position.

Even more remarkable was the fact that his training required
self-discipline that, in a four-year-old child, must have been almost a miracle. No mere mortal was supposed even to look upon
the living god, let alone give him an order. Thus if the child had

not wanted to study, no one could have made him do it. Nevertheless, except for Buddhist holidays on the fifteenth and thirtieth of each month, he had no rest from his daily routine. He worked an eight-hour day; three hours were devoted to prayers and ritual and five hours to study.

Fortunately the young God-King was studious. He applied himself diligently and without complaining to the long hours of daily instruction under the kindly monks. He rarely saw his parents now, and he did not seem to miss them. He still had his older brother as a companion, and together the boys had brief moments of healthy play typical of any normal child. But what preoccupied him the most was the responsibility that he realized, even at an early age, he had for the people. The downcast, tear-filled eyes of those who approached him, the deference he was shown, and the great joy that the mere touch of his hand in blessing gave to the people taught him how much they depended on him. Thus, while his family enjoyed the lofty titles and rich estates they had received, the Dalai Lama himself prepared for a life of devotion to his subjects through devotion to the faith he represented for them.

His studies began at nine in the morning, when the servants escorted him to the classroom. The room was comfortable but large and sparsely furnished. Besides the great volumes of the holy books, the room had only five cushioned benches and five small tables. Each table, with its corresponding bench, was at a different height. The highest was for the child Incarnation. The next highest was for the Retring Rimpoche, who was head tutor as well as Regent. Two still lower tables were for the assistant tutors who were lamas, also from Retring Monastery. The lowest table was for the Dalai Lama's seven-year-old brother Lobsang Samten, who was the holy child's companion for the first years at the school.

The tutors and Lobsang bowed low when the boy Incarnation entered the classroom. The Regent helped him onto the high bench. Sometimes, if the weather outside was inviting, the child sighed wistfully—for he was a human as well as a divine boy—

but he always picked up the bamboo pen, sharpened it carefully with a small knife, dipped it into the bowl of indelible ink made from berry juice, and waited patiently for the tutors to begin their instruction.

At first the tutors did not push the boy too hard. He studied the Lhasan tongue and copied letters from the holy books. Mostly his wise teacher gave every encouragement to his child's normal curiosity. When, for example, the boy learned to shape the letters for "tea," the Regent told him how tea was grown. He described the rich caravans of ancient times when the Chinese Emperor sent an annual gift of a million pounds of tea to the Dalai Lama and the monasteries. If the child asked about the carvings on one of the hall pillars, he was told the significance of the religious symbols.

Even the child's few leisure hours were directed toward the proper training for his position. The young Fourteenth showed an aptitude for art. Whenever he expressed a wish to paint or draw, an art tutor was immediately available with the proper materials to give him instruction; invariably the subjects for his art work were religious scenes or symbols. He learned from artisans how to work in jade, wood, ivory, stone, and metal. Even when he played with simple building blocks, the houses he constructed were Lamaist monasteries.

He had little time for more active play but, of course, he was not discouraged from it. During the lunch period from noon until three-thirty he romped or rested as he wished. He and his brother Lobsang often ran through the halls of the Potala, exploring the vast palace or playing tag or hide-and-seek. On these occasions one of the ten servants who always attended him went ahead to send everyone away from the rooms that the children wanted to use.

The Dalai Lama was given no training in sports. The child did enjoy the beautiful circular stables at Norbulingka; the Thirteenth Incarnation had been a keen horseman and had built up a stable of several hundred fine-blooded animals. The young Fourteenth learned how to ride—an absolute necessity in Tibet

where all travel was done on mule or horseback—and he tried
his hand at archery. Nevertheless, he showed little real enthusiasm
for either pastime.

His favorite pastime was kiteflying. The high roof of the Potala
was an ideal place for the sport. Also, on the windy air of the
Tibetan plateau kites could be made to reach great heights; in
fact, they were often flown so high that they could be seen only
with binoculars.

The kites used by Tibetan children were of the Indian type
rather than the Chinese, and the special string for them was
imported from India. Also Indian was the Tibetan sport of kite
fighting. The string was treated with a mixture of glue and ground
glass. The boys maneuvered their flying kites in order to cut the
opponent's string, thereby sending the "enemy" kite fluttering to
the ground. The young Dalai Lama became adept at this sport
and often engaged kites flown by his youthful subjects in the city
below. The Lhasan boy who found a "defeated" kite from the
Potala roof had a treasure indeed. No one would admit that such
a kite actually belonged to the Dalai Lama—he could not be
defeated even in such a small matter; instead the assumption
was that the kite's string had been cut by the Dalai's string, and
thus the cut string itself became a blessed object of auspicious
omen.

Little attention was paid to the Dalai Lama's physical development. Priests trained in Tibetan medicine watched his general
health. He was given simple and nutritious food, cooked more in
the Chinese way than in what might be called typically Tibetan.
He received no regular exercise, however, except a unique course
in special breathing. The Tibetan word for this exercise meant
"air thinking," and its purpose was to increase the powers of
concentration.

By the time the Fourteenth was six he needed exceptional
powers of concentration. The number of tutors was being gradually increased. He began his study of the holy books in earnest.
He was taught no foreign language or geography. Modern science
was taboo. He did not even learn history, although the story of

Lamaism was essentially the history of Tibet. Besides his religious training, however, he did study arithmetic. He learned the Tibetan computing system. A compartmentalized tray was used together with bits of rock, coal, dry berries, and twigs, each of which had a traditional numerical value and function. By shuffling selected counters in another tray he could work out basic mathematical problems. The system lacked the speed of the abacus, but with practice the boy learned to do quickly the limited computations he needed in his duties.

The training for his duties kept the Dalai Lama almost wholly protected from the world outside his two palaces. Nevertheless, in the year of his enthronement the whole world outside Tibet was inflamed with violence and disaster. World War II, however, had little effect on the mountain kingdom. Tibetans had no need to coin new words for four-engine bombers, rationing, propaganda, or war bonds. The caravans moved as they had for centuries, but the shrewd merchants soon learned the trick of turning the price fluctuations of war economy into a profit.

Also, the war occasioned the first formal contact between the United States and Tibetan governments. In 1942 the Kashag agreed to allow an American Army expedition to cross Tibet in search of a supply route to China. An alternative was wanted for the risky and expensive air lift of war supplies over the "hump." Two U. S. Army officers, Ilya Tolstoi and Brooke Dolan II (who had made a previous exploration trip through the eastern part of Tibet), undertook the mission. They carried a letter from President Roosevelt and after a difficult journey of several months arrived in Lhasa. All along the journey through Tibet they were warmly received, and they had complete co-operation from the officials and the people alike. The officers made many friends, and the American government later sent an appreciation gift of equipment for several radio stations.

The objective of the expedition was to find a supply route for the aid to China, but the Chinese authorities were not enthusiastic about the trip. When Tolstoi and Dolan left Delhi for Lhasa late in September 1942, they still had not obtained Chinese permission

to enter China through Tibet. Later the permission was received
and, once in China, the officers were well treated. The fact was
obvious, however, that the Chinese government did not want a
direct contact between Tibetans and American military representatives.

The idea of an overland supply route proved impractical, and
American planes continued to fly the formidable Himalayan
"hump." In January 1944 one of the U.S. planes wandered off
course and ran out of fuel among the cloud-fogged snow peaks.
The five crew members bailed out before the plane crashed into a
mountainside. Three of the group came down near a village; the
other two were isolated and one was injured. Friendly Tibetans,
however, came to their aid. Two days after the crash all five
airmen were brought together at the village of Tsetang, southeast
of Lhasa. Here a Bhutanese monk who spoke some English was
summoned to their aid. He told them that they had parachuted
into the "forbidden land." Nevertheless, their welcome could not
have been more sincere. With true hospitality the villagers out-
fitted the airmen with warm clothes and gave them gifts of food,
blankets, and every comfort which their simple homes could
provide. The monk contacted a Tibetan official who arranged for
mounts and escorted the young airmen to Lhasa. Here, too, they
were well received. After a rest, a little sight-seeing, and more
generous outfitting the men were given guides and transport
animals to take them to the Indian border.

Normally the only Westerners in Tibet were the British representatives. Also, Reginald Fox, a British radio technician, was
employed by the Tibetan government to establish a radio communications system for the country. Later Robert Ford, another
English radio technician, came to assist Fox. Finally the war was
responsible for the entrance of two other Europeans into Tibet.
The Austrian mountaineers, Heinrich Harrer and Peter Aufschnaiter, had been on a climbing expedition in Kashmir in the
summer of 1939. When they came down from the mountains that
fall, World War II had begun and enemy nationals in India had
been interned. The two mountaineers were detained and were

sent to a camp at Dehra Dun in the Himalayan foothills. In the spring of 1944 they escaped with several other internees and headed across the mountains for Tibet. The Austrians also were well received in Tibet but were always politely, and firmly, ordered back to the Indian border. Aufschnaiter and Harrer, however, were more persistent and resourceful. They managed to remain in Tibet. The rugged Tibetans respected the Austrians' mountain-climbing ability. Local officials found them pleasant and likable and did not hurry them on. Eventually the two Austrians settled in a village not far from the Nepalese border. They made friends among the Tibetans, learned the language, and eked out a living through their skills. Later they were accepted in Lhasa and were employed by the Tibetan government.

When my father and I visited Lhasa in 1949, Harrer was working with the Tibetans on map making and Aufschnaiter was planning improvement of the canal system. Both men were doing useful work and seemed entirely happy. They had been completely accepted by the Tibetans. Harrer had frequent contact with the young Dalai Lama to whom he was introducing the mysteries of photography and other aspects of Western civilization.

Eventually the Dalai Lama's tutors faced the fact that some exposure to modern civilization was unavoidable, and they broadened his training slightly. Officials in the Foreign Department were assigned to give him some idea of world affairs. The boy's natural inquisitiveness had made him thirsty for wider knowledge. His secretary told him about magazines, and the Dalai Lama expressed a wish to see some. After several months a supply of magazines was procured through India. The boy's favorite was *Life,* and his second choice was *The National Geographic.* He awaited eagerly the arrival of new issues. After poring over the pictures he told his secretary which ones especially puzzled him. The magazine then was sent to the Foreign Department where an English translator wrote down a Tibetan translation of the picture captions in the margins of the pages. This interest in magazines was not considered a part of the Dalai Lama's education; it was merely a diversion for which he had expressed a wish, but through it he picked up stray bits of information about the changing world outside.

A new menace was growing in China, the perennial source of most of Tibet's troubles. And this time the trouble was being fomented by the Chinese Communists. The Dalai Lama was already familiar with what Communism would mean to Tibetans. His predecessor had lived during the days when the Russian Soviets took over part of Mongolia. The Mongolians, also Lamaists, had been ruled by an Ulan Bator incarnation who was regarded as the third highest in the Lamaist hierarchy. After the Russians took over the Mongolians were prohibited from practicing their religion and were not allowed to seek a new incarnation. Even at the time the Thirteenth Dalai had written that the real threat to Tibet was from the "manner of working among the Red people." In his Political Testament, written two years before his death, he had made a prophecy about the effect of Communism on Lamaist culture.

"The continuous kingdom of the Three Ancestral Religious Rulers will be degraded," he had written. "All the servants of these rulers will find themselves powerless in the hands of the enemy. Their inheritance and wealth will be torn up by the roots. All living beings will live in fear of torture." He then exhorted his people to unity, and after beseeching them not to forget his dire prophecy, he counseled them to "give prayer day and night to the Exalted Chenrezi."

CHAPTER VI

The Red Wave Advances

Eat according to the height of your meal-bag,
Walk according to the width of your track.

—TIBETAN PROVERB

TIBETANS had their first contact with the Chinese Communists in 1934. Chiang Kai-shek's China had recently sent a "condolence mission" to Lhasa after the Thirteenth Dalai Lama's death. The mission stayed but did not interfere in Tibetan affairs. At the same time, however, Communist armies of the "long march," escaping battle with Chiang Kai-shek to reach a haven in the interior of China, crossed into the Tibetan-populated Sikang Province. These troops, under Chu Teh, were like a swarm of locusts. They took every bit of food and every possession of any value from the residents. They looted the monasteries and murdered anyone who stood in their way. What was worse, much of the devastation they wrought was pointless. Many invaluable books and art treasures in the monasteries were destroyed. They even shot down or mutilated women and children. Chinese and Tibetans alike suffered under the Communists. The Sikang governor, a Chinese Buddhist named Liu Wen-hui, finally appealed to Lhasa and was given military help to expel the common enemy.

Meanwhile another Communist army of the "long march" crossed the Tibetan border to the north. These troops were under Mao Tse-tung and Chou En-lai. They too marauded and looted whenever they could, but this area was peopled by the fierce Mantzu and Golok tribes. These Tibetans put up ferocious resistance, and the Communists, in fact, lost half their men in this wild area. The Communists who did escape managed to live only by looting the Tibetans' meager stocks of food.

"This is our only foreign debt," Mao later told Edgar Snow, "and some day we must pay the Mantzu and Tibetans for the provisions we were obliged to take from them." At the time of the conversation Mao must have slipped up in referring to this debt to Tibet as a "foreign debt"; today the Chinese Communists categorically claim that Tibet has been historically a part of China.

The brutality of the Communist armies awakened Tibetans to the need for a more adequate national defense. The first problem, they felt, was leadership. The Thirteenth Dalai had passed on. The search for the Fourteenth was being intensified, but even when found at least fifteen years must pass before he could reach majority. The Panchen Lama, Tibet's second highest incarnate lama, was still alive. He was living in China, however, where he had been exiled years before for political intrigue by some of his followers. There had been no conflict between him and the Thirteenth Dalai Lama, who, in fact, had tried several times to bring about the Panchen's return. The Chinese were willing to allow the Panchen's return only if they could provide an army to escort him. Nevertheless his return was important to supply spiritual leadership which Tibetans found so necessary in times of crisis.

The next aspect of the Tibetan defense problem was a better army.

To solve these problems the Lhasa government turned westward for help. In 1936 a British mission was invited. The mission made recommendations for enlarging and modernizing the Tibetan forces. The British also agreed to help the Tibetans obtain the release of the Panchen Lama, and again they began the slow process of pressuring the stubborn Chinese.

Both efforts unfortunately were frustrated. A year later the Panchen died, still in exile. World War II became imminent, and soon the British were too preoccupied to give much attention to Tibet's problems. Nevertheless the British did prod China periodically on the subject of a settlement of the Chinese-Tibetan border conflicts. In 1943, for example, Mr. Anthony Eden presented a memorandum to Mr. T. V. Soong, recalling Lord Curzon's words in 1921 to the effect that His Majesty's Government "would welcome any amicable arrangement which the Chinese Government might be disposed to make with Tibet whereby the latter recognized Chinese suzerainty in return for an agreed frontier and an undertaking to recognize Tibetan autonomy . . ."

In 1947, however, even the help of Britain's intervention disappeared. The Indian subcontinent south of Tibet and the Burma peninsula to the southeast gained independence, and the British no longer spoke with full authority in Asian affairs. The change was made suddenly and without the slow process of transition whereby four hundred million people might have eased painlessly from colonial rule to parliamentary democracy. Thus internal strife weakened and divided the new Asian countries. India inherited the fruits of the trade-seeking Younghusband Expedition. In Tibet the British flags at their Lhasa Mission and at the trade agencies were lowered; the Indian flag was raised. The British representative at Lhasa agreed to stay on at his post for a time, responsible to the new government in India. The small garrisons at the trade agencies, made up of Indian troops, now came under the command of their own free Indian Army.

India's leaders had little time to consider the rights and wrongs of their inherited position in Tibet. Their only hope for immediate progress in their country was a secure peace with all their neighbors. Thus the Indians, like the British, were anxious to maintain the peaceful status quo on their long northern frontier with Tibet.

To Tibetans also, the status quo was satisfactory—if it could be maintained. The Chinese, despite British pressure, had pushed their control relentlessly westward. Tibet's own little buffer of semiautonomous states, ruled by local chieftains and princes who owed their fealty to the Dalai Lama, had been absorbed into the Chinese provinces and their populations had been diluted by an influx of Chinese settlers. The de facto boundary between Chinese and Lhasan authority now was defined by the steep cliffs of the Yangtze, although less than fifty years ago Tatsienlu, two hundred miles to the east, had been a Tibetan border town. The Chinese "condolence mission," admitted into Lhasa after the Thirteenth Dalai Lama's death, had become a permanent official mission. After the Panchen Lama died in exile the Chinese supported a Panchen Incarnation "discovered" in China. In short, the Chinese were stubbornly holding onto any thread of possible influence and, as always, they were alert to any opportunity for reestablishing a foothold in independent Tibet. The British, when still a power in Asian affairs, had helped to keep the Chinese designs in check. The new government of India, however, was relatively without power and the country was torn by internal strife; few believed that the Indians would be able to influence the Chinese.

The Tibetans therefore tried direct negotiations with China. In the year of Indian independence the Tibetan government sent a mission to Nanking in the hope of reaching a definite settlement on the border demarcation and of securing recognition of Tibet's independence. Upon reaching Nanking the mission was refused access to the Minister for Foreign Affairs and was referred to the Commission for Tibetan and Mongolian Affairs. This Commission in turn referred the Tibetan group to the Chinese National Assembly. The Tibetan delegates were told that their requests had been forwarded to the National Assembly and that they would be welcome to attend its next session. They did attend—to be seated among the Chinese delegates and photographed; the next day they read in the illustrated Chinese newspapers that they were the elected delegates from the Tibetan area of China.

The Tibetans reacted philosophically to this new Chinese attempt to make their independence illegal. They were aware that the Nationalist government in China was failing fast and might expire altogether before any agreement could be reached. The Communist armies were making spectacular gains over Chiang Kai-shek's demoralized forces. The Tibetans turned their attention to the "Red Chinese." They remembered the prophecy of their Thirteenth Incarnation. They also remembered the brutality of Mao Tse-tung and Chu Teh. Tibetan workers now chanted anti-

Communist songs at their tasks. Monks intoned scriptures which might encourage divine intervention against the "Red" cause. In 1948 the Dalai Lama decreed a three-day prayer service in the great Jokhang Temple for the defeat of the Communists in the civil war. In the same year the Tibetan government sent a five-man trade delegation to Great Britain and the United States; the mission explored possibilities for direct trade that could provide sufficient dollar and sterling exchange to modernize Tibet's army.

As Tibet was forced increasingly into awareness of international affairs, the Dalai Lama's education on world problems was intensified. Despite his youth his opinion was sought on important decisions. Normally in Tibet major decisions were postponed during the Dalai Lama's minority; temporal matters were seldom so urgent that decisions could not wait. But the red tide was moving fast; decisions now were necessary, and the God-King who was still a boy began to share the burden of making them.

An important decision was made in the summer of 1949 when all the Chinese representatives were requested to leave Tibet. The request was made with the traditional courtesies, but a time limit of two weeks for the departure was enforced. The Chinese officials and their families were entertained before leaving. A traditional escort party bade the visitors farewell. Even a band to provide music for the beginning of the auspicious journey was on hand. The world press was confused by this sudden emergence of Tibet as a participant in international politics. The first reports speculated that a "Communist uprising" in Tibet had brought about the expulsion of the Nationalist representatives. Tibetan officials, however, finally explained to India's envoy that the Tibetan government feared the possibility of Communists being among the Chinese representatives.

China's acting president appealed to the Kashag to allow the representatives to remain in Lhasa, but the Tibetan government refused. The Chinese departed through India, and my father and I met a straggler or two from the ousted group on the trail when we entered Tibet a few months later.

The dismissal of the Chinese mission served two purposes for Tibet. First, with no Chinese representation in Lhasa, the victorious Communists could have no excuse to "take over" the Nationalist position there, and, second, the act was one more evidence of Tibet's independence. With the Chinese expelled, only two foreign representatives remained in Lhasa—the Indian and the Nepalese, good neighbors to the south and west.

The Tibetan government finished off its house cleaning by expelling a number of Tibetans who were suspected of Communist sympathies or who had been too long or too closely associated with the Chinese. Some of these went to the eastern border areas where they later joined Chinese Communists who were preparing for the invasion of Tibet.

This was the Tibet we visited in the fall of 1949—an independent Tibet, determined to safeguard its religion and its way of life, but by no means blind to the threatening dangers. My father and I were allowed to come, with cameras and microphones, because we might be useful. Tibet had no press. Her books were holy books. Her communications system was millions of prayer flags whose message was borne to the gods by the high winds of the plateau. Yet Tibet's story needed to be told. During the previous year, when the trade delegation went abroad, the Tibetan officials began to understand how little their country was known. We learned later that these officials were primarily responsible for convincing their government that my father should be allowed to come to Tibet.

Thus we were permitted to join that tiny and exclusive group of Westerners who have visited the roof of the world. We were received with warm hospitality and good will; we tried, through the press and radio, which were foreign to Tibet, to give our world a picture of the one place on the globe where religion came first in each man's life. We felt the need to explain to outsiders the intense desire of all Tibetans to maintain their national independence.

To Tibetans, their history for the past several centuries has centered on their struggle to maintain independence from China.

Thus, when the Communists drove Chiang Kai-shek's forces out of China late in 1949, the Tibetans expected no real change in the Chinese policy toward their country. They knew only that their traditional enemy, under the new regime, had more strength and fewer scruples than before.

In recent years Tibetans had relied on the British to check Chinese aggression. Now that India had inherited Britain's "special interest" in the mountain kingdom, Tibetans looked hopefully to Delhi for the same backing. They believed that the Chinese were waiting anxiously for an indication of India's attitude on the subject. The Chinese were aware that India was militarily weak but they knew that she had the backing of the great Western powers in any real emergency. Thus, if India insisted firmly on a "hands off" policy on Tibet, in much the same way Britain had done, the Chinese would listen respectfully. At the time the Chinese were mainly interested in Taiwan and in the Korean war. At the very least, therefore, a positive statement from India on Tibet would give the Tibetans more time to prepare for the attack they expected.

The Indian government, however, was one of the first to recognize the new regime in China. In addition, the Indian officials offered to help Communist China gain admittance to the United Nations. In fact, the Indians made such an effort to be friendly that the Chinese could have no reason to fear that they would take a firm stand against any Chinese action. Tibetan leaders felt that the Indians were acting without courage, and before long most Tibetans believed bitterly that India had deserted them.

The Tibetans, however, could not appreciate that the Indian government had little choice in the matter. India was contending with internal conflicts that threatened to push the whole subcontinent into utter chaos. Peace was essential to the country's very existence, and India, at the time, was ready to buy it at almost any price.

Moreover, still uppermost in the minds of the Indian leaders was the independence for which they had fought most of their lives and which they had won only recently. To admit now that they had to depend on the Western powers in the case of an emergency meant facing the fact that independence was only half won. Understandably such an admission was psychologically difficult. Even more difficult to face was the possibility of having to accept help from the erstwhile European colonialists against a brother Asian nation. Indeed, the Indian nationalists had considered that an important advantage of independence would be the chance it offered for friendly co-operation between all Asian nations in a common effort toward progress. Most Indians regarded the new China as Asian first and Communist second.

Finally the Indians were still dedicated sincerely to Gandhian principles. As leaders themselves in a new country, the Indian officials believed that they understood better the feeling of the new leaders in China. If the new China were treated as a criminal among nations, she might be inclined to act as one. Conversely, if the Chinese were given sympathy and understanding, they might be persuaded to co-operative behavior within the world community. Gandhi had always believed that one should look for and believe in the best of a person or a people. Most Indians were by no means naïve about Communism. In their position, however, they felt that there was everything to gain and nothing to lose—not only for themselves but for the rest of the world, including Tibet—in a friendly relationship with China. In short, they hoped to win the co-operation of the Chinese, not because of Communism, but in spite of it.

The Tibetans had no such hopes. They remembered the warning of the Thirteenth Incarnation and the brutality of the Communists who had entered eastern Tibet only fifteen years before. Early in January 1950, only a few days after India recognized Communist China, General Chu Teh, Vice-Chairman of the People's Republic, announced that the "liberation of Tibet" was a forthcoming assignment for the army.

India immediately asked for an explanation. Peking assured Delhi, however, that any problems between China and Tibet would be solved solely by peaceful negotiation.

At the same time, however, the Peking radio beamed at Lhasa

was carrying on a propaganda campaign intended to reduce the Tibetan will to resist military attack. The Tibetans were told to remember what had happened to them when the Communist armies of the "long march" had entered their country. They were informed that the People's Army was now much stronger and could take the "roof of the world" with ease.

Simultaneously a Communist army was pushing westward rapidly. In March of 1950 Tatsienlu, in the buffer area between China and Tibet, was occupied. Thereafter one local government after another was inundated by the Chinese Communists. More than ten thousand laborers were working day and night to improve the roads. Bridge steel was being moved in barges up-river from Shanghai. Special troops were being acclimatized by months-long training periods at high altitudes where they also learned to subsist on *tsamba*, the barley-flour staple of Tibet.

And if these indications of the Chinese intentions were not enough, there were the border incidents. Chinese troops frequently ambushed Tibetan patrols and shot to kill. If the Tibetans returned the fire, the Chinese accused the Tibetans of an unprovoked assault. Once the Chinese troops crossed the border and attacked a Tibetan border post. After killing the men at the post the Chinese removed the arms and radio equipment. When Tibetan army units tried to recapture their post, the Chinese used mountain guns and bazookas to drive them back. Meanwhile the Peking radio was accusing the Tibetans of barbarism and banditry.

Although the Chinese used the border incidents in cynical propaganda exercises, they presumably meant the attacks primarily as a probe and test of the Tibetan defenses. Also, in these small engagements, they frequently employed the latest types of military equipment, evidently with the idea of impressing the Tibetans with the futility of resistance. In any case, the mass army moved westward relentlessly. Ten-wheeled trucks in mile-long lines were used over improved sections of the new road; beyond the improved portions supplies were dropped by plane.

The Tibetans, understandably, were becoming panicky. The facts were told to the Indian government, which again asked

Peking for a clarification of Chinese intentions. The Chinese still insisted that they would solve the Tibet problem by peaceful negotiation and not by military force. Because India's policy was to maintain friendly relations with Communist China, India could not assume evil intention until China proved it by evil deeds. Moreover, in May of 1950, Peking radio called upon the Dalai Lama to submit to the "peaceful liberation" of his country. In June 1950, however, Mao Tse-tung stated publicly that, while some demobilization of the army was taking place, "sufficient manpower will be guaranteed for the liberation of Taiwan and Tibet." By now, even in that lost corner of the world, the Chinese military build-up was becoming difficult to hide. Nevertheless, anyone who listened to the Tibetan side of the story was accused by the Chinese of being a stooge of the imperialist warmongers. When questions about the Tibet situation were asked in the Indian parliament, India came in for sharp abuse from the Chinese press.

Oddly enough, the Tibetans had equal difficulty in making Westerners listen to their story. The consensus of armchair military strategists was that the Chinese forces, no matter how large, would become bogged down in the wild Tibetan passes where even the small Tibetan army could shoot them to pieces.

Thus the Tibetans slowly realized with dismay that they were completely alone in their predicament. The Indian government knew the facts of the situation but could do nothing without reversing its policy toward China. The Western nations were deluding themselves. Nothing was left for the Tibetans except a reappraisal of their own fighting forces.

Although individual Tibetans can be, and are, tough fighters, they have been historically apathetic toward organized belligerence. In a Buddhist theocracy the professional soldier naturally rates low. Aside from the two commanders-in-chief, one a monk and one a thoroughly non-military nobleman, the highest Tibetan military rank was the *depon*. He commanded a "regiment" of five hundred men. The *depon* was only a fourth-grade official who had neither military experience nor aspirations. His *depon*-ship was merely a step to some superior, and non-military, official position. No higher place for him existed in the military organization. He had no co-ordinating influence above him and no ability or incentive to work out a plan of co-operation with the other *depons* on his own level.

Below a *depon*, two *rupons* commanded two hundred and fifty men each in a regiment. These men were the real officers of the army. They were trained and experienced. Often they were older than the *depons*. Some *rupons* rose from the ranks. They had often shown outstanding ability. Some had been given training under the British at Gyantse. The *rupons* could fight and they commanded the respect of their men. They lacked, however, either the authority or the temerity ever to question their superiors.

The Tibetan private soldier was called *makme*. Prior to 1910, when Tibet's whole army numbered some three thousand, recruits were drawn only from certain feudal estates with a military tradition. An estate contributed soldier material as a tax; the number of men was set according to acreage owned by the noble. Nevertheless, morale in the army was good and reasonable efficiency was maintained. After 1912, however, when the Chinese revolution provided an opportunity for Tibet to drive out all the Chinese forces in her territory, the need to expand the Tibetan army grew. As World War II approached, Tibet had some nine thousand men under arms. Most of them had seen action in sporadic small engagements along the eastern frontier. The new regiments, both regular and militia, suffered under incompetent *depons*, poor living conditions, and lack of equipment and training. The morale and efficiency, therefore, were low.

Even so, the loyalty of the army was never in question. Every Tibetan soldier, from the joint commanders-in-chief to the lowest *makme*, realized that armies were not of first importance. A man would fight to defend his shrine and his home; an army would fight to defend the home of the gods. But one built up merit with prayers, not pistols. Faced with an emergency, most Tibetans would reach for a prayer wheel first. Lack of discipline was not the reason that a Tibetan soldier was permitted to miss drill for a turn around the Gora Path (holy walk) of the nearest monastery; it was a question of agreed values.

A handful of enlightened Tibetan officials, however, knew that much of the world did not accept these values. In 1936 the presence of Communist marauders on Tibet's eastern frontier prompted the Tibetan government to ask for military advice from Great Britain. A military mission visited Lhasa and studied the Tibetan army. The mission recommended the formation of a brigade with headquarters at Lhasa. The various units would be rotated for training under Indian Army instructors at the Brigade Headquarters. Modern weapons were to be procured through India. By the time these recommendations made their slow way through the Kashag and the National Assembly, and the request had gone out to the government of India, World War II was in progress and neither instructors nor arms could be obtained.

Tibet's army therefore remained unchanged. The officers continued to be young nobles of no experience. The men continued to serve unpaid, billeted in tents of nomads or huts of peasants, while they fought their small border engagements and tried to hold the frontier line. In 1949 a few military moves were made to match the diplomatic move of expelling Chinese officials. A Defense Minister was appointed—once again an inexperienced, although senior, official; troops were given regular pay; new recruits were put into training at Lhasa; the import of arms and ammunition from India grew from a trickle to a small stream.

For a time the Tibetan people were proud of the military improvements and they had much confidence in their new "modern" army. The officials, however, could not be deluded that the country was adequately prepared to stand off a Chinese invasion. While long convoys of Chinese trucks headed west with cargoes of the latest weapons, Tibetan recruits lacked the ammunition for elementary target practice. In the Kashag and National Assembly discussions on the situation went on far into the nights.

In May 1950 a three-man Communist delegation arrived in Lhasa from Sining. Tension throughout Tibet increased sharply. The delegates tried to "sell" Communism to the Tibetan officials, but they were not successful. Moreover, they bore no credentials from Peking. Thus, after a few fruitless talks, they were sent back to Sining. The Tibetans breathed easier. Nevertheless the delegation did spark the officials to action.

The Tibetans felt that the time had come to negotiate with China in a final effort to prevent actual invasion. Most of the officials now realized that outside help was unlikely, but they could not resist making another attempt to get it. Delegations, therefore, were organized to be sent to China, Nepal, India, Great Britain, and the U.S.A.

Unfortunately no one in Lhasa checked on whether the delegations would be received in all these countries. As soon as the Tibetan plans became known, Peking Radio began to speak loudly against the delegations. The Chinese took the attitude that Tibet was in no position to send its own representatives to foreign governments. Thus the Chinese called the delegations "illegal" and stated that reception of the delegates would indicate "hostile intention." The threat could have meaning only for India. Nevertheless, the Western powers declined to receive missions at this time and the delegates did not leave Lhasa.

The Chinese, however, did encourage the Tibetan mission intended for Peking to continue. The trouble was that now the Tibetan delegates no longer wanted to go. It was clear that the delegates to Peking would not be accepted as representatives of a free and independent nation. Instead, the mission would become merely a committee to receive a statement of Chinese terms. In the hope of still being able to negotiate with the Chinese, therefore, the delegates stated that they wanted to hold talks in neutral territory. They suggested Hong Kong. The British, however, refused the Tibetans entry permits for Hong Kong. The delegates, who had left Lhasa before final plans were made, lingered in India and tried to obtain Hong Kong visas. The Chinese continued to press the delegates to go to Peking. Finally a seeming compromise was reached. A newly appointed Chinese ambassador to India arrived in Delhi and was empowered to talk to the Tibetan delegates. The discussions began.

In Lhasa the officials had been watching these developments with increasing dismay. The hope of preventing invasion was fading, and the alarm spread to the people. Prayers were intensified. More incense was burned. The holy walks were crowded with prostrate pilgrims.

At the same time, however, defense preparations were stepped up. Levies of fierce Khambas from the eastern districts were recruited to bolster the frontier force. Stocks of grain were moved from monastery strongholds to eastern outposts. The meager communications equipment was dispersed among half-trained technicians. Ammunition was hoarded.

The Tibetans had a vague military plan. Their available forces were split between Nagchuka, north of Lhasa, and Chamdo near the eastern frontier. About five thousand troops were stationed at each of these centers. In addition, small mobile units were deployed along the northern and eastern borders to watch for Chinese infiltration.

The Defense Minister and the monk commander-in-chief had their headquarters in Nagchuka, which dominated the main caravan route from Chinese-controlled Tsinghai Province in Inner Tibet to the north. Although this route was considered the least likely for invasion, the Tibetans regarded it as the most dangerous. In Tsinghai the Chinese had organized a "provisional government" for Tibet under the young Panchen Lama; the most important of the Panchen's followers shared his exile and were under Communist domination. If the Chinese should send this provisional government into Tibet with an army, the route through Nagchuka would be their likely choice. By using this route the force could bypass Lhasa and continue on to Shigatse, site of the Panchen's home monastery of Tashi Lhunpo, which would be the Panchen's seat of government.

The most likely invasion route, however, was from the east through Chamdo. If the Chinese did attack from this quarter, the Nagchuka forces would move east and north to form a defense line west of the Jyekundo-Riwoche area. The Chamdo garrison troops had the most difficult assignment. In addition to defending the important frontier town they had to protect the southern fork of the main track to Lhasa. If they were pushed out of Chamdo, they would retreat westward along a difficult road through high passes toward Lho Dzong, where they hoped to have the backing of the Tibetan force from Nagchuka to help defend the track to Lhasa.

Although no better alternative was available, the plan had a serious flaw. The north prong of the main trail to Lhasa ran in a north-south direction from Jyekundo in Chinese-occupied Inner Tibet. It passed through Riwoche and joined with the Lhasa road west of the high mountains back of Chamdo. It was a relatively easy road. Thus if the Chinese entered Tibet along this road as well, they would reach Lho Dzong long before the retreating garrison from Chamdo could get there. The Tibetan army would be cut in half. Only the Nagchuka garrison would be left to block the Lhasa track. The Chamdo troops would have to retreat south. They would enter Assam in India at Sadiya, make their way to Gangtok in Sikkim, re-enter Tibet, and return to the front through Lhasa. Such an expedition would be fantastically difficult in those violent mountains and would take many weeks or even months. It represented last-measure desperation.

If the Chinese attacked through Nagchuka and along both prongs of the Lhasa road, as they were capable of doing, the Tibetans had no plan. Defeat would be inevitable. Outside strategy experts were still saying that the Chinese would not make the attack because the Tibetans could cut the invading forces to ribbons in the mountain passes. It was true that the Tibetans could ambush and inflict many casualties on the aggressor, but a well-armed enemy who was willing to take heavy losses would have to win eventually.

Meanwhile the presence of the Tibetan mission in Delhi, negotiating with the Chinese ambassador, was having one hopeful effect. By working so hard to prevent a Chinese attack on their country the Tibetan delegates began to convince some Indian officials that such an attack must be imminent. Questions in the Indian parliament and press became more pointed. This called for much abuse of India in the Chinese press, but on the official level the Chinese continued to give the Indian government unofficial assurances that they would not use military force in Tibet. At the same time Indian officials were projecting the Chinese viewpoint on the crossing of the 38th parallel by United Nations forces in Korea. The Indian government was also pressing for China's admission into the U.N. In return for this help Tibetans hoped that India would receive Chinese favors that would benefit Tibet. India's own security required—just as it did under the British—a demilitarized Tibet as a buffer. If India could win such a concession, Tibetans might retain at least some of their freedom.

In India the Chinese were exceedingly polite to the Tibetan delegates. Gradually, however, the delegates realized that the Chinese had no intention of negotiating. The Chinese still insisted that the Tibetan mission must go to Peking. Finally, by the end of September 1950, the talks ended inconclusively. The Tibetans would have to accept invasion of their country or accede to the demand for further talks in Peking. The delegates felt that, once in the enemy stronghold, they would have no bargaining position whatever and the Chinese mask of politeness would drop. Nevertheless talking was preferable to fighting. The British now allowed the Tibetan delegates visas for transit through Hong Kong to Peking. The Tibetans proceeded to Calcutta where they reluctantly prepared for the trip to China.

And then the blow fell. While the Tibetan delegation waited in Calcutta for the chance to talk peace, and while the Chinese ambassador in Delhi was assuring Indian officials that his country had only peaceful intentions, Tibet was attacked.

CHAPTER VII

Attack

Words are bubbles of water;
Deeds are drops of gold—or blood.
—TIBETAN PROVERB

ON OCTOBER 7, 1950, forty thousand troops of the 18th and 62nd Chinese armies crossed the eastern border and engaged the brave little Tibetan army. It seemed now that the Chinese Communists had never intended to do anything else. They had made their elaborate plans, organized the military build-up, and had moved in to attack the moment they were ready. The assurances to the Indians and the pretense at negotiation were merely talk.

The attack was made at three points simultaneously along Tibet's eastern frontier. The smallest enemy force—but still larger than the entire Tibetan army—entered at the southeast corner of Tibet to occupy Yakalo. Another and larger prong crossed the river further to the north but still south of Chamdo. The small Tibetan garrison in this area—a few hundred men at Markham—was soon overwhelmed. Finally the largest Chinese spearhead came from Dege and was thrown at Chamdo itself.

The Tibetan resistance could be described only as ferocious. The tough Khamba levies with their great warrior tradition were especially effective. They were defending their homelands and they inflicted such severe losses on the enemy that the Chinese were at first stopped in their tracks.

The vastly superior fire power of the Chinese, however, rather than the size of their forces, soon overcame Tibetan resistance. On a purely military basis, in the face of such a massive assault, the Chamdo garrison should have fallen back immediately toward a more easily defended spot, perhaps even as far as Lho Dzong. If they had done so, however, they would have abandoned the Khambas, the Kham lands, and the largest Kham monastery to the enemy. This would have alienated the touchy Khambas and might even have turned them against the Tibetan army. Thus the decision was made to hold off the enemy as long as possible at Chamdo. When the time for retreat did come, it was the fierce Khambas who held off the Chinese while the government troops withdrew.

Unfortunately at this moment the Tibetans received the news that they dreaded most. Still another Chinese force had entered Tibet from the north and was moving quickly against little opposition on Riwoche. Under these circumstances, according to the plan, the Chamdo garrison should have made its way south, entered India, and returned to Tibet by the southern trade route to Lhasa. Panic, however, gripped the Tibetan forces. The troops took a chance on reaching the junction with the Riwoche track before the Chinese. There was a scramble for transportation. Ngapho Shape, the recently appointed commissioner-general for Kham, took the best horses for himself and for lesser officials with their families, friends, and possessions—some three thousand people in all—and fled toward Lhasa. The troops had to destroy their arsenal, and many began to retreat on foot. Most of the people who remained in Chamdo gathered what possessions they could carry and sought refuge in the local monastery. Some of the remaining Khamba levies, for whom there was no transport and now not even leadership, turned in bitterness to looting and wanton destruction.

The retreating Tibetans, of course, did not have a chance. The Chinese reached the junction two days ahead of the most forward elements of the Tibetans from Chamdo. A messenger from the west brought the news to the Chamdo party. The Shape Ngapho sought refuge in a nearby monastery. He had already asked Lhasa for permission to surrender and had been refused. Nevertheless when Chinese troops, with some disgruntled Khambas acting as guides and interpreters, arrived at the monastery, Ngapho Shape did surrender. He returned with the enemy to Chamdo to negotiate terms.

It is clear now that many men in the Shape's party were not in accord with the decision to surrender. On the other hand, these men were not in the habit of questioning the decision of any high official. Thus they accepted Ngapho Shape's order to lay down their arms and return to their homes. In retrospect, further resistance plainly was useless. General Dege Sey also was given orders to fight on at Markham, but he too surrendered; he stated, however, that the decision was his own and that he had made it in order to save the lives of his men.

As for the troops themselves, they were full of resistance. Given a semblance of competent leadership, they would have added their own lives to the heavy casualties of the first frontier engagements. Untrained civilian officials, however, did not constitute adequate military leadership. The troops were bewildered by the debacle on the eastern front, and most of them obeyed orders; they turned over their arms and went home. Others, disarmed but still determined, made their way over little-known passes and joined with forces who were lightly holding the main track two hundred and fifty miles east of Lhasa.

At this point the Chinese armies paused. The initial phase of the invasion, although costly in casualties, had been a success. Less than two weeks after crossing the river they had taken Chamdo. By October 22, 1950, they were in control of Lho Dzong where the Salween River cuts across the main track and is the major obstacle on the road to Lhasa. Nevertheless, at noon on October 25, 1950, the Peking government released an official announcement to the press which read: "Units of the Chinese People's Army have been ordered to cross over into Tibet in order to free three million Tibetans from Western Imperialist oppression and to consolidate national defenses on China's western borders."

In Lhasa, meanwhile, the attack, although expected, still came as a shock. The officials had tried so hard to find some alternative to invasion. Even after the assault began they hoped to find a formula for placating the Chinese while still retaining a semblance of independence for their country. Thus, with the idea of giving the Chinese a face-saving device in case negotiation was still possible, the Tibetans did not broadcast the story of their plight to the rest of the world.

In India, however, news of the trouble in Tibet began to leak out. On October 12, several days after forty thousand Chinese troops were well within Tibetan territory, a Calcutta paper carried a months-old garbled version of border incidents. The article served the purpose of arousing Indian public opinion and of focusing Indian attention on the Tibet situation. The questions in the Indian parliament now became sharply pointed; the government could answer only that the Chinese still promised peace in Tibet. The Indian press speculated daily on the possibilities of Chinese military aggression in Tibet but generally followed the lead of Western military experts who still maintained that the Chinese army could get nowhere in the mountain kingdom. The Chinese ambassador in Delhi had no comment to make on the situation other than platitudes about the peace-loving Chinese people and the warmongering of the Western imperialists. Even the Tibetan delegates, still in Calcutta waiting passage to Peking, knew nothing of the real situation in their country.

Thus the Peking announcement of October 25, 1950, caught everyone outside Tibet off guard. In India the Chinese ambassador was in Agra to see the Taj Mahal and other cultural monuments; he had no statement to make on the press reports. The Indian government, unable to get an official version of the facts from their representatives in either Lhasa or Peking, framed a blunt query to the Chinese government, expressing "surprise and concern" at the reports. Finally India's Peking ambassador reported that the Chinese had given the military "order to advance," but he added that he could not find out if anything had really happened. On October 28, 1950, three full weeks after the invasion had taken place, Delhi received confirmation from the Indian representative in Lhasa.

The confirmation carried reasonably up-to-date information of the tragic situation. The press in India and in the West now reversed itself on Tibet. Instead of flippancy or indifference the news reports contained a note of hysteria. Rumors were wild, and for a while the "front" was said to be at the outskirts of Lhasa. Unhappily the American press was one of the worst offenders. The most tragic aspect of the free-press attitude was that it belittled the gallantry of the Tibetan defenders. For many months the Tibetans had been using every means within their power to make outsiders understand the true situation. No one had listened to them. The Chinese, whose propaganda effort was to belittle the whole attack, admitted that they had inflicted four thousand casualties on the Tibetans at Chamdo alone. These Tibetans fought with World War I equipment and a shortage of ammunition against a vastly superior force armed with modern automatic weapons, flame throwers, bazookas, and artillery. They fought magnificently and died defending their homes and their way of life. Yet in effect the free press, rather than admit an error in judgment, denied to the Tibetans the heroism they had proven. The denial helped the Chinese propaganda claim that the Tibetans jubilantly welcomed the "liberation."

The Indian officials, however, were not affected by the Chinese propaganda claim, but they were rendered helpless by their official policy that accepted the Chinese at face value. For days Peking did not bother to answer Delhi's blunt query on the Tibet situation. During this period the Chinese were presumably studying the world reaction to their aggression and deciding on a line to take; there was an almost complete blackout of news on Tibet either on their radio or in their press. When they did answer Delhi's note, they were scarcely polite. Their reply stated flatly that what went on in Tibet was entirely a Chinese internal affair and "no foreign interference shall be tolerated." India was accused of being merely a tool of "foreign influence hostile to China." Delhi replied immediately and firmly, to "categorically repudiate" the allegation that India was a tool of anyone and to repeat that she had no imperialist designs on Tibet. The Chinese did not reply for weeks; when they did the note, in effect, told India to keep her nose out of China's internal affairs.

Chinese news media suddenly began to mention the subject of Tibet again, but the propaganda line was changed. The Chinese army was still in the role of liberators, but now the army had entered Tibet in answer to the great need and demand of the Tibetan people to be freed of foreign oppression and to reunite with the motherland. Prime Minister Nehru stated publicly that it was not at all clear who were the oppressors from whom the Chinese were liberating the Tibetans. The British radio technician, Robert Ford, who was captured by the Chinese at Chamdo, was the only Westerner in the entire area. Nevertheless, Peking Radio stories on Tibet featured mainly the wild enthusiasm with which the Chinese "saviors" were welcomed by the Tibetans. The radio reports from other Communist countries described the corrupt and vicious rule of the Tibetan monk officials. And, as always, anyone who even tried to hear the Tibetan side of the story was an imperialist warmonger.

In Tibet itself, however, the Chinese did not waste words on such subjects as "popular demand" or "the liberation of the proletariat." They did their talking at the council table with Ngapho Shape and the officials who had been captured with him. They would make their deal with the Tibetan government; the Tibetan people would do as they were told.

While the talks between the Chinese and the Tibetans captured at Chamdo were going on, the government officials in Lhasa, frightened and uninformed, thought of the United Nations. They asked for India's diplomatic help in presenting a U.N. appeal. This put India in an awkward position. The Indian government was still bound by its policy of open friendship with the Chinese Communists, who had just told India sharply not to interfere in the Tibetan problem. The Indians, therefore, hedged; they refused to sponsor the U.N. appeal but pointed out that Tibet was free to submit an appeal in her own behalf.

Nevertheless, the Indian government was still pressing China for a peaceful solution to the Tibet problem. At this late date the idea of a peaceful solution may have been wishful thinking, but the Indian officials evidently wanted to give the Chinese every opportunity to behave decently.

Moreover, at the moment there was peace in Tibet—even if it was the peace of defeat. The Chinese were holding off the final push to Lhasa. They occupied strategic positions in eastern Tibet; they were improving roads and bringing up supplies, but they were poised to move again at will. A Tibetan in India told the press, "China can do what she likes. Tibet is a small slice of bread for which a double-edged sword has been sharpened carefully on both sides." Indians were sensitive to the fact that the sword had been sharpened while Peking was giving Delhi assurances of peaceful negotiation. Nevertheless, the situation in Tibet was far from clear and India was understandably confused.

In the rest of the world confusion about Tibet was even worse. Western military experts were still of the opinion that troop movement over the Tibetan passes in October was impossible. They were skeptical of the idea that whole armies of men could fight battles at altitudes in which the breath comes in gasps and the heart is strained to the bursting point.

To bolster the skeptical opinion the bewildered Tibetan delegates in India went ahead with their plans to proceed to Peking. They had received no other orders. They felt that perhaps the invasion talk was "propaganda stuff." When reporters asked them what they would talk about in Peking, if the confirmed invasion were true, they said they were trying to get in touch with the Chinese ambassador in Delhi to ask him what the "liberation of Tibet" meant. When clarified, this would be the subject of their discussion.

The Indian government meanwhile was trying to contact Lhasa, but without success. Rumors from Tibet said that the people in Lhasa were panic-stricken and that the Dalai Lama was preparing to flee. On November 5, 1950, communication between Delhi and Lhasa was re-established. The Dalai Lama was still at the Potala, but transportation was being organized for his possible flight. The situation in the Tibetan capital was tense, and the National Assembly was sitting in constant session. The Tibetan government sent orders to their delegation in India to cancel the Peking trip as useless. On November 8, Lhasa cabled an appeal direct to the U. N. Secretary-General.

Two days later, in the Indian press, a news item from Kalimpong quoted a Peking radio broadcast to the effect that China and Tibet had reached agreement and that a cease-fire order had been given. No other details were supplied, and no mention was made of who had signed the agreement on behalf of Tibet. Thus the Kalimpong rumor probably did not affect the attitude of the United Nations toward the Tibet appeal. Nevertheless the appeal had all the odds against it from the beginning. Tibet not only had no representative at the U.N.; the peacefully isolated religious state had no representatives anywhere. Her best hope was for Indian backing, and indeed some of the powers, including the U.S.A., announced their decision to follow India's lead. The Press Trust of India, in analyzing the U.N. opinion, said that most of the delegations, including Nationalist China, recognized Chinese suzerainty in Tibet. Pakistan already had put it on record that the whole affair was between Tibet and China. India, it was understood, would support the appeal to the extent of condemning the use of force as endangering world peace.

The U.N. member nations were preoccupied with the Korean war, which now was reaching a crisis. After the initial U.N. successes the Chinese Communist "volunteers" had come in and the U.N. had suffered disastrous reverses. President Truman had visited Wake Island for his meeting with General MacArthur; there was talk of complete withdrawal of U.N. forces after a large American contingent had had to be air-lifted out of a cut-off position. A delegation from Communist China had been invited to the U.N. to present a complaint against U.S. aggression as supposedly evidenced by 7th Fleet activities around Taiwan. Observers generally agreed, however, that the underlying importance of the delegation's visit was the opportunity it presented to reach some understanding on the extent of Chinese troop participation in the Korean war. Attention was focused on these negotiations.

The Tibet problem was secondary. A *Manchester Guardian* editorial commented: "By gratuitously invading Tibet the Chinese would seem to have provided the western powers with an important additional bargaining counter . . ."

Tibet's appeal did, however, find a sponsor in El Salvador, who introduced the complaint on November 18 and asked that it be placed on the Assembly agenda.

A few days later the Chinese Communist delegates, led by General Wu, arrived. They presented their credentials on November 24. On the same day the Steering Committee of the United Nations decided to defer consideration of whether to place the Tibet appeal on the agenda. Britain and India, it was reported, had asked for a postponement; the Indian delegates said that they understood China and Tibet were working on an agreement.

The Tibetan government, of course, was not negotiating with the Chinese invaders. On the contrary, because of the emergency the Dalai Lama was granted his full powers in a special ceremony. One of his first acts was to appoint a three-man delegation to go to the U.N. in personal support of the appeal. The delegation was in India on its way to Lake Success when the reversed policy became known.

What India gained by instigating the reversed policy was not clear. No one doubted that her efforts to preserve peace were sincere. In her efforts, however, she sacrificed a peaceful neighbor and, in effect, condoned aggression. Most Tibetans felt that India had betrayed them once again and henceforth viewed with suspicion all policies of India's government. Even the Chinese, who gained the most from India's stand, seemed unappreciative; their press and some of their official notes continued to express what amounted to contempt for India's policies. At the time India's Mr. Krishna Menon commented, "They (the Chinese Communists) appear to be very angry with us, but we must not be angry with them . . ."

Finally, India lost a bit of the high respect she had won from the Western democracies. Admittedly, at the time, India's reversed policy on Tibet was convenient to the West. Most of the Western nations had committed themselves to following India's lead on the subject. The fact that India, in effect, took the side of the Chinese Communists with regard to Tibet enabled the Indian U.N. delegates to negotiate with the visiting Chinese military commission on the subject of Korea. India's Sir Benegal Rao was the only non-Communist U.N. member to hold private conversations with Chinese General Wu. President Truman, in a press conference, revealed that the conversations concerned Chinese intervention in the Korean war. Nevertheless, when India abandoned Tibet, the suspicion did arise in many parts of the Western world that India was not so vehement against aggression and colonialism when committed by Asians or Communists.

The fact was, however, that India was motivated chiefly by the danger to world peace from the Korean war. At the time the war threatened seriously to become a world-wide holocaust, the center of which would be Asia. India was working desperately to keep the war from spreading.

Moreover, at this point openly accusing Communist China of aggression in Tibet could result in a direct threat to India's own security. The conflict between India and Pakistan over Kashmir had not been settled, and Kashmir's district of Ladakh had a long common frontier with western Tibet. The Ladakhis were Lamaist and economically as well as ethnically were closer to the Tibetans. Furthermore, the independent state of Nepal, which shared five hundred miles of Tibet's southern borders and acted as a buffer between India and Tibet, was suffering internal unrest; Communist maps already showed Nepal as part of China. Thus, if India provoked China on the subject of Tibet, the Chinese might retaliate by "liberating" Ladakh and Nepal. In that case India would no longer have the Himalayan barrier to protect her frontier.

The isolated Tibetans, however, knew little of the infinite complexities that made international affairs so difficult. "We understand that the United Nations have decided to stop aggression whenever it takes place," the Tibetan appeal had stated. On December 4, 1950, the Tibetan officials sent a further appeal to the U.N., expressing concern that the discussion of their plight had been set aside. They repeated that they would abide by any U.N. decision on their problem. The Tibetan delegation, however, was told to wait in India. The Tibetan officials realized that their cause was lost.

The Chinese Communists also realized that they were not going to have outside interference. Peking Radio now boasted openly that reinforcements were pouring into Tibet "in a never-ending stream." The Chinese began to enter Tibet at other points along the border. A few Tibetan garrisons in the northwest part of the country were taken by Chinese who came down from Sinkiang. Southern outposts along India's Assam border also fell to the Communists.

On December 7, 1950, Lhasa learned from Peking Radio that "peace talks" were going on. The Tibetan government, at first incredulous, could only conclude that talks were being conducted in Tibet's name by the officials captured and returned to Chamdo. The situation was further confused next day when a party of three arrived from the Kumbum Monastery in Sining. Leader of the party was Takster Rimpoche, older brother of the Dalai Lama and a high incarnation lama of the monastery. He was accompanied by two other lamas. The Chinese Communists apparently believed that they had successfully indoctrinated the brother. Who could better place their terms before the Dalai?

The terms they brought were tempting on their face value. The shrewd Tibetan officials, however, were not taken in by them. In any case, the lama emissary sought private audience with his brother and, according to another brother, immediately dropped his Communist-tutored front. He evidently spoke at bitter length of his experiences under Communist rule. The other two lama emissaries were kept out of the way while the brother talked daily with the officials. A course of action was planned.

The plan accepted the fact that Tibetans would be left with little but their faith and its symbol, the Dalai Lama. Without him, however, the enemy's conquest could never be complete. He must escape, therefore, to a place of safety before negotiations con-

tinued. The Chinese Communists had asked for a reply to their
terms by December 16, 1950. A delegation was to proceed to
China overland through Kham. The Tibetans were in no position
to refuse, but they had the temerity not to be hurried despite the
overwhelming military power which they knew was poised to
strike again. The National Assembly deliberated and settled upon
a negotiating delegation which would leave only after the Dalai
Lama was installed in a safe place. His emissary brother and
other family members would accompany him.

Before he left the young God-King ordered the release of all
political prisoners. Intrigues of the past were forgotten in the new
urgency. All Tibetans now stood together to resist, with faith if
not with arms, the godless invader.

Early in the morning of December 18, 1950, the boy ruler
secluded himself for prayers and meditation. Then he took tea
with his officials. Some were to accompany him; others were to
remain behind to keep the machinery of government going as
long as possible. The Dalai Lama's final cup of tea was left on the
low table untouched. This was a symbol meaning that he would
return.

The destination of the caravan was Yatung, just inside Tibet's
southern border, not far from the Natu La which led into the
Indian border state of Sikkim. Rumors said that the Dalai Lama
would seek asylum in India. In Kalimpong the Tibetan residents
had a throne prepared for his reception. The Dalai chose, however, to stay inside Tibet's borders, for the time being at least.
All along the route of the sixteen-day journey throngs of his
worshiping subjects lined the way and prostrated themselves in
his path. Blessing his subjects from his sedan chair, he may have
remembered his journey to Lhasa as a small boy. His people's
tears then had been tears of joy. There was joy even now at his
presence, but there was also fear of an unknown future.

Blizzards swept across the plateau as the caravan journeyed
south. The Dalai Lama used his sedan chair mainly when entering
a settlement where he would be called upon to accept official
greetings. On much of the journey he rode a horse or mule, as did

his family and the officials who accompanied him. Often he would dismount and walk for long distances. If the Dalai Lama walked everyone in the caravan also walked; thus even the most pampered officials arrived quite fit at the Chumbi Valley headquarters of the district governor. Here a provisional capital was set up. The Dalai Lama occupied the governor's house, and the officials were quartered in the houses of nearby peasants. Some families were sent on into India to ease the housing problem. All of the valley approaches were guarded by the hand-picked troops who had formed the escort party for the caravan. A courier service to Lhasa was established. The government-in-exile settled down to business.

The negotiating party now could depart for Peking. Tibet's only real bargaining power lay in the fact that the young Dalai Lama stood at the border. If he crossed the border the heart of the people would go with him. The devotion he commanded was unquestioning. He could lead his subjects where no army could force them to go. If the Communists did not know this they would have to learn it before they could expect to dominate the mountain kingdom.

The Dalai Lama moved to the nearby Dungkar Monastery, where he lived in semi-isolation. He spent hours each day in meditation and prayer. Tibet was quiet as winter closed the passes and isolated the holy country once again. But it was now a pseudo-isolation. Inside the borders were godless foreigners, heavily armed. Altar fires burned in every peasant's hut and nomad's tent; in the smoky firelight prayer wheels turned. The people waited in fear.

CHAPTER VIII

The Communist Panchen Lama

A tiger's skin clothes and identifies him,
A man's robes only clothe him.

—TIBETAN PROVERB

WHEN the spring of 1951 cleared the passes of deep snow, the Chinese did not strike again as the Tibetans feared. Instead the invaders were content merely to consolidate their position. They concentrated on building and improving roads. They did capture a number of other small garrisons, but only when they were sure that the Tibetans would not resist strenuously. The Chinese troops did not loot or kill. Captured Tibetan soldiers were given a short indoctrination course in Communism but then were sent home, often with a silver piece for traveling expenses.

Thus the fear of violence in Tibet slowly subsided. Nevertheless tension mounted over the question of the terms that the Han now would impose on the mountain kingdom. As official negotiator, the Kashag realistically appointed Ngapho Shape who had been with the Communists ever since the fall of Chamdo. Two minor officials and the two commanders-in-chief were sent from Tibet to join the Shape in Peking and make up the negotiating committee. These delegates were politely received in Peking; they were given an elaborate reception. They even dined with Mao Tse-tung. Also, the Tibetans saw that the Chinese were more than a little nervous about the situation in Tibet. For this reason the Chinese were willing to make a few minor concessions, but they refused to bargain over the terms. Within a week the delegates realized the futility of further negotiation and they signed the treaty.

The most important provisions of the treaty—and the worst ones for the Tibetans—concerned the rights and privileges of the Chinese forces in occupied Tibet. The provisions spelled out complete military domination of Tibet by the Communists. Even the Tibetan army was to be "reorganized by stages into the People's Liberation Army and become a part of the national defense forces of the People's Republic of China." The provisions were a shock to the delegates, who knew that they would arouse great antagonism in Tibet. Finally, therefore, the military aspects of the treaty —with the exception of the terms dealing with the Tibetan army —were made into a separate agreement that was kept secret for many months.

Although the delegates argued vehemently to prevent Communist military domination of their country, they still regarded the matter as temporal and therefore of lesser importance than religious affairs. The Chinese in their terms, however, also interfered with Tibetan religious tradition, and on this point the delegates objected so violently that the Chinese compromised. The point concerned the status of the Panchen Lama.

The boy whom the Chinese recognized as the Ninth Panchen had been chosen in China by a pro-Chinese Panchen follower whom the Tibetans regarded as a traitor. The traditional procedure for identifying the incarnation had not been followed. Moreover, Panchen followers in Tibet had identified a true incarnation, even though this child was still studying and had not been officially proclaimed. Nevertheless, the Chinese had trained their Panchen as a Communist, and they wanted to ensure that he would acquire political authority in Tibet. Thus the original treaty contained terms that would enforce Tibetan recognition of new power and status for the Panchen.

By tradition, however, the Panchen's position was religious only. He was never entitled to authority in temporal affairs. When the delegates took a firm stand against these terms, the matter was referred back to the Dalai Lama. His Holiness replied that the status of the Panchen was defined explicitly in historical religious writings and could not be changed. The Dalai Lama, however, compromised by offering to allow the Chinese-chosen Panchen to "return" to Tibet without opposition.

This was an enormous concession. On the surface it might seem that allowing a false Panchen to occupy the second highest position in the Lamaist hierarchy was to defile that position. Nevertheless recognition of the false Panchen was considered by many in Lhasa to be the cleverest possible piece of anti-Chinese strategy. The Tibetans, although they show respect for the office of a high incarnation, have their real reverence for the "body" himself who is the living god. If forced, they would have no compunction about going through the motions of showing respect for a false incarnation. But every time they made obeisance they would be reminded of the godlessness and arrogance of their conquerors. The real Panchen would become a true martyr, revered even more highly because he had to be worshiped in secret. The usurper became known contemptuously as "Mao's Panchen," even though Articles Five and Six of the treaty gave him the status of the true incarnation.

Aside from the articles in the treaty concerning the Panchen and the one that defined the reorganization of the Tibetan army, the so-called 17-Point Agreement seemed almost generous. The Chinese maintained the fiction, in Article One, that imperialists were the sole reason for their intervention. The article provided that "The Tibetan people shall unite and drive out imperialist aggressive forces from Tibet." The first Soviet broadcast in which the agreement was publicized naïvely quoted the Tibetan delegates as thanking "the Chinese leaders for their patient explanations which showed the delegation that the imperialist aggressors were Tibet's worst enemy."

Most of the other terms made the Chinese Communists appear to be Tibet's best friends. The Han would not alter the existing political system in Tibet. Religious freedom was to be guaranteed; the religious beliefs, customs, and habits of the Tibetan people were to be respected; the Lamaist monasteries would be protected, and no changes would be made in their income. The development of Tibetan language and education would be encouraged. Agriculture, animal husbandry, industry, and commerce would be improved so as to raise the Tibetan living standard. There was to be no compulsion, however, about these reforms; reforms would be instituted only upon the demand of the people and would be worked out in consultation with Tibetan leaders. Finally the Chinese agreed to be completely fair in their economic dealings with the Tibetans and would "not arbitrarily take a single needle or thread from the people."

On the other hand, the "Tibetan right of exercising national regional autonomy" was allowed to exist only under "the unified leadership of the Chinese Central People's Government." The Central Government also took on responsibility for all Tibetan external affairs. Moreover, Article Fifteen of the agreement stated that in order to implement the agreement the Chinese government would set up a military and administrative committee and a military area headquarters in Tibet. In short, the agreement, despite the glowing but vague promises it made, was explicit only in establishing complete Chinese authority over Tibet.

No one in the mountain kingdom was fooled by the true meaning of the terms. The agreement confirmed the Tibetans' worst fears and came as a shock to the whole nation. Nevertheless, neither the officials nor the people could do much about it. They waited, bitter and sullen, to see how the Han would implement the terms.

The first act of the Chinese, after the agreement was signed, was to send their administrator to Lhasa as quickly as possible. The administrator, therefore, went from China to Tibet via India.

It is an interesting piece of irony that even today, with the improved roads from China to the roof of the world, travelers in a hurry still reach Tibet through India. The Chinese refer to India as "Tibet's back door." The Tibetans, however, with geographical and historic logic on their side, have always considered India as the honored guest at their front door, while China was the thief trying to break in through the back door.

In any case, the administrator was a forty-five-year-old Chinese general named Chang Ching-wu. He made an effort to be jovial and friendly, but such virtues were foreign to his nature. He was really pompous, arrogant, short-tempered, and extremely sensitive about the prerogatives of his position. He was the sort of person whom the Tibetans delight in deflating. Thus a welcoming party of Tibetan officials met him at Kalimpong. The officials were polite and even friendly. In short, the general was not met with humility as a conqueror but was greeted with proud dignity as a guest. This implied that the Tibetans still regarded themselves as independent and that they expected the visitor's stay to be impermanent. The general made it clear to the officials that he was not pleased with the nature of his reception.

To make matters worse for him, the general stopped in Yatung to pay proper respects to the Dalai Lama. We can assume that he had orders from Peking to make this gesture. The Tibetans lost no opportunity of publicizing the picture of the general showing humble obeisance to the God-King. In effect, this punctuated the general's status as merely a guest in Tibet.

General Chang Ching-wu hurried to Lhasa. He established himself in an imposing house where he avoided all but the necessary receptions and busied himself with the arrangements for the entry of his administrative assistants into the capital.

One of his assistants was General Wang Ching-ming, the "hero of Chamdo." He began the long trek to Lhasa from occupied eastern Tibet. With him were five thousand troops. General Fan Ming, a secretary of the Chinese Communist Party, traveled toward Lhasa along the northern route through Nagchuka; another five thousand troops accompanied him. Ngapho Shape, the treaty negotiations finished, began the months-long overland journey from Peking. He was escorted by the Chinese general Chang Kuo-hua with three thousand more Han soldiers. "Mao's Panchen" also prepared to make a triumphal "return" to Tibet; he traveled with General Fan Ming and, of course, had his own escort of Chinese troops.

In addition, tens of thousands of road laborers worked ahead of the advancing Chinese fighting forces in order to give the occupation army a secure supply line in the rear. Thus the Chinese forces moved slowly. To the Tibetans their advance seemed ominous, like the slow flexing of the arms of an octopus that intended to crush the holy kingdom.

In Lhasa itself the people waited and watched in silence. They saw Chinese technicians string wire through the streets. Loudspeakers were installed, and the Lhasans began to get their first taste of concentrated propaganda.

Once the treaty had been signed and plans were made for receiving the Chinese troops into the capital, the Dalai Lama no longer had reason to remain in Yatung. He returned, therefore, to the Holy City, where he could be closer to his people in the ordeals all Tibetans felt they would soon face. His journey was leisurely; he stopped at numerous monasteries along the route for sermons and prayers. In the Holy City the entire populace turned out, suddenly joyful to have their God-King with them again and hopeful once more that he might find some means of protecting them.

Even from his high apartments in the Potala the Dalai Lama could hear the loud-speakers in the streets of Lhasa far below. The speakers now were instructing the Tibetans on how to act when the Han troops entered the city. "The Liberation Army comes as your friend," the Lhasans were told. "The troops will not harm you; they will not interfere with your religion or customs. You may watch them as they enter, but you must not shout or be disorderly. You will receive the troops quietly. This is an order of your officials."

One night the Han soldiers by the thousands appeared seemingly from nowhere. They camped outside the city until morning. An advance guard entered Lhasa first and patrolled both sides of the line of march. They kept back the people and watched for weapons. Spectators who carried swords were motioned away from the front line. Behind the advance guard came five thousand troops, following the Chinese flag and huge banners bearing the likeness of Mao Tse-tung. Between formations of troops who marched with bayoneted rifles held forward were units of horse-drawn field artillery. There were also many machine-gun companies whose weapons were slung on poles and carried by four men.

About twenty thousand Tibetans came to watch the parade and see their fears confirmed. Among them were thousands of monks. All the spectators were quiet, as they had been told to be. No face showed joy at being liberated from "imperialist aggressors." Every face was grim. A few showed bitterness and resentment. Many of the older men wept unashamedly.

The parade ended at a small park where the Chinese had erected a reviewing stand decorated in their own pagoda style. Here high Tibetan officials were on hand to make the addresses of official welcome. Their speeches had been carefully prepared and Chinese "suggestions" had been incorporated in them. Standing under the portrait of Mao Tse-tung and speaking into a microphone that carried their words throughout the city, many of them participated for the first time in a public ceremony in which religion had no part.

Although not seen in the parade or at the official reception, a greatly enlarged staff for the propaganda department, along with additional equipment, arrived with the troops. The loud-speaker system was now put into daily use. The people were constantly reassured about the 17-Point Agreement. They were told over and over again that the Chinese would not oppress them and would not interfere with them in any way. The Chinese had come as friends and helpers. The Chinese would respect the Tibetan people. The Chinese would pay for all supplies and services. The great Mao Tse-tung wanted to free Tibet and to make all Tibetans happy.

To the surprise of the skeptical Tibetan listeners, these fine promises seemed to be kept. Lhasa hummed with activity as the Chinese settled in. Many new construction jobs were begun, and Tibetan workers were paid high wages in silver. The Chinese troops were not allowed to commandeer transport; they hired work animals and paid a good rate, again in silver. They showed outward respect to the monks and monasteries. In the bazaar stalls they spent freely and did not quibble over prices with the traders. Farmers and nomads who brought produce into the Lhasa market found an immediate demand and high prices for their wares; they also went off with silver jingling in their pockets. The people began to wonder if the Communists were such monsters after all.

In the monasteries also there were second thoughts. Many monks had seen the arrival of the Chinese army with guns, banners, and huge pictures of Mao Tse-tung. But the Dalai Lama's guard still marched under the sacred flag. Prayer flags still fluttered from the Potala's roof. The monasteries were not disturbed. A few high Chinese officials did visit the larger institutions, but they came by proper appointment; they brought gifts and were correct and respectful. They showed a flattering interest in the holy objects which the monasteries prized, and they distributed lavish quantities of brick tea and silver among the monk congregations.

In Lhasa the Chinese officials bought or rented at high prices unoccupied houses of the Lhasa nobles. Here they feasted and feted the Tibetan officials. Around the banquet tables they did not speak of land reform or of the redistribution of wealth.

At first the Tibetans remained suspicious. They reminded each other of their proverb, "Beware of honey offered on a sharp knife." Nevertheless, much of their apprehension faded; it began to seem a little foolish.

Less than three months after the arrival of the first troops in Lhasa the second large contingent came. Again the official welcome included parades and speeches. Also, more propaganda workers with more printing presses and more loud-speakers arrived. Dancers and entertainers to amuse the growing Chinese colony appeared. In addition, Chinese artisans and shopkeepers came to settle in Lhasa. Chinese sweetmakers catered to the troops and drew business away from the Tibetan stalls. Chinese shoemakers began to take over the trade on which Tibetan craftsmen had prospered. The prices of produce went still higher—so high that the Tibetan who did not live on the food that he himself raised found that his increased silver earnings could not feed his family.

The Tibetans in Lhasa looked around and suddenly found that they were living in a Chinese city. Chinese troops were everywhere. Chinese officials occupied more and more of the houses and offices, and Chinese merchants took over the best shops.

And still more Chinese troops poured in. Like their predecessors they came with only "chopsticks and empty rice bowls." Finally the Tibetan officials expressed grave concern over the problem of feeding all these troops. The Chinese authorities replied that the bulk of the troops was intended for the area along the Indian border. True, the Chinese forces soon left Lhasa to take up new positions in the south—but almost immediately new contingents arrived in Lhasa to take their place. Inflation and food shortages became serious first in Lhasa and then, following the occupation troops, throughout Tibet.

Everywhere in Tibet resentment began to replace the first novelty of pleased surprise at fair treatment, generous pay, and non-interference. Tibetans, meeting in their homes, at their temples, and in the market places, discussed the meaning of these new developments. They asked each other and their lama leaders how many Chinese would come. Would they bring no food with their caravans but only more weapons and printing presses?

The answer eventually was supplied through Radio Peking. The Communists intended to send sufficient Chinese settlers to increase Tibet's population to ten million. This would mean that for every Tibetan in his own country there would be two Chinese colonists along with an untold number of permanently stationed Chinese troops.

Meanwhile the Chinese were quietly buying up supplies of all kinds. They searched the country for stored grains and purchased the surplus stocks. Even worse, they bought dung for fuel. In Tibet, despite the frigid winters, the majority could not afford the luxury of fuel used simply to keep themselves warm or for light at night. The only available fuel was dung, and it had to be used for fertilizer as well as for cooking fires. The countryside was dotted with windbreak walls of dung in the shelter of which a traveler could pitch his tent. He used the dried fuel from these walls and replaced it with a fresh supply from his own animals. Now that the Chinese bought the fuel these walls became rare. A traveler in sub-zero weather could no longer expect even the meager comfort of hot buttered tea. Many fields were insufficiently fertilized. Few other aspects of the occupation caused more hardship.

Nevertheless, the Chinese troops behaved properly; obviously their correct behavior was by military order. On the rare occasions when a Chinese interfered with a Tibetan he was severely punished. A few cases of violence in Lhasa between Tibetans and the Han troops did occur; several murders were recorded. In these cases, however, the occupation authorities handed over the guilty Chinese to the Tibetan court without argument. The Chinese offenders lost their hands or their eyes in accordance with the old books of Tibetan justice. The Chinese authorities wanted the Tibetan government to inaugurate new laws, but they could not force the change; the Agreement decreed that the local government could carry out reforms only when the Tibetan people raised demands for them. The Tibetans did not demand a new law system. Their laws had been written down in the sacred books by former incarnations of the living god. Moreover, Tibetans themselves took punishment under their own law system without complaint. When a Tibetan killed a Chinese he did not ask for mercy from the court or for different laws. He did not even try to deny his crime. "I killed him," he would say simply, and he would submit stoically to the decreed punishment.

But the Communist troops were afraid of Tibetan law and because of it they maintained a respectful attitude toward the Tibetans. Seeing this fear in the eyes of the enemy, the Tibetans were tempted to resistance. They were proud of their countrymen who committed acts of heroic defiance against the invader. At the same time, however, the Tibetans knew that if they started a really large-scale revolt against their oppressors they would not only lose their lives but would bring about the destruction of their temples and their sacred relics; they might even endanger the life of their beloved Dalai Lama. Talk of defiance was food for pride, but it was not the way of the Buddha. Instead they prayed to Chenrezi, walked the Gora Path, and trusted their gods to bring deliverance.

The Tibetans were heartened by the approach of the February 1952 New Year's celebration when, traditionally, the Drepung monks for three weeks take over all authority for law and order in the city of Lhasa. The Chinese administrator tried to have this privilege of the monks canceled. His request, of course, was refused; Article Seven of the Agreement provided that "the religious beliefs, customs, and habits of the Tibetan people shall be respected."

Nevertheless, in preparation for the new year the Han authorities called back troops from Gyantse to Lhasa. The troops dug trenches outside the city and set up field artillery near the Chinese barracks. They installed machine guns to guard Chinese Communist offices and houses within the city. The monks who descended on Lhasa found a well-fortified city but no Chinese troops in evidence. All Chinese troops had been ordered to stay within their barracks. No Chinese soldier could show himself in Lhasa unless he carried a special pass from his commanding officer. Few troops asked for passes. They missed a sight which several foreign travelers in the past had risked their lives to see. The Han could hardly be blamed for avoiding these red-robed, dedicated men who carried swords and held their lives cheap but their religion dear.

Scattered incidents occurred, but on the whole the monks maintained discipline. The celebration was not on the usual large scale. Many monks had been detailed to remain within the monasteries. With the enemy so near the head lamas did not want to leave unguarded the treasures and the precious stores of grain and guns kept in the monasteries.

The people, whose custom was to celebrate for three days after the lamas had gone, had small heart for festivity this year. Few had grain to offer to the gods or barley for *chang;* many Tibetans had their first experience with hunger. The people still sang, but now their songs had subtle words of disrespect for the Chinese troops and officials.

Tibetans consider their songs gifts from the gods. The tunes are traditional, but new words seem to come from nowhere as they are needed. News is passed around through the medium of song.

The news now concerned the new "devil" in their midst. The verses told of the devil's evil deeds and described the forms he took.

Shortly after the New Year's celebration in 1952 the Tibetan folk songs began to announce the impending arrival of "Mao's Panchen." Some of the verses described the unfortunate boy as worse than the lowest animal. Most of the verses mentioned that he would bring with him more of the devil's hungry helpers to take the people's food and more printing machines to print more leaflets for the monks; the songs advised the monks to burn the leaflets like an incense offering because destruction of the godless words would please the gods.

In Shigatse, however, the stronghold of Panchen followers, some enthusiasm for the "return" of Mao's Panchen was worked up. This was done by Che Jigme, the long-exiled Tibetan opportunist and collaborator who had found the false Panchen. In Shigatse most of the people revered their own choice for the incarnation, the studious boy who was being given rigorous training in a Lhasa monastery and whom my father and I met briefly in 1949. Nevertheless, the Chinese authorities offered a high reward for recognition of their Panchen. They promised many improvements and new prosperity to the Shigatse area. A new clinic, for example, was hastily built and was to be opened when Mao's Panchen arrived. The Chinese erected other new buildings and renovated old ones. Even more important, lands that had been confiscated by the Lhasa government ever since the exile of the previous Panchen Lama were to be returned to the traditional landlords. Finally the Chinese said that in the Shigatse area their Panchen would be granted some political powers in addition to his religious authority; Shigatse Tibetans who did not co-operate fully, therefore, might find themselves in difficult circumstances. Thus a meeting party from Shigatse's Tashi Lhunpo Monastery was sent to Nagchuka as part of the escort for the false Panchen.

Tibetans outside Shigatse, however, had no such incentives for accepting a false incarnation. As the time approached for his arrival, their indignation grew. The Chinese posters announcing the arrival were defaced with offal. Crude, handmade Tibetan posters, quoting the Thirteenth Dalai Lama's warnings against Communism, appeared. The Chinese authorities ordered the Tibetan government to put a stop to these activities. A curfew was imposed. The Lhasans defied the curfew. More posters appeared, demanding that the Chinese should leave Tibet; the campaign was similar to the "Quit India" action against the British in the subcontinent nine years before. Groups of Tibetans courted arrest by publicly requesting their officials to expel the Chinese or to arm the people so that the Tibetans themselves could drive out the invaders. Several small and spontaneous riots had to be suppressed with Chinese troops.

Nevertheless, the Chinese adopted a policy of restraint and their troops were ordered to take no action against the Tibetans. As tension mounted, the Chinese feared that even a small incident of suppression or reprisal might light a spark that could fire the whole country into revolt. Thus the Chinese authorities worked through the Tibetan government, making "suggestions" by day and feasting susceptible Tibetan officials by night.

At one such feast, a few nights before the scheduled arrival of Mao's Panchen, a serious revolt did almost break out. A crowd of Tibetans collected in front of the house where the party was going on. They stoned the house. The Chinese guards panicked and opened fire. Immediately the crowd rushed the guards. The Chinese called for reinforcements, and hand-to-hand street fighting took place during most of the night. The casualties were few, but the temper of the people was clearly revealed. The Panchen's arrival was delayed. The Chinese strengthened their patrols and alerted reinforcements. They imposed strict censorship; even the couriers and traders between Tibet and India were detained and questioned by Chinese troops along the border.

Across the border in India the interest in Tibet's plight was increasing. Many officials and most journalists there believed that the arrival of the false Panchen in Tibet would mark an important turning point in the situation. So far Article 15 of the Agreement had not been fully carried out; the Chinese had not yet organized the "Military and Administrative Committee," the means whereby they would hold all political power in the mountain kingdom. The Kashag, and especially the Dalai Lama, had used evasion and delaying tactics to prevent the Chinese from taking this final step. Such tactics could not be used indefinitely, however, and the arrival of Mao's Panchen—and another contingent of Chinese troops—was expected to signal a stronger stand by the Chinese.

Moreover, the Panchen's usefulness to the Chinese was clearer now. He was to become, in effect, the head of the government for western Tibet. Ngapho, regarded as a Chinese puppet, was to head the eastern Tibet area from Chamdo. The Dalai Lama nominally would lead the whole country, but his political powers would be limited to Tibet's central zone—where the Chinese Military Area Headquarters as well as their Military and Administrative Committee could see that his policies were kept in line with theirs.

In short, the Chinese had adopted the old system of divide and rule. No one was more familiar with the system than the Indians. The British had once developed it into an art. In India the British many times had used their troops, ostensibly to protect one raja's land against the aggressive ambitions of another. Once in, the troops did not leave. In these instances the British laid great stress on treaties in which their duty to bring about reforms was stated and promises not to interfere with local religion, customs, and traditions were made. By the process of divide and rule a comparative handful of British had been able to rule millions of Indians, until the Indians themselves managed to unite. Now, in the Western countries, the idea that a people of one culture should arbitrarily rule the people of another against their will was no longer accepted as practical, moral, or even legal. For this reason the Indians had been able successfully to use logical argument and moral pressure against the British.

The Chinese, however, despite unity and strength under their new ideology, had not learned what the old Western imperialist nations had discovered the hard way. The Indians had won freedom from colonialism only four and one half years before; but now on their northern frontier they were seeing their big Asian neighbor copying the British techniques of two centuries earlier. Even worse, the Chinese were committing their acts of colonial domination with cynicism; two centuries before power politics and colonialism were everywhere accepted as a legitimate—and even moral aspect of international relations. The British merely had been the most successful with their domination and exploitation. The Chinese, however, were committing imperialist aggression on the excuse of opposing imperialist aggression. Thus Indians who thought that the worst of this evil had been removed from the world four and one half years before, when the British officials left their country, now saw the evil looming larger and more virulent than ever.

The Indians could hardly be impressed with China's legal claim on Tibet; if they accepted the legality of that claim, they would also have to accept that Britain had an even stronger legal claim on the subcontinent, that Portugal was legally entitled to rule Goa, and that, in short, colonialism was not dead.

Nor were many Indians taken in by the Chinese promises of reforms, autonomy, and non-interference in culture. The same promises could be found in dozens of treaties between the British and the old rulers of India, but the Indians had not been free.

Thus thoughtful Indians watched the developments on their northern frontier with increasing dismay. The key to the immediate situation seemed to be the arrival of Mao's Panchen. If the Chinese succeeded in forcing him down Tibet's political throat, the country would be successfully divided—and lost. There seemed no way, however, for the Tibetans to avoid accepting him.

When Mao's Panchen finally arrived in Lhasa, he was accompanied by an impressive entourage. The highest Tibetan officials received him. Men of such importance, of course, could not really accept a false incarnation. Thus going through the form of acceptance appeared to be an act forced upon them by the Chinese invaders. The Tibetan officials did not lose face by this act, but all the Chinese propaganda concerning good intentions was immediately invalidated. If the Chinese forced the highest Tibetans to accept a false incarnation, they were depriving Tibet of the promised autonomy and they were interfering with the country's religion and customs.

Although the Tibetan leaders went through the form of accepting Mao's Panchen, they absolutely refused to accept him as *more* than the Panchen. Traditionally the Panchen's status was limited solely to spiritual matters. The Chinese were not interested in him as a high ecclesiastic; as such he was useless to them. They wanted his authority over Tibetans on spiritual matters to be extended to administrative affairs as well, but this the Tibetan officials would not acknowledge. And they had excellent authority for their refusal. The most ancient and holy books in the country defined explicitly the limits of the Panchen's responsibilities and status. The Chinese were bound officially by the agreement not to interfere in the religion. They could do nothing, therefore, to enforce the further recognition without which their created incarnation was useless.

To make matters easier for the Tibetans, Mao's Panchen was not very bright. Moreover, the Chinese had not taken full advantage of their opportunity to educate him adequately. He was literate, and he had a vague command of elementary Communist slogans. Otherwise he seemed to have been taught little except that he was a person of almost limitless importance. When he was not paid the deference that he had been taught was due to him, he did not become angry or petulant; he was merely reduced to utter confusion. He deserved sympathy rather than criticism, because he was barely more than a child and he was caught in the middle of infinitely complicated intrigues.

There was nothing complicated, however, about his reception in Lhasa. It was a mere two-tent affair. In one tent the Chinese greeted the child as an important political figure such as the governor of a large state. In the other tent Tibetan officials accepted him as they would a high ecclesiastic.

The Dalai Lama, however, was gentle with the boy. Mao's Panchen was even younger than the Dalai Lama; he was coming to his homeland for the first time and he was finding that his own people were quietly hostile to him. During the formal reception at the Potala the only Chinese allowed to be present were newsmen and photographers. They were not anxious to publicize their Panchen's subservience to the Dalai Lama. One of the Tibetan officials, however, had a movie camera and filmed complete pictures of the Panchen making the customary obeisance, including three complete kowtows, to the Dalai Lama. Within a week these pictures found their way to a Lhasa screen and the Tibetans learned that Mao's Panchen had behaved with proper respect.

After the formal reception the two incarnations dined together and talked of religious matters while officials of the Dalai's court were hosts to leading Tibetan members of the Panchen's entourage. Not only did the Dalai Lama enjoy vastly superior status; he was older and far more wise than the poor Panchen. By the time the official and unofficial receptions were over Mao's Panchen was visibly baffled and crushed at having to recognize and accept an authority greater than his own.

Thus the Chinese plans to use their Panchen as a means to divide Tibet failed. The Panchen remained in Lhasa for more than a month while heated negotiations went on between the Chinese authorities and the Tibetan officials.

During this period many songs about Mao's Panchen were sung in the streets of Lhasa. None were complimentary to him. The words of the most popular song, roughly translated, were:

"In holy quarters in Lhasa
There dwells a young pretender.
He is as tall in body as he is conceited in ignorance.
If the dawn had not broken
The thief would have committed robbery."

The last two lines meant that the thief (Mao's Panchen) would have robbed the Dalai Lama of power if the dawn of enlightenment had not awakened in time the Tibetan people to the evil plan of the Chinese.

If the Chinese were frustrated for the present in the three-zone partitioning of Tibet, they meant to achieve at least the administrative control of Tibet as mentioned in Article 15 of the Agreement. At the time only the Tibet Military District Headquarters had been established under General Chang Kuo-hua. The administrative aspect of the Chinese "guidance" was handled through two military "vice-commanders," who were Ngapho, the defector from Chamdo, and Ragashar, the former Defense Minister of Tibet. These men were also Shapes in the Kashag. Thus, unofficially, close liaison was maintained between the Chinese military and the Tibetan government.

By the time the Panchen was ready to depart for Shigatse, however, the Chinese were able to force further concessions from the Tibetans. The two prime ministers, who were the link between the Dalai Lama and the Kashag, were forced to resign. One of the prime ministers, Lukhang, was greatly loved by the Tibetans as a man of exceptional integrity and patriotism. He had headed the government during the Dalai Lama's retreat in Yatung. Recently, however, he had incurred Chinese disapproval when he failed to take stern measures against the Tibetan groups who had petitioned the government to expel the Han.

When the two prime ministers were gone, this important post was abolished and the membership of the Kashag was increased from four to six. Moreover, the Kashag's authority was extended to cover the ecclesiastical court whose four top secretaries had held traditional authority over all monk officials. The Dalai Lama was urged to take personal lead of the new Kashag. He delayed acceptance—and thus authorization of the change—by pointing out that such activities were inconsistent with his religious responsibilities. Finally he was made to agree to act as nominal head of the new Kashag, but he did not attend the meetings; instead he sent a relatively minor monk to represent him. The new Kashag, according to Radio Peking, was to be "guided in all matters by General Chang Ching-wu."

CHAPTER IX

The "New" Tibet

Where there is life, there is death.
—TIBETAN PROVERB

THE Chinese military and civil officials in Tibet were finding the road to reform slow and difficult; the now huge propaganda department was having even more trouble. Despite the almost constant loud-speaker broadcasts and the deluge of leaflets, no friends for China or for Communism had been made. The propagandists were particularly sensitive to the fact that, despite their prodigious efforts, the Tibetan people were not demanding socialization; on the contrary, Tibetans were sulkily opposing it. Finally General Chang Ching-wu himself called for a great mass meeting of the Lhasan proletariat. The assembled Tibetans were served tea and cake. Every worker who came was given a silver dollar. Then the general spoke to them seriously about their becoming conscious of themselves as a working class. At the end he asked them to speak freely about their grievances. The workers' spokesman told Chang Ching-wu that the people had no grievances but that they would like to express the hope that the doctrines of Lord Buddha would be encouraged and that the Dalai Lama and their great monasteries would keep their sacred position.

The Chinese had more understanding of the position of the Tibetan peasants. The largest single difficulty of the peasants concerned an adequate supply of seed grain. When a farmer could not keep enough seed grain from his share of the crop to resow his fields, he would have to borrow money from his landlord or monastery to buy more at the planting season. The interest rates on such loans were high, and many farmers were in debt. The Chinese, at the suggestion of their propagandists, inaugurated an interest-free loan policy for the Tibetan peasants. The loans of seed grain were to benefit the Chinese in several ways. They would encourage larger crops and thereby help to feed the ever-growing army of occupation. They would drive a wedge between the land workers and the landowners. And, most of all, the loans would win the popular support of the largest segment of the Tibetan population.

To the surprise of the Chinese, the loans did not win over the peasants. When the propagandists who accompanied the seed-loan teams called for expressions of popular opinion, the reply was invariably the same, "We take your seed and we thank you. But we prefer our own ways. Our fathers always managed to get seed for the land and so will our children. Although we accept your seed we would be happier if you had not come."

Moreover, the seed-loan program often had a boomerang effect on the Chinese. The seed they lent to needy peasants came from stocks that they had purchased from landowners and monasteries. These stocks sometimes contained very old grain. In Tibet's climate thirty- and even forty-year-old grain remained edible but was hardly ideal for seed. Thus much of the seed lent by the Chinese did not germinate. A farmer who recognized that his seed was bad could return it and get a fresh supply. If he planted his field and nothing grew, however, he was in a bad financial position, even though the authorities canceled his debt. In such cases the Chinese were careful to point out to the unlucky farmer, "We gave you Tibetan seed. Therefore complain to your Tibetan landlords, not to us." But the peasants stubbornly refused to blame the landlords. They could not help but feel that the landowners and lamas had been very clever to sell bad grain for good silver to the invaders. And if the farmer could not eat from his barren

field that winter he had the satisfaction of knowing that the Han
soldiers could not eat from it either.

Thus, although the Chinese distributed the seed loans widely
and with great fanfare, they achieved little. Before long the
Tibetan government announced an interest ceiling on all loans,
and the Tibetan peasants returned happily to the old system. If
the peasants thought that the interest ceiling was a benefit from
the Chinese invaders, they did not admit it. They were learning
that any seemingly good action by the Chinese was done for a
bad reason.

The Tibetan merchant class learned this truth even more
thoroughly than did the peasants. At first the traders fared well
under the occupation. The Chinese needed many products which
India manufactured in quantity but which were hardly obtainable
in China. Thus the Chinese bought heavily through the traders,
advising them of their needs and allowing them handsome profits
on the goods brought in. Caravans moved along the trade trails,
bringing in thousands of loads of pickaxes, shovels, blankets,
cigarettes, sugar—even noodles which had been made by Chinese
restaurant keepers in Calcutta. All these goods, the Chinese told
the Tibetans, were made in the factories of the Soviet Union. This
became a joke among even the poorest Tibetans—to whom an
Indian cigarette might be a luxury but not a mystery. A number
of witty songs on the subject were sung by the muleteers who
guided the loads over the familiar trails.

Before long the Chinese attitude toward the Tibetan traders
changed. While the roads into Tibet were being built the Chinese
desperately needed the supplies that the traders could get from
India. As the roads neared completion, however, the need was
not so great and the Chinese began to eye the trade profits.
They set up a Sino-Tibetan trading agency through which many
of the imports were channeled. They limited the profit margin
for all traders. In many cases they discouraged the trader from
pursuing his business, suggesting that he lend his capital to the
Chinese at a modest interest rate and not bother about making
the tiresome trade trips at all. Individual traders who persisted in

moving their caravans found that they were held up at frequent intervals along the route while Chinese-controlled caravans took priority on the path. Chinese check posts at the border passes found other ways of delaying and discouraging the independent traders.

The chief item of export for these traders was a coarse variety of wool used mainly in carpets. The wool passed through India and much of it was shipped to the United States. After the Chinese occupation the United States prohibited the import of the wool. This drop in demand, combined with a general fall in the world market price of wool, was a blow to the Tibetan traders and suppliers. Large stocks accumulated both in Tibet and in Kalimpong, the Indian entry point for the wool. In 1952 the Chinese made large wool purchases. They paid good prices and made much propaganda about it. The following year Soviet experts took samplings of the wool and made an offer, but the price was less than the Tibetans could afford to accept. The Chinese then continued to buy wool at a set price. Some of it they shipped back to China, via India, and some they sold to Czechoslovakia. Tibetan traders, however, disliked dealing with a monopoly at a set price; many continued to sell as much of their wool as possible to the Indian traders in the traditional pattern.

The Chinese, then, found other ways to discourage private trade with India. After the original free use of silver they set up a Bank of China in Lhasa. The bank did not accept Tibetan currency for remittances to India. Only traders who could show legitimate possession of Chinese silver, obtained through sales to the Chinese, secured drafts for further purchases. At the same time the Chinese encouraged Sino-Tibetan trade by allowing Tibetan traders higher profits on Chinese imports and by making motor transport for Chinese imports available to the Tibetan traders for a part of the journey. Except for the traditional imports of brick tea and silks, however, the Tibetan traders had little enthusiasm for Chinese manufactured articles.

Many of the preferred Indian-manufactured articles were brought into western Tibet by Indian traders. At certain seasons these traders crossed into Tibet and overnight whole cities blossomed in the wilderness. Tibetan sheepherders brought their flocks to these *mandis* (markets), and the merchants who bought the wool sheared the sheep as well. Most of the trade was on a barter basis. The Tibetans offered wool, musk, salt, borax, and livestock in exchange for cloth, sugar, and tools.

The *mandis* were social centers as well as trading posts. The atmosphere of a fair prevailed, as old friends met year after year at the colorful tent encampments. Religion was also a part of the seasonal fete. A Hindu trader might leave his goods in care of a Tibetan friend while he went on pilgrimage to Mt. Kailas. Holy men from India talked philosophy with trading lamas from Tibet's western monasteries.

Gradually, however, the Chinese completely altered the traditional trading pattern. Only three authorized *mandis* were open for trade. Chinese garrisons "guarded" the traders against bandits and kept a sharp watch on activities. The Chinese banned free trading in salt, grain, and wool and held monopoly rights on all these commodities. They discouraged the old barter system and propagandized each visiting trader on the merits of dealing with the Chinese official trade agencies. Finally the Tibetans themselves began to be forced out of business entirely. Much of the "free trade" still permitted was given to Chinese colonists whom the authorities had already begun to bring in, now that their garrisons were large enough to guarantee protection.

The Chinese colonists were a miserable lot, but the Tibetans had no sympathy for them. The Tibetans had been told they could expect many millions of the colonists. The interlopers had not chosen to settle in Tibet; they had been sent. Moreover, they did not come from the borderlands. They were sent from China's overcrowded eastern cities. They knew nothing of the Tibetan language or customs. Many knew little about farming, and none were familiar with the farming methods required on the high plateau. All of them suffered because of the altitude. They were given seed, work animals, a little cash, and small plots of unused government land. And they worked hard, for they worked under the eyes of the same soldiers who protected them from their resentful Tibetan neighbors. They lived in tents until they could build huts or until a Chinese labor crew came through to build houses for them.

These laborers also had not chosen to come to Tibet. They were ill-clad, underfed, and they lived crowded into tents. They worked at gun point under heavy guard. At first the Chinese had not used their forced labor battalions in Tibetan cities. Tibetans heard about the laborers when refugees from the east brought stories of the thousands of Chinese who broke stone for the new roads. The laborers worked with torn hands on which the blood was frozen; they carried heavy loads on their backs although the rags they wore did not cover their bleeding shoulders; many had no shoes, but still they worked with frozen feet wrapped in rags. They died in untold numbers, but more were always brought in— human supplies for the great road program.

At first the Tibetan laborers who were recruited for road work did not work alongside the Chinese labor battalions. The Tibetans were well paid and well treated. The propaganda advantage of this good treatment would be offset if the Tibetans saw the plight of their brother workers from the motherland. But as the roads pushed westward the Chinese authorities grew less particular. The forced laborers worked wherever they were needed. Even in the capital itself these miserable men broke and carried stone for the foundations of "New Lhasa," the all-Chinese city which began to grow on the outskirts of the Holy City. The Tibetans were beginning to see the true picture of what their life would be under colonial domination.

"We licked a very little honey from the knife," they told each other, "before the blade was exposed."

Moreover, the always present hope for outside help was fading fast. In the spring of 1954 India and China negotiated an agreement on "Trade and Intercourse between the Tibet Region of China and India." This put a formal seal on Indian recognition of China's supremacy in Tibet. Tibet's borders were strongly garrisoned by Chinese troops. The road links between China and

Tibet had progressed to a point that ensured security of military supply.

The Dalai Lama had done all that he could do, the people knew. He was a youth only in the years of his body; in his mind and spirit he had shown the wisdom and faith of the Incarnate Chenrezi. He had blocked and delayed with finesse. He had protected the monasteries and the priesthood. But the time he had bought was running out. He counseled unity and peace and faith. The people listened and, on the whole, obeyed.

The temper of the people was best illustrated in the petitions they submitted through their officials to the Chinese. A typical petition said in effect, "You have told us repeatedly that the reason—and the only reason—your troops entered our country was to save us from the imperialist aggressors who were taking over our country. We thank you very much. But, as you can see, your soldiers have now driven out all the imperialist aggressors. Your armies therefore are no longer needed here and should be sent back into China. Should we be threatened again by the imperialist aggressors, we shall be pleased to call for your help . . ."

Such petitions infuriated the Chinese. The Tibetan officials who failed to take disciplinary action against the people who submitted them were apt to be relieved of their duties.

The petitions had the effect of unmasking the true designs of the Chinese in Tibet. As a result, some Tibetans could not resist the temptation to open defiance.

For example, a group of Tibetan laborers who were assigned to clearing a wooded area for Chinese barracks set a little forest fire. The troops who were called in to fight the fire worked all night to bring it under control, and eight of them lost their lives. Many Tibetans were arrested, but for many others the blaze was a symbol of hope.

In Kham, although several of the important chieftains of the fierce Khambas had been bribed and were collaborating with the Chinese, sporadic uprisings delayed bridgebuilding on the roads and forced the Chinese to keep heavy guard detachments at supply posts.

On the northern portion of the Sining-Lhasa road Tsinghai Tibetans gave help and support to guerrilla bands of anti-Communist Chinese Muslims. For several months guerrillas carried out night attacks on Chinese installations along the roadway. The Chinese tried to enlist Tibetan militia to fight the guerrillas; they encouraged Tibetans to inform on the resisting groups. They wooed the Tibetan population with free medical and veterinary aid, propaganda shows, good pay, and the promise of government posts for local Tibetan leaders. The Tibetans took what was offered, but very few informed on the guerrillas in their midst. Chinese bombers from Sian were required to scatter and destroy the guerrilla forces in the hills.

The bombers came when they were needed. That was the Communist way, and few Tibetans tried to fool themselves about it. It was the "way of working among the Red people," as the Thirteenth Dalai Lama had written it down. The silver dollars and soft words had been spent with little effect. Tibetans awaited the harsher measures which they knew must come.

Although the Tibetans knew that eventually the Han would resort to harsh force, they did not realize how effectively their passive resistance and stubbornness were frustrating the invaders' aims. Despite propaganda claims to the contrary, the Chinese were behind their originally announced schedule for making Tibet into a Chinese Communist province. They moved slowly and cautiously, because they were afraid to do otherwise. Although their military forces were large, the Chinese in Tibet felt cut off from their homeland and isolated among a hostile and unpredictable people. Communication was the key to their problem. As long as access to Tibet from China was easier and faster through India, the Chinese had difficulty convincing themselves, let alone the rest of the world, that India was the "back door to Tibet" and that the mountain kingdom was an integral part only of China.

Communications between China and Tibet, therefore, became a preoccupation of the Han authorities. By 1953 telegraph wires connected China and all the important cities in Tibet. At least two airfields in Tibet were in use, and many more were under construction; garrisons to protect these fields were already established. All the Chinese garrisons in Tibet were linked efficiently by radiotelephone.

Early in 1954 the Chinese acquired an important addition for their communications system inside Tibet. With the signing of the Sino-Indian Agreement on Tibet, India gave up the communications facilities installed by the British and inherited by the Indians. The facilities included posts, telegraph and telephone installations, and a chain of resthouses along the trade route. When questioned in the Indian parliament about this aspect of the agreement, Indian officials replied that the installations were objects of British imperialism and therefore should be eschewed by Indians. The Chinese occupying force took over all the installations. The Tibetans, who were beginning to perceive the importance of communications to the invaders, felt that the Indians had given one more proof of being pro-Communist.

The most important aspect of the communications problem, however, was the roads. The Chinese Communists expected to complete two roads from China into Tibet by the end of 1954. One came from Sining. For several hundred miles it followed a westerly direction, passing south of the Tsaidam Swamp, and then joined the caravan track which led south to Nagchuka. The whole of this road, some twelve hundred miles in length and crossing terrifying terrain, would be ready for motor traffic by 1955.

The other road, from Tatsienlu via Kantze and Chamdo to Lhasa, followed a new route that had been surveyed and laid out by Soviet engineers. It was more southerly than the old Chamdo-Lhasa caravan track and it cut close to the Indian border before branching north to Chamdo. It crossed a dozen mountain ranges, countless rivers and gorges, but was also expected to take motor traffic by 1955. Finally, inside Tibet itself, rapid progress on roads was linking the important centers.

Outside Tibet, and particularly in the Western press, the consensus was that the task could not be accomplished in three years. Nevertheless, it was accomplished on schedule. Chinese propaganda credited the success to the "invincible spirit of dedicated workers," the "road heroes." Neutral journalists surmised that success was the result of "the frenzy of overpowering political propaganda that whipped these half-frozen men into a state of fanatical determination." The Tibetans, who watched with concern as the roads pushed rapidly through their land, invariably said that the success should be claimed by the bayonets of Chinese troops who literally worked the road laborers to death.

In any case, the roads now tied Tibet to China. Immediately the Chinese increased their pressure on the Dalai Lama and high officials; they wanted no more delay about the establishment of the administrative committee that would give them formal control of the country. The formal control was necessary in order to force the independent Tibetans to accept Chinese authority.

The Tibetan leaders, however, still managed to stall. Finally the Chinese turned their attention from the top echelons of the Tibetan government to the bottom. They began with the organization of a Reforms Office which was nominally Tibetan but was headed by the collaborator Ngapho who took his instructions from the Han. The office studied the operations of the Tibetan government and recommended improvements.

One such "improvement" was the alteration of the status of the *dzongpon*. Since ancient times Tibet was divided into *dzongs*, which were comparable to a county. The *dzongpon* was the head official, above the village leaders but below the regional governor. Traditionally the *dzongpon* had great power, particularly in the outlying areas. He was appointed for no definite period and often held the post for life. He was obligated to pay a fixed revenue from his *dzong* to Lhasa. Whatever he could collect in excess of the fixed amount was his own profit. He was not salaried and was subject to only loose control from higher authority.

Under the reform the *dzongpon* was paid a fixed monthly salary and forwarded all revenues to Lhasa. Also, he was appointed for a fixed term of three or four years. The reform, however, did not stop here. Older *dzongpons* now were pensioned off and new *dzongpons* were appointed. And all *dzongpons*, whether new or old, were to perform their official functions "only after consultation with and advice from the local Chinese military commander." The notice which informed the *dzongpons* of their new status pointed out that the Dalai Lama himself was governing "with the advice of the Chinese Commander-in-Chief." Thus the Chinese hoped to enforce co-operation of the Tibetans at the *dzong* level.

The Tibetans reacted sharply to this change. Previously the individual's personal contact with government was through his *dzongpon*. As long as the *dzongpon* reported through higher Tibetan officials ultimately to the Dalai Lama, the individual felt that he was living securely under his own traditional government. Now, however, the *dzongpon* was really subservient to the local Chinese military commander. Thus the individual's contact with his own government was broken; he felt that his God-King, the Dalai Lama, would no longer be able to hear of his problems and to help him. His tendency, therefore, was to attempt bypassing the new Chinese-controlled *dzongpon* in order to reach his Lhasa government and the Potala directly. The attempt required some kind of an organization in which his chosen and trusted representative would speak for him in the capital. The average Tibetans, however, had no real experience with organizing themselves on their own initiative into political parties or, indeed, with any organization that was not a traditional aspect of either the religious or civil hierarchy.

Fortunately, however, one small exception did exist. During the early days of the Thirteenth Dalai Lama a group of young Tibetan noblemen took the unprecedented step of forming a secret society. The Chinese Ambans intended to murder the Dalai Lama before he reached his majority and took over his rightful power. The secret society conspired to prevent the murder. Because the coup staged by the society was successful the members acquired prestige. The organization, although it had the unique feature of being associated with neither the government nor the monasteries, and although it now had no real function, continued to exist. It ultimately became known as the *Mimang Tshogpa*, or "People's Party."

The Mimang began to grow immediately after the first Chinese attacks on the eastern border. It still served little purpose other than to satisfy an instinctive desire of the people to band together in adversity. Soon, however, the Mimang began to take vaguely organized political action. Mimang members, for example, were the ones who had courted arrest by petitioning the Kashag to expel the Chinese.

The Mimang found that it had a definite purpose when the Chinese took over the *dzongpons*. At first the people began asking some local Mimang member to take up their grievances with the Tibetan officials in Lhasa. Before long, however, Tibetan groups in every part of the country had their own member representatives. Some of these members represented a small district. Others spoke for a group of people belonging to one profession—for example, the wool traders from a certain area. Even lamas and government officials had their representatives. Finally the Mimang acquired more than four thousand members and almost every part of Tibet and every segment of Tibetan society were represented.

At this point the Mimang began calling national meetings. The meetings, known as *Mimang Tsongdu* (People's Assembly), were not held regularly; the assembly convened in Lhasa on the eve of an important event or because of an emergency. Moreover, not all of the members attended; only those came who might be directly affected by the problem at hand. Finally, once the problem had been discussed, a solution could not always be found.

One must avoid the temptation to overemphasize either the efficiency or effectiveness of the Mimang. It lacked any real authority to make its demands considered, even by the Tibetan government. It did not have the brilliant leadership or statesmanship of the members of India's nationalist movement, the Congress Party. And its organization was too loose for the Mimang to be called properly a political party. Nevertheless it was an organization; it enabled the Tibetans to isolate the Chinese-controlled *dzongpon*, and above all it represented the instinctive striving, among all civilized people, for democratic forms and institutions.

Thus the Mimang became the greatest single threat to the

Chinese Communist aims for Tibet and was quickly recognized as such. At first the Han did not dare oppose it openly; this would have driven it underground where it would have been even more dangerous. In propaganda broadcasts beamed abroad the Chinese authorities tried to associate themselves with the Mimang, suggesting even that the idea for it had been theirs and that they had started it in order to encourage democratic practice among the Tibetans. The falsehood was soon exposed by the many Tibetan refugees who escaped into India.

At the same time the Chinese made a concerted effort to subvert the Mimang to their purposes. If successful, they would have a really powerful instrument for the complete control of the mountain kingdom; their planted "demands for reforms" in a body that seemed truly to speak with the voice of the people would give the Han the authority they needed for rapid communization of the country.

Thus persuasion and bribery were used constantly against Mimang members. According to a few refugees, several of the members were "bought," but they were quickly identified by the other members and isolated.

When the Han finally faced the fact that they could not pervert the Mimang, they moved against it. Several of its more important members were jailed. This called for another violent reaction from almost the entire Tibetan population. The monasteries particularly fought hard to save the lives of these members. Fearing a mass uprising, the Chinese soon released the prisoners.

Finally the Chinese turned their effort to minimizing the Mimang's effectiveness. The attempts to bribe the members still went on, but the propaganda now belittled Mimang activities. Rumors meant to cast doubt on the integrity of the members were spread. Important members sometimes found that they were delayed en route to Lhasa, usually by a polite Chinese military patrol who "mistakenly" held them until the meeting was over. And almost always the Chinese authorities called for huge mass meetings to take place while the *Mimang Tsongdu* was in session. The Chinese-sponsored mass meetings were a colorful farce. After

lavish teas and even feasts the Han authorities made dramatic
announcements of new wonders that they planned to introduce at
once to their Tibetan brothers—electricity for every village in
Tibet, for example. Following the announcements, the Tibetans
made flowery speeches expressing delight and gratitude at the
generosity of their Chinese brothers. Finally even more flowery
speeches exchanging compliments were made until the meeting
of the People's Assembly was over. The news broadcasts next day
were filled with the details of the mass meeting, and the generally
less colorful achievements of the *Mimang Tsongdu* somehow did
not rate mention. No Tibetan was so boorish as to expect the
Chinese to implement their plans for the promised wonders, but
the mass meetings seemed to delight everyone, and they saved
face all around.

The Chinese, of course, were not content merely to save face.
Their failures to persuade, subvert, or trick the Tibetans into
giving up the country made them turn their thoughts again to
military force. The Chinese armies now in Tibet were strong but
they were playing no real part in the battle of wits for Tibet.

The Chinese troops were afraid. According to the fiction maintained by their officials, their purpose in Tibet was to protect the
Tibetans from imperialist aggressors. The mountain kingdom was
supposed to be autonomous until the people themselves made
demands for the reforms that would enable the Chinese Communists to take over the country's administration. Meanwhile, as
protectors of the Tibetans, the Chinese troops were ordered to
respect Tibetans. A Chinese soldier who committed a misdemeanor
against a Tibetan was subject to trial in a Tibetan court. The
old-fashioned Tibetan law carried such ferocious punishments that
the Chinese troops were understandably terrified of it. Thus they
avoided Tibetans whenever possible, and when contact was necessary they were exceedingly polite. The Tibetans were losing all
fear of the troops and, as a result, their respect for the Chinese
authorities was also diminishing. To change this tendency the
Chinese realized that their troops, in order to command more respect from the Tibetans, must be free of the harsh Tibetan law.

Working through their collaborators, therefore, the Chinese now brought forward a "popular demand" of the Tibetans for modernization of the legal system.

No Tibetans to whom I talked were sentimental about their legal system or were against legal reform in itself. All Tibetans, however, realized the importance of their harsh laws in keeping the Chinese troops polite. Thus another clamor was raised in Tibet against the change. According to the Agreement, the Chinese could not arbitrarily make such a basic change in the face of united Tibetan resistance to it. The reform had to be abandoned, but the Chinese did manage to win their main point. Chinese personnel who committed offenses against Tibetan citizens were still tried in Tibetan courts, but if found guilty they were turned over to the Chinese authorities for punishment.

Almost immediately the Chinese soldiers developed an arrogance more befitting an occupation force in a conquered country. The Tibetans did acquire some fear of the Han troops. The effect, however, was to increase the unity of all Tibetans. The Mimang became more powerful, and part of its operations now became secret.

The increased unity of Tibetans turned the Chinese thoughts back to their British-inspired policy of divide and rule. Moreover, their Panchen Lama had now been in Shigatse for many months without doing anything for their cause other than to quote publicly a few Communist slogans. The subject of the three-zonal government for Tibet, therefore, was heard again in the propaganda broadcasts. The Dalai Lama and the Kashag were subjected to renewed pressure to accept the "reform." The Tibetan leaders objected as vehemently as before.

The Chinese then attempted to work through the National Assembly, that body of appointed minor officials whose duty was to advise the Kashag. Some of its members were collaborators. The Chinese had a pro-Communist Tibet group circulate a petition demanding the three-zonal government. The group then approached the National Assembly collaborators, who were to sign the petition themselves and push it through for presentation to the

Kashag. The Kashag members, however, got wind of the trick; they confiscated the petition papers and gave them to the Dalai Lama.

The Chinese lost much face over this incident, and they responded with a direct move that involved their Panchen Lama. Shortly after the failure of the petition approach a so-called Panchen Lama Kanpo Lija (Panchen Lama's Administrative Council) was established in Shigatse. Theoretically it had complete administrative authority over a large area in the west. Later on Che Jigme, the collaborator who had sponsored the Panchen for the Chinese, stated in a report that the council had been formed "after reporting to and requesting the permission of the Central Government's Representative and of the Central Government." To Mao's Panchen, of course, the "central government" was at Peking.

This was a wholly arbitrary act on the part of the Chinese; according to the Agreement, legal authority for Tibet's administration was still in the hands of the Dalai Lama and the Kashag members, all of whom had been emphatically against the partitioning of their country.

Moreover, the far eastern zone of Tibet, the center of which was Chamdo, had been administered by a Chinese People's Liberation Committee ever since the area was captured in 1950. Thus, in theory, the partitioning of Tibet was achieved. Chinese broadcasts no longer referred to "The Tibetan Government." Instead they mentioned laboriously "The Panchen Lama Kanpo Lija, the Tibet Local Government, and the People's Liberation Committee of the Chamdo Area."

The only trouble was that all Tibetans except the few collaborators simply refused to accept the partitioning. They would not recognize the status of the appointed officials in the western and eastern committee governments. They paid no attention to the decrees of the committees. Instead they relied even more on the Mimang and followed only the dictates of their Lhasan officials. The Chinese-appointed committee officials drew their salaries but soon found that they had nothing to do.

The lamas had been the most incensed by the Chinese use of the false Panchen as a political power. It was mainly the lamas, therefore, who guided the people in resisting effectively the committee rule. Thus when the Chinese found that, for all practical purposes, their partitioning of Tibet existed only on their paper and in their propaganda, they turned in anger against the monasteries.

The Chinese Military District Headquarters in Lhasa was expanded to include a new Public Security Department. This department made the first real move against monastery authority. At the end of 1953, when plans for the Great Prayer Festival of the New Year were being made, the Public Security Department issued a proclamation that denied the Drepung Monastery proctors the traditional right to control law and order in Lhasa during the celebration. All loyal Tibetans objected, but the Chinese, with the signatures of their two collaborators who were both Military District vice-commanders and Kashag Shapes, overrode the objections. Thus in February 1954, during the three-week festival, the Lhasa streets were patrolled by Chinese and Tibetan soldiers together. Offenders picked up by these troops were turned over to a committee made up of three groups—Tibetan officials, Chinese military authorities, and monastery representatives. An offender was questioned by his own group—Tibetan laymen by their officials, Chinese by their officers, and monks by their high lamas. If a monk was judged guilty, he was held by the military until the end of the festival and then turned over to civil authorities for trial. This very limited jurisdiction of the monasteries over their monks was all that remained of their wide powers during the Great Prayer.

On the surface the Great Prayer ceremonies were begun with the customary color and spirit. To ease the blow of lost prestige the Chinese gave each monk who entered Lhasa a gift of silver comparable in value to two American dollars. The monks accepted the money without any show of appreciation. It was soon evident that, under the surface, resentments seethed. Tension mounted. On the fifth night of the festival two patrol groups were ambushed and chopped to pieces with swords. The next morning an unscheduled procession of "warrior monks" demonstrated against the new oppressions. A full-sized battle was avoided only by letting the demonstrators proceed without interference. Thereafter, however, the Chinese patrols were strengthened and increased. A strict curfew was imposed. All the festive spirit was now gone from the celebration; it was replaced with fear and hatred. Both Chinese and practical-minded Tibetans lived in terror of the possible consequences of some impulsive action by the more headstrong and reckless monks.

The monastery heads tried to keep their people under control. They had warned the monks in advance that self-imposed discipline was their only timely weapon; open defiance of the Communist power was useless and dangerous. Yet even some of the higher lamas, speaking in the temples to their own monks and to pilgrim monks who had come from distant parts of Tibet to see the changes they had heard about, spoke out against the new enemies of Buddhism. They hinted that the time might come when prayers would not be enough. When they spoke of protecting the treasures of the monasteries their listeners knew that they meant not only the images and holy vessels and the books of the Doctrine; they meant also the guns and the precious ammunition.

The Chinese also knew about these arms held by the monasteries. Further, they knew that in the secret meetings of the Mimang talk of an uprising was growing more frequent. The Chinese did not dare risk an open breach with the monasteries—that would mean violent revolt from the whole country—but they tried to infiltrate suspected monasteries.

Thus many new pilgrims from the eastern monasteries, in land under complete Chinese domination, were suddenly seen in the streets of Lhasa. They mixed with the Lhasa lamas and sought shelter in the great monasteries. They were courteously received, for they wore the cloth of the religion and they knew the doctrine and forms. But the Lhasa monks had means of ascertaining the patriotism of loyal Tibetans. Almost none of the visitors passed the test. Thus in the presence of these pilgrims from the east the

Lhasan monks talked only of religion and politely sent the visitors on their way.

Not long after their failure to get at the monastery secrets with spies the Chinese suggested a fiscal reform for the monasteries. The monasteries were to keep detailed accounts of their receipts and expenditures. The records were to be available for audit by the proper office of the Tibetan government. Tibetan officials pointed out the complete impropriety of questioning the monasteries' financial affairs. All tradition was against it. But the Chinese persisted.

The Chinese already suspected that monastery funds were supporting the resistance group of the Mimang. An audit of the funds, therefore, would give the Chinese an idea of the size of the resistance movement. They would be able to curtail the movement by cutting off the supporting funds. They would get an accurate picture of the monasteries' wealth. And they would have an opening wedge with which to cut deeper into lama authority.

The lamas, of course, were perfectly aware of the Chinese intentions. They knew that sooner or later the Han would try to get his hands on their wealth. The Thirteenth Incarnation had written fully on this subject. He told, for example, of the Mongolian monastery which the Communists had insisted on infiltrating with their own group as a "new order." The new members demanded a share of the monastery treasures and eventually took out and sent away all the objects of value. Having robbed the monastery, they mistreated the original resident lamas so brutally that the residents were forced to flee. Whereupon the Communist authorities pursued and arrested them—charging the real lamas with theft of the monastery's wealth. This was the "way of working among the Red people," and the lamas understood it well. They offered prayers of thanks for the wisdom of the Great Thirteenth.

And they refused flatly to show their books to any temporal authority.

The Chinese mentioned fiscal reforms no more, and they closed their eyes to monastery participation in the resistance movement. The lamas were too dangerous to handle; a false step by the

Chinese could bring about the very conflagration that their interference in the monasteries was meant to prevent. The Chinese in
Tibet knew that liberation heroes were not made by the death of
a million Tibetan fanatics. Moreover, despite the endless frustration, their superiors in Peking had told them that only caution, compromise, and patience could build a really secure Communist military base on the roof of the world.

The Han authorities, however, brought additional pressure on
the civilian officials to identify and apprehend the resistance
workers. Several suspected leaders were arrested in Lhasa. The
lamas among these suspects were allowed to be confined in their
own monasteries, while the others were put in the custody of the
Tibetan police. The men, however, were not brought to trial. The
monasteries kept up constant pressure on the authorities either
to try or to release the men.

While the Chinese had their hands full dealing with the lamas,
they suddenly found that the group from whom they expected
the least difficulty—the working classes—was showing distinct
signs of unrest. The trouble was the result of recently implemented labor-conscription regulations. During the early days of
the occupation—before the bulk of the Chinese troops had arrived
—the Chinese had paid good wages for Tibetan road laborers.
With the arrival of the troops the wage scale fell abruptly. The
Tibetan workers quit, and no amount of propaganda could persuade them to go back to the jobs. Meanwhile the road-construc-
tion program was reaching its frenzied climax and local workers
were needed desperately. The Chinese therefore resorted to conscript labor.

Conscript labor was traditional in Tibet as a form of tax to the
government, but normal requirements were not great and no individual was overburdened. Now the demands were colossal—
seven thousand men for the Lhasa airport; twenty thousand for
the western reaches of the Shigatse-Gartok road; eight thousand
for the roads of the Chumbi Valley; five thousand to clear timber for a Chinese rest camp in the forested hills to the east of

Lhasa; more thousands for the forts and landing fields of southwest Tibet and all along the Indian border.

In giving his traditional work tribute the Tibetan was unpaid but he worked near his home and his length of service was short. Generally he was allowed to give his service at a time when he was not occupied with planting or harvesting or with the demands of his craft or trade. Now the workers were summarily called up and dispatched to any area where they were needed. They might be required to go great distances on foot to reach their assigned work area. They might be transported *to* the scene, but they were on their own for the return journey. Usually they were given rations only while working; sometimes they were supplied with no rations if they were working within a reasonable distance from their homes. They were paid only for working days, and the pay was less than one third the amount they had received in the early days of the occupation. This pay was further reduced by fines levied for the slightest dalliance or disobedience. The men were forced to work on Buddhist holy days. Their overseers sneered openly at their religious practices.

Tibetan laborers who had fulfilled their assignments, usually after months of hard work, were issued cards which attested to their labor and which were "safe conduct" passes for their return home. Military patrols stopped and questioned all workers who traveled; if the worker could not show the card he was taken in custody and assigned to a work project, often with a part of his pay deducted as a fine.

The local Tibetan officials whose job was to conscript the labor were caught between two fires. To fill the demands meant risking revengeful action from their people; to refuse meant trouble from the Chinese military. Either course could lead to the loss of official position. The high Tibetan officials, on complaints through Mimang, could insist on his dismissal, or the Chinese could see that he was fired for failing to act "in co-operation with and on advice from" the local Chinese military authorities. The wiser officials tried to compromise, even as they knew their Dalai Lama was compromising in Lhasa.

"Go to the task," they would say. "It is the wish of the Precious One. If we do not find the workers they ask for, the Chinese will take the monks from our monasteries. We will have no one to turn to for counsel. We will become one with the enemies of religion." And with the Chinese authorities the official would plead for a reduction in the demands, for the exemption of a few who were old or sick or were badly needed by their families. "The head lama at the monastery," he might say, "is concerned about the welfare of the people. He is a religious man who cannot understand the importance of your great projects. Many of his monks come from the local families. If they should become unruly . . ."

It was not too hard to play on the Chinese fears of the lamas, and some concessions therefore could be won. If the official showed signs of becoming too easy on his people, however, the military authorities had a clever means of hardening him. Instead of imposing their own fines and punishments on reluctant workers they brought back such laborers and made the local official impose fines and mete out punishments. The money from the fines might add to the treasury of the *dzong*, but it was small compensation for the new hostility which the *dzongpon* received from his own people.

Under such conditions the proud Tibetan workers grew bitterly restive. Trouble from them broke out after an incident late in 1954. Two elderly men, who made up part of a group of ninety workers conscripted from a village, died of exhaustion during their term of labor. They were working many days' journey from home, and the Chinese overseer troops would not allow the bodies to be taken back for traditional disposal and the religious rites, all-important to an auspicious rebirth. When the village work group returned home, bearing this news, the people were at first sick with grief. Two nights later, however, they attacked the camp of a military patrol near the village. Three Chinese soldiers were killed.

More Chinese troops came at once and surrounded the village. Their officer demanded that the villagers identify the attackers and that all arms of the village be brought out and relinquished.

The villagers refused. The Chinese then threatened that if the villagers did not obey they would take ten young men and exile them for forced labor outside of Tibet. A spokesman for the villagers said that they would like to refer to the monastery. A messenger was allowed to go to the monastery and bring a lama. After hearing the story of the action and the threat the lama said that the village should stand firm in its refusal and that the young men should go into exile if necessary. "We have a saying here," the lama told the Chinese officer, "that where there is life there is death."

The threat was not carried out. Troop reinforcements camped near the village and Chinese soldiers patrolled the streets in armed groups. The people were sullen. They hid their arms carefully.

Chinese attempts to confiscate arms met with stoic resistance throughout Tibet. Every Tibetan who could afford a gun had one, and families of any substance had a number of firearms. The weapons could be old and faulty or they could be fine examples of craftsmanship. Whatever they were, they were highly prized and jealously guarded. No action of the Chinese Communists was resisted so unanimously as the sporadic attempts to disarm the public. The attempts were repeatedly begun, postponed, and abandoned.

CHAPTER X

Honey on the Knife

Beware of honey offered on a sharp knife.
—TIBETAN PROVERB

THE Chinese increased their efforts at building good will. Every private owner whose land was diminished by the new roads was scrupulously reimbursed at a good rate for his loss. The Chinese opened a three hundred-bed hospital in Lhasa; it was well staffed and well stocked. They treated outpatients at the hospital and also sent out mobile teams of hygienists to look after the medical needs of the people in outlying districts. They opened a few clinics in other important centers as well. They undertook inoculation programs against smallpox. They advised mothers in child care. All the medical services were free.

The Chinese opened a few schools in Lhasa and in Shigatse, Gyantse, and Yatung. Children from six to eighteen years of age were accepted and the medium of education was Tibetan, although Chinese was a compulsory subject after a certain age. The Tibetans, however, were suspicious of the schools; traditionally education was given in the monasteries. The enrollment in the Chinese schools, therefore, was small.

More appealing was the "youth movement," which the Communists inaugurated in 1953. Within two years youth centers were established in almost every *dzong*. At first membership was more than half Chinese and Chinese Muslim and most of the "members" were imported cadres. The organization, however, was well supplied with funds, and the authorities soon found ways to appeal to the Tibetan young people.

The original title was the Cultural Association for Patriotic Youth. Quarters were assigned by the military officers. Reading and study rooms, sports fields, game rooms, and theaters were provided. The children were told, "Form study groups; decide what you want, ask for it, and it will be supplied." Well-trained Chinese cadres participated in study-group discussions on Tibetan art, folklore, and music. They also guided the study of such subjects as "Mao Tse-tung and Chinese Policies toward Minorities" and "Monasteries as an Obstacle to Progress." Cadres suggested that some of the old Tibetan songs needed new words and they fashioned "progressive" lyrics for ancient tunes. Astonished Tibetan parents heard their children singing of "Mao Tse-tung, Ten Thousand Years." Much worse, they found their children asking to go to China, the motherland of great progress. To the Tibetan children the youth centers were places of wonder and excitement— with film shows, sports, entertainments, and free sweets. Everything was free. The humblest Tibetan child could mingle here with the sons and daughters of the high officials. And all this, the children were told, was nothing compared to China. Naturally the children wanted to go to China.

And they did go. When the roads in the east were ready for traffic, trucks came to the road terminals. Children who had gathered at the youth centers climbed aboard, singing and shouting and happy. The tears of their parents had little effect; the children had been taught thoroughly that the way of the Tibetan lamas was difficult and slow but that the way of the great Mao Tse-tung was easy. They were promised new clothes and fine schools in China. They might become high officials, no matter how humble their background. Families who had gladly given one son to a monastery now lost all their children to the strange non-religion of Communism. More than twenty thousand Tibetan children from eight to sixteen years of age followed the rough new roads to China. Few of the Chinese efforts to communize Tibet were as successful, but none embittered the adult Tibetans more.

The palace of the Dalai Lama in Lhasa, one of the most extraordinary and dramatic structures in the world, from which the Dalai Lama escaped from the Communists in 1959. *Below,* the Communist barracks in the field before the palace.

Above, the old road to Tibet over which the author and his father, Lowell Thomas, Sr., traveled on their visit in 1949. *Below,* the same road, rebuilt by the Communists as a military artery to Lhasa, the capital.

The famed Khamba tribesmen, fierce and loyal fighters for autonomous Tibet, who have recaptured great areas from the Communists. *Below*, the old Tibetan army, wiped out in the battle at Chamdo in October 1950.

Lowell Thomas, Sr., chatting with the true Panchen Lama in 1949. *Below,* the Dalai Lama (right) and the false Panchen Lama (left), foisted on Tibet by the Communists, and now the puppet religious leader since the Dalai Lama fled.

Above, the Dalai Lama in India for the 2500th anniversary of Buddhism in 1956. *Below,* some months later, in his capital, in a last vain attempt to preserve peace under communism.

Under the old Tibetan order. These giant monks were the Dalai Lama's personal bodyguard. *Below,* one of the distant mountain monasteries. Those which were centers of resistance were bombed by the Communists.

Above, Communist buildings at Lhasa. LOWER LEFT, People's Civilian Hospital. RIGHT CENTER, Tibetan Foreign Bureau. LEFT CENTER, Chinese Weather Observatory. *Below,* the new Communist-built bridge across Kyi Chu River.

Refugee Tibetans at the refugee centers across the border inside India. *Below,* Lowell Thomas, Sr., with the Dalai Lama's family in 1949. In 1959 they escaped with the Dalai Lama as the world waited news of their safety.

The Chinese were less successful with a "women's movement" that they started at the same time. The sponsors were the wives of General Chang Ching-wu and of Ngapho Shape. These ladies entertained at a few social functions and sponsored group study in child care and homemaking. Tibetan women, however, showed a minimum of interest in learning about the writings of Mao. They were not enthused when they were told about the "equal privileges" women could enjoy under Communism or the great part they could play in Tibetan progress. Tibetan women had always enjoyed independence and their contribution to their country was great. They refused to believe that raising children who failed to respect the family altar and who clamored to leave their homes for the wonders of a foreign land could be called progress. They were not anxious either to mix "equally" with a Chinese general's wife or with the wives of collaboration officials and traitors.

Although the Chinese were perturbed by the failure of such projects, they expected ultimate success in a long-range program to engulf the Tibetan population. Tibetans knew that the Communist leaders had promised to increase Tibet's population to ten million people. They gave a cool reception to the families of Chinese settlers, whom they called "the grafted ones." The settlers were allowed to cultivate the fallow lands of the fertile Chumbi Valley and to break new land on the reserved government acreages. Chinese agricultural settlers were safe only near Chinese garrisons, and even here their fields were sometimes laid waste by night or their small new flocks were spirited mysteriously away. They came in sufficient numbers to disturb the Tibetans and to upset the economy, especially in areas where they were allowed to take over certain trades. Even so, these numbers were not enough to fulfill the promise of ten million. Briefly the fears of overwhelming colonization were allayed.

Then Muslim refugees from the north brought the answer. The Chinese settlers were taking over the great grazing lands of the Tsaidam Basin. In the tall-grass steppes west of Sining tens of thousands of Han followed the progress of the new Sining-Lhasa road. They were brought by the truckload to the point of road completion, where they were unloaded, with tents and a few implements, and told to make themselves a home.

It was a hard country, where the tall grass grew each summer and where herds of antelope and wild yak made their home. In winter deep snow buried the land and icy gales swept across the steppes. In springtime the melting snow made treacherous torrents of the streams. Flash floods imperiled traffic on the caravan track. Tsaidam Mongols and nomadic Tibetan herders traditionally led their flocks to these grasslands in late summer, after the streams subsided, and led them out again before the winter set in. This year, however, they found not only the thousands of road workers, with their army guards, but also the tent towns of settlers who had come to stay.

Tibetans believed that the settlers would be unable to stay. No one had ever farmed the northern grasslands. No one thought that crops could grow in the short season or that the settlers could live through the arctic winter. But Soviet experts had come first, it was said; the experts had tested the soil and reported that it could be farmed. The Russians also said that oil and perhaps valuable minerals might be found in the area. Nevertheless, the herders expected that the cruel winter would drive out the settlers and that next year the tents would be gone.

Next year the tents were gone, but they had been replaced by huts. Moreover, the land was divided into cultivated fields that supplied a living—although a miserable one—for the settlers. On ahead, following the road, were new tents which next year would become huts while more tents would spring up still further ahead. Even south of the Tsaidam, on the road to Lhasa, near the military road posts were areas which had been staked out for future settlement. This, then, was the fulfillment of the promise. An ever-growing horde, inching down from the north, establishing cities with Chinese names, setting up Chinese shops, living off the wild life which no Tibetan herder ever had disturbed.

The Chinese called it a "reclamation-of-wastelands" program. This had been a land of beauty and inspiration, of silence and

wide plains under wider skies. It was a land which fed the tame
herds of thousands of Tibetan nomads each summer and where
great herds of untamed creatures lived in sanctuary the year
around. This, of course, would constitute a wasteland to the
colonizing Communists.

At the edge of the Tsaidam, where the road turned south to
Lhasa, a huge Chinese city was growing. A large airfield was already in operation. Electric power was being installed for small
factories that were uprooted from China's crowded east coast and
transported to the new site, along with their managers and workers,
willing or unwilling. Russian scientists explored for mineral wealth
and blueprinted plans for communications to connect this new
center with the Chinese cities of Kansu and with Sinkiang. The
Chinese in Lhasa often spoke of this new city. They called the
Tsaidam Basin area the "treasure house of Tibet." But it was
strictly a Chinese treasure house, to be exploited by Chinese
colonists who would become part of the new ten-million population of the "Tibet area of China."

Tibetans could take some slight comfort from the fact that the
new population was neither happy nor entirely reliable. While
the Propaganda Department worked to indoctrinate the Tibetans, the Chinese also required indoctrination. Daily lectures exhorted the troops and cadres to give up "unreliable thinking" and
to work steadfastly at their tasks for the greater glory of the
motherland. Periodically large groups of Chinese—troops, cadres,
settlers, and artisans—were returned to China. They had been
found "politically unreliable." Those who remained lived in an
atmosphere of mutual distrust. No one knew who might be an
informer. Cadres were urged to learn the Tibetan language well,
yet if they learned it well enough to carry on any easy conversation
they might be suspected of overfriendliness to the Tibetan people.
Among the troops any personal grudge could be revenged by
hinting that a certain soldier leaned toward the KMT or had a
relative among the guerrilla bands on the eastern border. Respect
for the Tibetans' religious beliefs was a part of the Chinese policy,
but a construction overseer who allowed his conscript laborers to

observe the holy days risked a reprimand for slackness. Every word or act had its political implications. Even the labor-battalion workers, whose lot was so miserable that one could not imagine a worse fate for them, were combed for "dissenters" and groups regularly were sent back. Cases of sabotage were not always of Tibetan inspiration, although a Tibetan scapegoat generally could be found while the real culprits were re-exported.

Some of the Chinese, particularly the troops, tried to escape into India. A few succeeded, and many lost their lives in the little-known passes that had no border guards. Indian traders and pilgrims often were approached for help in smuggling Chinese defectors out of Tibet, but the Indians were closely watched and few were willing to take the risk.

Faced with engulfment of their population, the "education" of their children in the godless ways of Communism, the loss of political independence, the subversion of their culture, and the increased brutality of foreign troops in their land, the Tibetan will to resist grew rapidly. Some of the hotheads committed spontaneous acts of violence in revenge against the hated aggressors. These acts helped little and only called for more repressive measures from the Chinese. Other Tibetans, therefore, began to meet secretly to plan more effective means of united revolt. Nevertheless, the mass of Tibetans, at least by instinct and at the most under the guidance of their lamas, worked out methods of passive resistance that continually frustrated the Communists.

Perhaps the most remarkable aspect of the passive resistance was the ability that the Tibetans acquired to see through Chinese propaganda. The Chinese underestimated the natural intelligence of the Tibetans, and their propaganda depended more on sheer quantity than on subtlety. Nevertheless, the Tibetan shrewdness at separating fact from fiction in Chinese propaganda and at "reading between the lines" to arrive at an accurate estimate of the Communists' real intentions—indeed, the very fact that the Tibetans made such an effort—would have done much credit to a far more sophisticated people.

The Tibetans even learned eventually to counteract the worst of the Communist efforts against the children. It was not difficult for Tibetan parents to show their children how often the Chinese invaders lied and broke their promises. After a few years of the occupation all intelligent Tibetans realized that when the invaders seemingly offered something good the offer invariably proved to be motivated by an evil intention. The children were taught to understand this. They were also taught pride of country and culture so that they came to despise and ostracize children whose families permitted too close association with the enemy. Finally the children were instructed to enjoy the facilities of the youth centers but to avoid and not to believe the Chinese who supervised them. In this connection the children were reminded of an old Tibetan saying, "If profit comes to me, why worry about who takes the loss?"

The same saying was applied by older Tibetans in accepting the good-will gestures of the Chinese. When the Chinese came to the rescue of the wool trade, for example, the Tibetan merchants sold their accumulated stocks at the original high prices. But later, when the wool price was controlled at a low figure and the trade threatened to become a Chinese monopoly, most merchants refused to sell. Traditionally the buyer in the Western markets did his own shearing, on either side of the border. The Tibetans now ignored the Chinese advice to bring their wool to Chinese offices for weighing and sale. They simply left it on the sheep and bided their time. In some areas the Chinese sent their own men out with shearing scissors to bring in the wool. Reluctantly then the Tibetan producer would sell, but he would leave the problems of the work and the transport entirely up to the buyer. Sheepherders refused to take advice or help from Chinese veterinary teams who came with suggestions for inoculations and crossbreeding for improvement of the product. "We do not care to improve our product," the Tibetans said. "It brought a higher price before you came. The Indians like our wool as it is. Go away and let us sell it to them."

Tibetans who had taken the seed loans, and the propaganda that went with them, were in no hurry to repay the debt. In order

to establish the ability to pay the Chinese had to send out in-
formers, disguised as merchants, to discuss purchases and thus
to determine the location and quantity of surplus stocks. This ruse
fooled few Tibetan farmers. When the Chinese authorities arrived
to collect the loan, the surplus stocks usually had been well hidden.
Many farmers took their surpluses to the local monastery rather
than repay the Chinese.

Despite the Chinese efforts aimed at weaning the people away
from their dependence on the monasteries, most Tibetans drew
closer to their lama leaders. In these difficult days the only real
comfort available to the Tibetans was prayer, and their only hope
and guidance came from the religious leaders. The Chinese tried
to teach the children that monasteries impeded progress, but
Tibetan adults believed that without religion life had no meaning.

The monasteries themselves had much to resist. Their own children—the young student monks—were primary targets of the Communist propaganda. In a barrage of talks and pamphlets these
young men were told of an exciting new religion. It was called
Buddho-Marxism; it was described as a good way and an easier
way. It did not demand the rigid behavior standards of the reformed sects of Lamaism. All young men were encouraged to enjoy the good things of life. Leave the monasteries, marry, and
raise families, the pamphlets suggested; forget the stodgy religious
books and contribute to the progress of the Tibet part of China.
A Buddho-Marxist could drink good wine, eat fine food, and have
silver in his pockets. Why should the fine young men of Tibet
be slaves to the higher priesthood—to which they could attain, if
lucky, only in their own old age?

Unquestionably such talk found listeners. The higher lamas,
however, had many ways to refute it. In one large monastery,
for example, where the young men appeared susceptible, the
monk leaders shortened the rations for everyone. "This is necessary because there is less food now that the Chinese have come,"
they said. "The Chinese share their opinions with us; we must
share our food with them." The older lamas described to their
young men the misery of the Chinese labor battalions. "The Chi-

nese are working for the progress which you have heard about,"
they said. "They would like you also to work for this progress."
The lamas emphasized to the young monks the importance of
trade to the support of the monasteries. "Many of you will take
part in this trade as an honor and a duty," they said, "unless the
Chinese make all trade their own monopoly. So far we have not
been molested, but our Tibetan private merchants have suffered
greatly. Unless we remain unified and strong, our trade, too, will
be taken over."

The older lamas patiently tried to help their men understand
the real contempt which Communists held for all religion. They
allowed the young monks to read the literature which the Propaganda Department supplied—extracts from speeches of Mao Tse-
tung and long treatises on the minority policies of the Communist
government. Then they gave the young men other material to
read—translations, for example, of Soviet blasts at the "poison of
Buddhism." All young monks were familiarized with the Thirteenth Dalai Lama's exposé of the unspeakable cruelties against
the lama priesthood of Mongolia, where the Communists brought
"deeds of sticky blood." In the Thirteenth Incarnation's writings
the young monks read how the clergy of one Mongolian monastery were called together to receive the "appreciation" of the new
masters. "We will grant you largesse; come at the signal." And
when the monks gathered at the signal within the temple, the
doors were closed, the building was set afire, and all the monks
were burned alive.

The learned lamas worked tirelessly to keep their own group
informed, united, and faithful; this was vital because they believed that their primary duty was to give aid, advice, comfort, and leadership to the Tibetan people. Thus the lamas patiently analyzed the actions of the Chinese authorities. They
learned when to counsel patience and restraint for the people or
when to suggest firm passive resistance. Monks were assigned to
attend Chinese-sponsored showings of propaganda films and to
report any specific points which might mislead the people and
which thus should be refuted.

A film running in Lhasa, for example, might show a smiling Tibetan family, dressed in new clothes and standing in front of their new house "somewhere in western Tibet," where the local people, according to the commentary, were co-operating happily with the People's Liberation Army. Thereafter people who went to the monastery for prayers or to hear a sermon would hear further comments on the film from the monks. The people might learn that a high lama pilgrim had recently come from a tour of all the monasteries of western Tibet. No Tibetan family in that area had a new house, although certainly a few new houses had been built for the Chinese "grafted ones." This film was being shown all over Tibet, the people were told by their monks. In western Tibet, however, the smiling family was described as coming from an eastern area. "But in each place where the film is shown," the lamas would say, "the new house will *not* be, because good Tibetans there are not co-operating. The smiling family in front of the new house has co-operated. They have silver in their pockets for putting on the fine clothes and standing in front of a new house which is not their house." Perhaps then the lama's eyes would twinkle. "And their smiles are real—who would not smile at such an easy way to earn a little silver? Many of our Tibetan people would do the same, but none of us can be fooled by this picture." The listeners, too, would smile. They would remember, and they would tell their friends and neighbors.

Thus the lamas, with their network of communications throughout Tibet and their constant pilgrimages, were able to give invaluable aid to the people. The most appreciated help was an effort made in conjunction with the Mimang. All the outlying monasteries were instructed to report any local example of injustice or hardship imposed by the occupation force on the people. High Lhasan monks, then, could bring such examples to the attention of the top Tibetan officials who had the authority to make demands for relief of the distress.

Nevertheless, the most important single contribution made by the lamas during this period of the occupation was the gathering of accurate information from every corner of the country. With this information they were able to keep all Tibetans informed on the true state of affairs. The lamas, therefore, continued to expand and improve their network. Eventually the network extended beyond the borders of Tibet into the neighboring countries. From the outside sources they were able to keep track of the Chinese propaganda on Tibet beamed to the rest of the world. These broadcasts occasionally contained news of Chinese intentions that was of vital importance to Tibetans.

Thus the Tibetan resistance still stood in the way of Chinese plans. The Tibetans whom they now officially dominated still refused to be subjected. The key to control of the Tibetans, the Chinese officials had learned, was the Dalai Lama. The Chinese did not dare to take open action against him, but the time had come for an all-out effort to subvert him.

CHAPTER XI

The Precious One in Red China

The sweet song of the devil-bird brings misfortune;
The sweet words of a devil bring benefit—but only to him.

—TIBETAN PROVERB

FROM the pragmatic viewpoint of the Chinese Communists the process of persuading the Dalai Lama to their way of thinking could not have seemed difficult. Undoubtedly they recognized that he was intelligent and that he was sincerely—even stubbornly —devoted to his people. Nevertheless he was only a boy. He was also unworldly and impressionable. If given time and the opportunity to "educate" him properly, therefore, he could be turned into an invaluable tool for the occupation force.

The trouble was that, in Lhasa, he did not have the time for the education process. His whole day was taken up with religious and state functions. He was sheltered by the Potala, held aloof by tradition from contact with foreigners, and protected not only by his bodyguard but, in effect, by every living Tibetan as well.

The obvious solution was to take the Dalai Lama to China for an extended visit. Here he would be separated from his people not only by thousands of miles but also by centuries in time. The impressionable boy, if carefully shown only the more glittering achievements of the People's Republic, could not fail to be awed. Moreover, in China some of the best Communist minds could concentrate on his indoctrination.

The Chinese began the project early in 1954 by announcing throughout Tibet that the Dalai and Panchen Lamas had been invited by Peking to participate in the Chinese People's Congress. The occasion was the ratification of the new Chinese Constitution on which the great lamas would be permitted to express their views. The announcement of the invitation was received in Tibet with an ominous silence. A few days later, in a new proclamation, the people were told that the Dalai Lama had accepted the invitation.

Immediately a storm of almost hysterical protest came from every corner of the country. Monasteries, large and small, dispatched fast couriers to Lhasa with messages pleading with the Precious One to remain with his people. At emergency meetings of the Mimang opinions were unanimous: the Dalai Lama must not go to China. Personal delegations arrived in the capital and begged for audiences with the Precious Protector so that the living god could see the tears and hear the entreaties of his worshipers. Khamba chieftains from the east galloped into Lhasa, their swords drawn, to proclaim their loyalty to the God-King and to state their opinion that he should not leave the Holy City.

The Chinese hurriedly ordered more troops. The Propaganda Department concentrated on reassuring the people and exhorting them to remain calm. But the Chinese were adamant about the trip. The Dalai Lama was made to issue a statement to the effect that he was going voluntarily. The date for his departure was made earlier. The Tibetan officials, knowing that if the people lost their self-control everyone would suffer and nothing would be gained, took to the loud-speakers. They told the people that the Holy One had promised to return within a year. They pleaded for patience and faith.

The people had faith in their God-King but not in the words which, they believed, the Han made him say. Thus when the Dalai Lama still persisted in leaving, despite the nationwide pleas for him to stay, the people assumed that the Chinese were forcing him to go. A wave of grief swept through the country. Few believed that the Fourteenth would ever return, and they mourned for him as though he were already dead. Thousands of people who lived near Lhasa dropped their work and made toward the Holy City, presumably hoping for a final glimpse of the Precious Protector.

On July 11, 1954, the Dalai Lama left the Potala to begin the journey to Peking. His entourage included his mother, sister, brother, personal servants, important lamas, and high Tibetan officials, some of whom were accompanied by their wives. In addition, top Chinese military personnel and a strong bodyguard of Han troops swelled the procession. When they entered Lhasa city they found that the streets were jammed with a crowd so huge that the troops had been unable to clear the way.

The moment the procession was sighted a terrible cry of anguish came from the crowd. The sound drowned out the shrieking of the loud-speakers, which were hysterically calling to the people to be calm. The crowd surged forward and, pushing the officials aside, surrounded the Dalai Lama's sedan chair. Every person in the throng was sobbing uncontrollably. Some screamed as though in unbearable anguish. Those nearest the Holy One knelt in the street, crying and pleading for him not to desert them. Others tugged at the chair-bearers, beseeching them not to carry the god away.

Those who witnessed the scene say it was an utter abandonment to grief beyond anything one could imagine. Every witness to whom I have spoken mentioned especially the terrible sound of the sobbing from many thousands of people against a background of the shrill loud-speakers.

The Chinese seemed stunned by the display of emotion and reverence that they could not understand. The troops especially were confused. They had been ordered to act with the utmost restraint. The people, however, showed complete indifference to the bayonets. Many threw themselves into the street, and their prostrate bodies had to be lifted out of the way. Thus the procession inched along, and hours were required to get through the city.

The climax of this dramatic scene came when the procession prepared to cross the river. In a final paroxysm of despair a group from the crowd suddenly rushed forward and broke through the guards. At first the Chinese thought the crowd was beginning to attack. Instead the people threw themselves from the stone embankment into the river to drown. Their action signaled a wave of suicidal frenzy in the great throng. Crowds pushed frantically toward the river. More troops were called hurriedly to line the embankment and to prevent the crowds from reaching the water. Some of the people tried to throw themselves onto the bayonets. The soldiers struggled with the people and kept most of them away. Other soldiers in boats, however, had to drag people forcibly from the water.

Fortunately, when the procession had crossed the river and moved on, the violent emotion in the crowd began to ebb. The people seemed listless and apathetic. Lhasa was like a dead city for many days.

A week after the tragic departure a Tibetan collaborator in Kalimpong made a statement to the Indian press. He said that opposition to the Dalai Lama's departure was merely "wishful thinking" on the part of "Western agents." He insisted that the Dalai Lama was going of his own free will and that the Tibetan oracle had predicted good results from the trip. He added that, far from being "forcibly removed," the Dalai Lama might even decide to proceed to China via India.

A few days later, however, the Indian newsmen showed no surprise when they learned that the Dalai Lama had departed a week before the collaborator's statement and that he was traveling with a large Chinese escort overland via the new Chamdo-Lhasa road.

By taking this route the Chinese expected to impress the Dalai Lama with their road-building achievement in Tibet. At this time, however, in July 1954, the road was motorable only a few hundred miles south and west of Chamdo. It was not expected to be ready for motor traffic to the river outside Lhasa until the end of the year. The two hundred miles from Lhasa to the present motorable point on the road, however, was supposed to be adequate for animal transport. Thus, although the party would have to make this part of the journey on foot or horseback, the traveling was expected to be easy. General Chang Ching-wu, the senior Chinese officer in the Dalai Lama's entourage, overestimated the efficiency of his road workers and underestimated the effects of the Tibetan weather. Nothing had really been done to the last two hundred miles of the road since the Russian surveyors had marked out the route some years before. Many of the road markings were washed out. Often the camp sites, which Chinese minor officials had carefully planned and laid out in advance, could not be found.

According to a Tibetan member of the traveling party, the journey that followed would have been amusingly ludicrous if it had not been so strenuous. Part of the time the whole party, amounting to several hundred people, was completely lost in the wild gorges of that country. The Chinese attempts to pretend they knew where they were going and, even more, to pretend that they were traveling along a well-marked roadway kept the Tibetans endlessly amused. The rigors of the traveling, however, were far from amusing. Often the party had to scramble over slippery ledges on hands and knees. A cold rain fell almost constantly. Frequent heavy mists made the precipitous paths even more hazardous. Twice the people had to climb dangerous cliffs. Camps were pitched whenever the travelers were too exhausted to go further. On some nights, despite the luxurious tents, the travelers bedded down in several inches of icy water.

By the tenth day the party was still more than a hundred miles from the motorable point on the road. The Dalai Lama was bearing the rigors well and without complaint. All the others, however, showed signs of the strain. The suffering of the women and older members of the party was especially acute.

On the eleventh day, therefore, the Tibetan officials approached General Chang Ching-wu and told him that they could not allow the Dalai Lama to proceed. The journey was too dangerous. The party must return to Lhasa and proceed by the old caravan route to Chamdo. Chang, famous for his temper, lost it now. The Chinese people in general, he said, and their road-building accomplishments in particular, had been insulted by the

Tibetan officials. He, and he alone, was responsible for the safety of the Dalai Lama. He had set the route. He and the Dalai Lama would follow it. The others could come along or go back to Lhasa. The Tibetans listened courteously but insisted on returning with the Dalai Lama.

The argument finally was settled by the Dalai Lama. He asked Chang how many days the rest of the trip to the motor point would require. He was told that the trip would take ten more days. In that case, the Dalai Lama said, they were beyond the point of no return. Going back to Lhasa would impose another eleven days of hardship on the women and older people. Thus they all might as well see the rest of the "new road." His inference that the rest of the road could not possibly be worse than what they had already seen amused the Tibetans and put them in the mood to accept the Chinese direction again. The Tibetans must have known also that the Chinese could hardly take lightly the loss of face that a return would entail, much less a repeat performance of the Lhasa departure drama; the unpleasantness of the Chinese in such circumstances might be worse than the journey.

Thus the party pushed on once more. Incredibly the rest of the journey was worse. The motorable point was not reached until two weeks later. By then the travelers were so exhausted that they were not even cheered by the sight of the jeeps. Even when Chang pointedly informed them that the Willys jeeps were made in the Soviet Union, the Tibetans were unable to enjoy the joke among themselves.

The jeeps took them through Chamdo to Chengtu, the capital of Szechwan. At this point half of the party returned to Lhasa. The important members of the remaining half were flown to Sian. Here they rested while they waited for the minor officials of the party who came on by train. They also waited for the Panchen Lama's entourage, which had left Tibet by the northern route through Sining along the other new road. When the two parties joined in Sian, the Chinese Minister of Communications arrived in person to escort the two great lamas to Peking.

Meanwhile, back in Tibet, the morale was sinking even lower. The people were despondent. Suicide, which normally was rare among the lively Tibetans, was becoming more common. Many of the older monks fell ill when the Dalai Lama departed. They had lost their guiding light. They would not take food and, unable to sustain hope or life, hundreds of them died in their monastery cells.

To make matters worse, a terrible catastrophe struck Tibet with a strangely fateful timing. The rains were unusually heavy that year, but almost from the moment the Dalai Lama left Lhasa they increased to a volume unequaled in Tibet's history. Within ten days of his departure the streams, rivers, and lakes began to overflow. Tibetans had never seen floods of the size that followed. Thousands died in the angry waters. Many more thousands lost their homes, all their possessions, and the crops on their lands. The floods were especially bad in the Shigatse-Gyantse area where almost the entire population was made destitute. When the waters receded, the survivors, starving and in rags, wandered through scenes of utter desolation, looking for their dead.

The Tibetans did not question the cause of this new misfortune. They knew. "The gods are angry because the Precious Protector has left the Holy City," they said. "We will all be destroyed."

Moreover, the gods had not struck blindly. The Holy City and the Potala were undamaged and secure. The wrath had descended on Shigatse where Mao's false lama defiled the residence of the Panchen Incarnation. One of his palaces collapsed in the flood, and two hundred people were buried in the debris. Nearby a barracks for the Chinese guard of the false Panchen was swept away and several hundred of the Han troops had drowned.

The first traveler from Tibet to India with the full story of the horror was, strangely enough, a Tibetan emissary from the Peking government. He was sent with a message for the older brother of the Dalai Lama, Gyalo Thondup, who was in Darjeeling. According to the press, the message was a "delicate request" to transfer the young sister and the niece and nephew of the Dalai Lama from their Darjeeling school to Peking where "the

Chinese Government promised to attend to their every comfort and well-being." Peking officials evidently felt that this was an auspicious moment to press once again for the removal of the children of Tibetan noble families from Indian schools. The Dalai Lama and his sister, who was the mother of two of the children, would soon arrive in Peking.

The time, however, was not auspicious. The Dalai Lama's brother ignored the "delicate request," but he set about at once to obtain help for the Tibetans who had survived the flood. The emissary estimated that at least fifteen hundred people had died (a figure which later turned out to be conservative), and he described the survivors as "half starved and near naked . . . about them all were endless empty fields of soggy earth. Above them crows and vultures . . ."

Gyalo Thondup organized a Tibet Flood Relief Committee in Kalimpong and appealed to representatives of all foreign governments for gifts of food, clothing, medicines, and money. Emergency relief supplies were sent in from Gangtok in Sikkim. The Indian Political Officer at Gangtok went to Gyantse to study the situation at first hand and to check up on the staff and properties of the Indian Trade Agency there. Some Indians also had lost their lives in the disaster.

The Chinese authorities at this point went into action. They announced that they did not require outside assistance and that they were distributing relief supplies. Orders totaling half a million rupees ($100,000) were reportedly placed in India, with the payment handled through Kalimpong's Bank of China. Chinese Communist troops, brought into the flood areas, were publicized as sharing their clothing and shoes as gifts to the suffering Tibetan people.

The Chinese Communists, again speaking through their Tibetan collaborator in Kalimpong, denied published reports of the extensive damage and said that the Panchen's palace had not collapsed, nor had any Chinese soldiers lost their lives. Later, however, the Chinese did not bother to deny published reports that the Panchen's followers were building a new palace for him.

The Tibetan people, miserable and frightened, looked for other evil omens and waited for some news of their God-King. Food shortages, aggravated by the loss of crops to the flood, became acute. Bitterly despondent, hungry men turned to low-paid jobs on the road construction. Frustration increased the number of incidents between Tibetans and the Chinese troops and settlers.

The incidents were increased by still another circumstance. As soon as the Dalai Lama was safely out of Tibet, the Chinese authorities in Lhasa made further attempts to establish their Military and Administrative Committee. During the Dalai Lama's absence the government was nominally headed by the Kashag members who had not accompanied their leader. In actual control was General Chang Kuo-hua, commander of the Chinese forces in Lhasa, who now took over Chang Ching-wu's duties as well. In the new attempt to establish the Military and Administrative Committee, Chang Kuo-hua used the Chinese-sponsored Development Department and a small group of Tibetan minor officials who collaborated with the invaders.

The minor Tibetan officials submitted a written memorandum to the Kashag, demanding the immediate formation of the Military and Administrative Committee in accordance with the 17-Point Agreement. The memorandum also contained a demand for government management of landed estates belonging to officials. The Kashag members, through personal pressure on their junior officials, persuaded them not to press such demands in the absence of their leader. Thus the Chinese attempt to win nominal control of the country failed again, and the Kashag avoided having to make a flat refusal.

Obviously the Chinese had counted on making big strides toward the final subjugation of Tibet during the Dalai Lama's absence. No one—not even the Tibetans themselves—however, had realized how demoralized the people would be by the Holy One's departure. The Chinese naturally feared that the people's deep despondency and bitterness might suddenly turn into equally intense hatred directed at them. They therefore heeded the warning of the increased instances of violence. Instead of pushing for more "reforms" their propaganda now concentrated on keeping the people reassured about their God-King. The Tibetans showed little interest in the Dalai Lama's activities in China; they wanted to know when he would return to them. Above all, they wanted the feeling of being in personal contact with him.

At this point some clever Chinese propagandist struck on the idea of using the recently completed network of telegraph communications between Tibet and China as a means of putting Tibetans in closer contact with their ruler. Distance, of course, is measured really in terms of time rather than miles. When the Holy One was many weeks of hard travel away, his subjects felt that he was separated from them by a great distance. If the people, however, could send him messages that would reach him within only a few hours, the distance would seem diminished. Previously private persons—usually important businessmen—had been permitted to send telegrams only on rare occasions of proven emergency. Now, however, the Chinese told the people that private telegrams, if addressed to the Dalai Lama and if paid for at the very high commercial rate, would be accepted.

The Tibetans responded with joy. The *dzongpons* collected the messages from the people in their districts and sent free official telegrams summarizing the greetings and requests. Groups of individuals banded together to contribute toward the cost of a telegram. The Mimang had funds with which to help deserving individuals pay for a private message. The monasteries also gave such help and, of course, sent their own telegrams. Petitions, tear-stained and bearing many signatures, were dispatched by courier to border cities where postal service into China was available.

By offering to put the Tibetans in close personal touch with the Dalai Lama the Chinese unquestionably scored an important propaganda victory. The effect of this victory, however, was lost through a grave propaganda mistake made at the same time. For release in India and in other free countries outside Tibet, the Peking authorities issued a news story describing the departure of the Dalai Lama from Lhasa. Newspaper cuttings of the release were obtained by the monastery contacts in the Indian border areas and before long were shown throughout Tibet.

Instead of describing the almost complete abandonment to grief that had accompanied the departure, the release said that Lhasa's streets had been crowded with people who had come in great joy "to celebrate and to pray for the health of Chairman Mao Tse-tung." The rest of the article suggested that the Tibetans were delighted to see their God-King off to visit such a great benefactor as the Chinese head of state.

The Chinese propagandists, however, were speaking the truth when they said that the Dalai Lama was being given a magnificent reception in China. His special train was stopped frequently along the route from Sian to Peking so that he could receive honors and ovations. In Peking itself he was met by the most important state officials, who greeted him as a great personage. He was installed in a special palace which had been suitably furnished and decorated for him.

From the Dalai Lama's viewpoint, according to a member of his entourage, the receptions were unique in that, for the first time, the God-King attended functions at which no other religious persons were present. Instead of obeisance, literal or symbolic, the high officials shook his hand.

For the first time, also, the Dalai Lama found himself being treated as an equal to the Panchen Lama. True, the Panchen and party were lodged in less impressive quarters than those given to the Dalai. Also, on formal occasions when protocol decreed a show of precedence, the Dalai received priority. The priority, however, was seldom more than a handshake offered to him first. Generally the distinctions between the two high lamas were carefully eradicated in public. The Panchen almost immediately developed a regal swagger, but the Dalai remained simple and dignified, showing no disapproval of the manners of his hosts.

His hosts kept him busy with a full schedule from the moment of his arrival. A few days after he reached Peking the National People's Congress opened, and the Dalai Lama attended all the meetings. During the meetings he made two speeches. Although he wrote his own speeches, they were edited by Central Government representatives who rewrote any portions that went beyond purely internal Tibetan concerns and touched on relationships between Tibet and China. Press coverage concentrated purely on quotes from the rewritten "relationship" portions. The Dalai's own words often touched on religion, for religion was both the life and the government of Tibet, but no hint of religion appeared in the press excerpts.

At the same time the Chinese officials were careful to see that the young God-King found evidence of religious freedom and respect for Buddhism in China. In Peking an ancient lama temple, which had long been in disrepair, was renovated soon after the "liberation" of Tibet; the lamas now were taken to this temple to speak and to hold audiences. Physically the temple was in excellent condition. Its occupants, however, had not been renovated; only fifty or sixty elderly monks, mostly Mongolians, were in residence. The temple had no school nor any young monks in training. The whole place had an atmosphere of decay.

When the Dalai Lama spoke at the temple, large crowds gathered to hear him, but many appeared to have come out of curiosity rather than in devotion. Even so, the large turnout was surprising because the sermons at the lama temple were never publicized in advance. The Dalai Lama's temporal activities, on the other hand, were widely publicized and large crowds were encouraged. Curiously enough, although the Chinese made much of their renovated lama temple, they warned the Dalai Lama and his party to exercise great care during the visits; the place was described as a hotbed of KMT agents and activity.

When the Dalai Lama spoke at the temple he did not use the government-supplied interpreter but personally hired a Chinese Buddhist who had studied at Drepung and who was fluent in Tibetan. Speaking the words of religion, even in this temple which might be only a showpiece, the Dalai Lama wanted to ensure that his words were truly interpreted. He spoke only on religious matters. According to his mother, he enjoyed the temple because it gave him a fleeting touch with the familiar.

At the same time, however, his youth and quick intelligence enabled him to enjoy new adventures as well. He had experienced his first train ride, first airplane flight, first view of a city of modern streets and buildings. A sleek motorcar whisked him from place to place. He participated in political meetings. He attended formal receptions, visited factories, hospitals, schools, and universities.

The Chinese were careful to see that the young Dalai's program, although full, was not overly formal. He met several times informally with Mao Tse-tung, who was always polite and friendly. Mao invited the Dalai Lama to his home, and he often went to the Dalai's residence. Chou En-lai also had informal friendly meetings with the Tibetan God-King.

The world press at the time, guessing at what might be going on in Peking, published stories about the lamas attending eight-hour-daily indoctrination courses. The Chinese, however, were not unsubtle with their potential puppet. The Dalai Lama was given concentrated indoctrination, but his tutor was Liu Ke-ping of the Committee of Nationalities Affairs. Liu accompanied the Dalai Lama everywhere. He filled odd moments with friendly discussion and instruction. He came several times a week for longer talks over tea and in an atmosphere of friendship at the Dalai's residence. Liu explained Communist theory and presented a picture of world affairs from the Communist viewpoint. He encouraged questions and made suggestions. The Dalai Lama was invited to sit in on meetings of high officials—often at the invitation of Mao himself—and to observe the way the Chinese rulers worked. Subtly, too, the Chinese leaders allowed him to see that they held him in higher esteem than their own sponsored Panchen. Publicly the two lamas were treated alike—but privately the Dalai Lama could infer that he was the chosen one to sit among the leaders if he would.

The Chinese were careful to keep outside influences from upsetting their indoctrination program for the Dalai Lama. Foreign ambassadors paid respectful calls at his residence and were politely received. Ambassadors from Communist countries were allowed to converse freely through the interpreter, and the Soviet ambassador came for long talks on more than one occasion. When the Indian ambassador called, however, a number of Chinese officials happened to be on hand at the same time. When Prime Minister Nehru visited Peking, a month after the Dalai Lama's arrival, the two met only at a large formal reception for the Indian leader and at a cocktail party given by the mayor of Peking. When Prime Minister Nehru left, the lamas were theoretically to be included in a seeing-off party at the airport. Through some mistake, however, the lamas' car took them to the airport at the wrong time, and they found themselves seeing off a planeload of Indian journalists.

Chinese control over the Dalai's contacts could not be extended to his own people. According to a Tibetan official who was with the Dalai Lama, the Peking authorities were reluctant to deliver the many telegrams, letters, pleas, and petitions that arrived daily for him. Evidently the Chinese wanted, to the fullest extent possible, to cut the bonds that bound the Dalai Lama to his country and people and to overawe the boy so that henceforth he would be more Chinese than Tibetan. The failure to deliver the messages, however, would have been too risky. Ultimately the Tibetans would have discovered the fact, and undoubtedly they would have been enraged. Thus the messages were delivered. The Dalai Lama not only read them all but personally answered each one. He told his people that he was being well treated and that he would return within the promised time. With the Chinese he showed polite interest in the tours, sight-seeing, and receptions. The fact was soon apparent, however, that the Dalai Lama was homesick. He showed real enthusiasm only when he was given news of Tibet and the Tibetans.

The big news in Tibet at the end of 1954 was the completion of the two motorable roads all the way to Lhasa. The Propaganda Department made plans for an extravagant road-opening ceremony. The streets were lavishly decorated. Youth groups practiced dances. Officials rehearsed speeches.

On December 25, 1954, more than a hundred trucks came in a

straggling line to the motor terminal that had been erected at a village across the river from Lhasa; a bridge over the river was not yet built. The trucks flew triumphant banners hailing the "road heroes" and Tibet's reunion with the motherland. The trucks also carried thirty-five tons of Chinese goods manufactured in Canton and Shanghai. The goods were supplies for the army of occupation.

The Tibetans gathered at the terminal in large but quiet crowds. The strange sound of motor traffic, heard for the first time in the Holy City, seemed to bewilder them rather than make them festive. They stared at the trucks curiously. The trucks had come from faraway China. Somewhere in that distant land to the east was their Dalai Lama. The words to a then current popular folk song asked sadly if the Precious One might one day return to his people over the new road.

The climax of the road-opening ceremony was an announcement that the Dalai Lama had sent a special message for his people on the occasion. The Tibetans listened tensely. "The opening of the roads," the loud-speakers quoted the Dalai Lama as saying, "will bring closer unity between the Chinese and Tibetan people."

The Tibetans turned from the loud-speakers and began to drift away. Many were weeping. To almost all Tibetans now the word "unity" in the propaganda broadcasts had become a clue to the bogus.

"Unity" was the theme of all the Dalai Lama's messages from China. "Unity between the Han and the Tibetans is growing day by day," one message said. "The return of the Panchen Lama has strengthened internal unity in Tibet," was another. To Tibetans such statements from any Dalai, but particularly from their Fourteenth, were beyond belief. They already had proof that no perversion of truth was too vile for the Communists. Thus, to the Tibetans, the Dalai Lama was being forced to speak the lies in his messages.

But, if the Han were telling lies and were using force on the Dalai Lama, they might really intend to hold the God-King indefinitely and the promises to return him might be false. It was a fact, despite constant assurances from the Propaganda Department, few Tibetans believed that their Fourteenth would ever see Lhasa again. Their reaction to this belief was a deep despondency, as though their country had suffered a terrible calamity. The reaction confused and even frightened the Chinese, who were never able to understand the real religious feelings of the Tibetans. The Chinese did appreciate, however, that when the Tibetans recovered from their grief the people's emotion might well turn into a blind and violent hatred toward them.

Moreover, some Tibetans did show signs of increasing hatred for their conquerors. In Lhasa and Shigatse especially, riots flared suddenly, frequently, and for no discernible reason. The houses of Chinese officials and Tibetan collaborators were often stoned. Chinese posters and proclamations were always defaced with offal or were torn down. And the cases of ambushed patrols were increasing steadily. One night tires on the trucks parked at the terminal across the river from Lhasa were slashed with swords to ribbons.

Nevertheless, the majority of the Tibetans still wanted only to have their Precious Protector back in Lhasa. In January 1955 a rumor was whispered through the country that a delegation had been formed to go to China and to bring back the Dalai Lama. The acts of violence stopped immediately, and the people pinned their hopes on the success of the mission.

Early in February 1955 a party of sixteen people arrived at the Dalai Lama's residence in Peking. The delegation was made up of Tibetan officials, monks, traders, Khambas, and even the fierce and individualistic Goloks. This was true unity—pure Tibetan unity. The strangely assorted travelers demanded an audience with the Dalai Lama. When they came into his presence they fell at his feet with tears and entreaties. The Dalai Lama blessed the supplicants, talked to them, and arranged for their care. He assured them that he was not a prisoner of the Chinese. He was well treated, as they could see, and he would return to his people within the promised time. He asked them to go back to Tibet and tell these facts to the people.

The delegates, however, did not altogether believe him. They still thought that the Chinese might be exerting some subtle pressure on their ruler here in this Peking palace. They demanded to see Mao Tse-tung.

An appointment was arranged, and Mao received the delegation politely. The delegates told him that he must release the Dalai Lama at once and allow him to return to Tibet. Mao reassured them. He told them of the honors that had been accorded to the Dalai Lama, of the extensive tours and the full program. He asked the delegates to go back, secure in the knowledge that the Dalai Lama soon would rejoin them in Tibet.

After a few days in Peking the delegation bid a tearful farewell to the Dalai Lama and set off. They did not, however, return all the way. When they reached Chengtu, capital of Szechwan, they settled down to await the arrival of the Dalai Lama's party. They sent a courier on to Lhasa to carry the news of their mission.

The Dalai Lama left Peking on March 12, 1955, with a planned itinerary that included a flight from Sian to Lanchow and a motor trip to Sining, where he would tour the area of his old home. He spent almost three weeks here, visiting monasteries and temples. He found that the house in which he had been born was unused and in disrepair. He arranged to give the land for a school. He established a fund for the building and maintenance of the school, which would take the children of Tsinghai Tibetans. On this tour, as on all his other tours in China, the friendly indoctrinator accompanied the Dalai Lama as the head Chinese official in the party. Chinese troops from local areas provided an escort.

On his return to Chengtu, however, the Dalai Lama said goodby to indoctrinator Liu. He joined the now jubilant Tibetan delegates. He was made the responsibility of the deputy governor of Szechwan. About two hundred Chinese party workers, going to Tibet, also joined the entourage here. The Chinese itinerary called for a direct and rather quick trip for the balance of the return journey. Cars, trucks, and jeeps were available; supplies had been efficiently arranged; the troop escort was ready.

The sixteen-man Tibetan delegation, however, had other ideas.

They had passed on to the Dalai Lama, in Peking, invitations from many monasteries of eastern Tibet and the West China border-lands. During the wait in Chengtu representatives of all these monasteries had repeatedly contacted the delegation to confirm and press their invitations. They were now awaiting the visit of the God-King.

The Dalai Lama reminded the delegation that he must return to Lhasa within the promised time or the people might take some unwise action. The delegates knew that this was true, but they had faced the importunate lamas of the eastern monasteries and they knew also the fervor of the lamas' desire for a visit from the god. The Chinese distinctly, although politely, favored a direct return with a minimum of monastery visits.

Before the question was resolved nature or the gods intervened. An earthquake to the west, near Tatsienlu, damaged the road and made travel impossible for some time. The Chinese, perhaps sur-prised to find nature on their side, reminded the Dalai Lama of the time limit he had imposed on his absence. He must not dis-appoint his people—he must set off directly for Lhasa as soon as the road was open.

Finally, during the three weeks of waiting for the road repairs, the question was resolved. The monasteries received messages saying that the Dalai Lama wanted to see the monks but because of the earthquake he could not reach all the monasteries. Arrange-ments, therefore, were made for representatives from the nearby monasteries to converge at "new bridge," a point where the road crossed a river about two days to the north and west of Tatsienlu. The Dalai Lama would greet his followers there.

When the Dalai Lama and his entourage reached "new bridge," they saw a wide-spreading tent city. More than fifteen thousand worshipers—including some from as far away as Lhasa who had been waiting here for weeks—welcomed the return. This was Chi-nese territory—not even "the Tibet region of China"—but the Chinese provincial official and his party workers and troops could hardly doubt that the Dalai Lama had come home.

Chinese propaganda, at the time of the opening of the new

roads, had said that the travel time from Peking to Lhasa had
been reduced to twenty days. And normally, with luck, this no
doubt was true. But the Dalai Lama's return was far from a normal
journey. No modern development project could take into account
the mass devotion of his subjects. Chinese bayonets had helped
to build the road, but they could not clear it when thousands of
monks decided to block the route with their bodies and keep
their god a little longer in their presence.

For almost six weeks the huge, unwieldy, and weirdly assorted
party lumbered along to the north and west, heading for
Chamdo. The traveling party alone numbered almost a thousand
people—nearly three hundred of the Dalai's group, two hundred
Chinese party workers, and never less than five hundred troops.
Transport included three hundred vehicles—closed motorcars,
jeeps, and trucks. But as they went from monastery stop to monastery stop the traveling party was swelled by "greeting parties"
from the next place to be visited and by "seeing off" parties from
the last. Many monks attached themselves to the group and went
along to all the stops. They went on foot, on mule, or on horseback. Laden yaks carried gifts for the God-King. Small flocks of
sheep and goats followed along with their herders. Fifteen Chinese newsmen and photographers were included in the party, but
no word or picture of this fantastic devotion ever appeared in the
Chinese press.

The Chinese found no way to cope with the mass demonstration of love and fealty. They made a few attempts at first to clear
the road by ordering troops to march forward with bayonets
ready. But a monk thus threatened would simply bare his chest
and walk toward the bayonet, inviting a thrust. Tibetan officials
who tried to help the Chinese establish order found that the
monks would attack them, often with the intent to kill. In such a
crisis only the Dalai Lama himself, with a gentle gesture and
kindly but firm words, could calm his people so that the journey
could continue.

At Chamdo many monastery representatives and officials had
come from Lhasa to greet the Dalai. This delegation was headed

by General Li, Chinese chief of staff in Lhasa, who took over responsibility for the Dalai Lama from the exhausted Szechwan official.

The final stop of the long journey was at a village southeast of Lhasa, where huge throngs converged to watch for the arrival. Many of these same people fifteen years ago had waited for the arrival of a small child from China. He had come in a sedan chair over a long, slow route into a strange land. He had looked at the people and said, "I know them all."

Now he was coming again from China, a man whose lama robes had brushed against the realities of the modern world. He had sat in conferences with Mao Tse-tung and cast his vote for the Chinese Constitution. He had joined with Chinese voices to condemn the atom bomb. He had traveled in trains and planes and river steamships. He returned now along the road that linked Tibet to China. His motorcar was flanked by jeeps of the Chinese army. He returned, according to Chinese pronouncement, to establish a "Preparatory Committee for the Autonomous Region of Tibet." The Tibetans never doubted that he was returning to them as their Precious Protector and that he would do all within his power to keep 'the Han from destroying their way of life. The Chinese officials were hoping that the indoctrination course had been successful and that the God-King was now merely a government worker in the Tibet Region of China.

The Chinese authorities arranged an elaborate official reception for the Dalai Lama's entry into Lhasa on June 29, 1955. As usual at such celebrations, Chinese officials praised the unity of all nationalities under the great motherland. On this occasion they also predicted the early and auspicious establishment of the Preparatory Committee for the Autonomous Region of Tibet. In reply the Dalai Lama praised the achievements of the Communist regime in China. He said that he "looked forward" to the establishment of the Preparatory Committee, which had been decided upon by China's State Council on March 9, only three days before the Dalai Lama left Peking.

The Tibetans who crowded the parade ground wore their best

clothes and happiest smiles. They were content to bask in the God-King's presence and to turn a deaf ear to his words. This was not because they were too dull to hear and comprehend; they were too wise to be fooled. Moreover, they had been warned to pay little heed to what the Dalai Lama was forced to say by the Chinese.

The warning had come from the Mimang, who had written down the crimes of the Chinese Communists. In a small crude booklet, which could have been printed only secretly by the monasteries' wood-block process for the holy books, Tibetans were told of Chinese plans and informed of which measures they must firmly oppose. They were instructed to be unified and hopeful and to support the resolutions which the Mimang set down.

The pamphlets had passed from hand to hand and, for those who could not read, the words were spoken softly in monastery courtyards, in the market places, and over the campfires of travelers. In speaking of the Dalai Lama the booklet said, "Even though His Holiness spoke from China as He did, do not be downhearted. He . . . has no option but to speak what is written for Him. More than this, when He returns to His capital, He in person is likely to speak more along the same lines. Even if He should do so, we are agreed that we shall not be discouraged nor be disillusioned nor lose our belief in Him."

The people kept their belief, and when their god blessed them they felt the gentle warmth of the Precious Protector. They refused to believe that he had become a regional officer under the Chinese. A Tibetan spat in disgust at the enormity of the Chinese in naming their God-King a "Vice-Chairman of the Standing Committee of the National People's Congress."

To the Chinese, however, there was nothing ridiculous in this title or in the Dalai Lama's announced chairmanship of the Preparatory Committee. All this was a logical sequence of liberation. The party workers who had joined the returning Dalai Lama's entourage were trained in administration and in the devious "ways of working among the Red people." They were here to do a job, and now was the time to start.

The Chinese also had seen the secret pamphlet. They knew that all of Tibet was united in opposition to this administrative move which would finally end the independence of the religious kingdom. They knew that the Tibetan collaborators had been called "unprincipled men, their bellies satiated with Chinese silver," who were being instructed and trained to "spread the vile practices and beliefs of the Communist Party." The Chinese believed that they must act quickly to establish the new government. While the resistance was still in the pamphlet stage and while the young Dalai Lama was confused by his recent experiences and still remembered the kindly attentions of his Chinese hosts, the Communists had their best—and perhaps their only—chance to take Tibet completely.

After the one speech at the return celebration, however, the Dalai Lama gave the Chinese no more help toward the establishment of the Preparatory Committee. Instead he surrounded himself with a few trusted Tibetans and retreated into meditation and prayer. The trusted men spread the word that these observances were necessary in order that the Dalai Lama could cleanse himself from the effects of a long absence from the Holy City.

Several weeks later the Dalai Lama came out of his isolation and addressed a large group of Tibetan monk and lay officials whom he had called together at the summer palace. His words no longer echoed Peking. He spoke of Tibet as a "country in which religion and political life are joined together," and he gave examples from history to show that Tibet prospered only under "joint development of political life and religion." The Chinese Communists came to Tibet, he said, to help the Tibetan people, "who lack political experience." They did not come to oppress or rule. But, he added, "If the Chinese are really to help Tibet, they must respect the Tibetan people's own social system, culture, customs, and habits" and not obstruct or damage the "high principles of our nation." "If the Chinese Communists do not do this," he said, "you should immediately report the facts to the government." And, "if the Communist men do not correct their ways our government can immediately ask for their removal."

The Dalai Lama thanked his officials for their hard work in behalf of the country's welfare. He told those officials who work "for their own selfish good and under the attraction of glittering gold" to reform their ways and atone by new effort in the right direction. He also chided those who, considering themselves to be progressives, "disregard their national culture and history." "I regard such ideas to be mistaken," he said, for progress "must be attained gradually in an ordered way."

Finally the Dalai Lama reminded his listeners that all the areas of Tibet were one and that all their people were one people. "Their spirit and way of living are so intimately connected that they cannot be separated from each other," he said. He expressed the hope that all the people of Tibet would co-operate to "increase our strength and put all their energies into the construction of a new Tibet based on the unity of political life and religion."

After the address the Dalai Lama again retired into meditation.

The nineteen-year-old newly indoctrinated youth required great courage to speak out in this manner. According to schedule, he was on the eve of heading a new administration for his country. The Preparatory Committee, although its planned membership would include monastery representatives, could hardly be calculated to "contruct a new Tibet based on the unity of political life and religion." Tibetans, as the Chinese knew well, viewed this inclusion of a minority of religious men in the administration as the weapon by which the Chinese meant to rob the monasteries of prestige and power. Thus the Chinese had every reason to be infuriated by the Dalai Lama's statement. The Dalai Lama, however, had worded his statement cleverly. It contained many typically Communist phrases, such as "the new Tibet," and therefore sounded as though the God-King had been successfully indoctrinated. Nevertheless, to the Tibetans the meaning of his statement was clearly that he did not approve of the new Chinese effort to win the country's subjugation.

Whatever their specific complaints, the Chinese did object to the Dalai's statement, and they later issued an altered version of it. Excerpts from the alterations then were broadcast locally. Chinese news agencies did not release, or even refer to, the speech. The original versions of the Dalai's statements, however, found their way to India and caused much speculation among Indian newsmen.

A number of Indian journalists, particularly those who had visited Peking at the time of Prime Minister Nehru's trip and had seen both of the lamas at the Chinese capital, had periodically questioned the whereabouts and activities of the Dalai. After the Peking announcement of the State Council's plan for the Preparatory Committee (on March 9) and the Dalai Lama's departure from Peking (on March 12), no news had been heard concerning the Tibetan God-King. During the last two months before his return to Lhasa, Indian readers knew only that he had visited his birthplace near Sining and was "said to be visiting monasteries in Kham and Amdo."

Thus when the Dalai Lama suddenly reappeared in the news, striking an independent note with his July statement, Indian journalists found new meaning in persistent rumors that were coming out of Tibet. These rumors said that a resistance movement had consolidated in Tibet during the Dalai Lama's absence; the huge delegation which greeted him on his return to the Holy City included Mimang leaders who urged him not to allow the establishment of the Preparatory Committee; plans for active opposition were in the making, with a Kham chieftain ready to rally guerrilla forces in the east. The hope of the resistance movement was that its fighting forces could disrupt Chinese communications and hold out long enough for the attention of the free world to focus on Tibet. Then perhaps a new appeal to the United Nations would receive a hearing.

Commentators in India agreed that such a plan, if in actual existence, would have to be implemented before the establishment of the Preparatory Committee. The new administration certainly would push through measures for the confiscation of weapons and would nullify the usefulness of the monasteries as message centers for the co-ordination of the resistance movement. Timing was of paramount importance and might explain the

Dalai Lama's delaying tactics of prolonged meditations. On the other hand, the fact that the Tibetans would attempt an uprising in the strongly garrisoned country whose new road links with China could enable the occupation force to bring in quick reinforcements and massive supplies was difficult to believe.

According to the Hong Kong press, twenty-two thousand fresh Chinese troops had already moved into Tibet by motor transport along the new roads. An artillery unit had crossed the border to take up a strategic position near the new southern road. It was estimated that reinforcements from Lanchow or Chengtu could reach Lhasa within two weeks along the new routes.

Chinese forces had taken Tibet without the roads. Surely they could hold it now. Only a desperate people could dream of opposing the Communist war machine. The Tibetan government might stall, as it had stalled successfully for several years, but the early establishment of the Preparatory Committee appeared unavoidable.

By September 1955, however, the committee still had not been established. The Dalai Lama continued to devote most of his time to religious observances. Frustrated, the Chinese authorities turned again to Ngapho Shape, their number-one collaborator. Ngapho Shape, the Chinese announced, would head a "preparatory office" whose duties would be to prepare for the Preparatory Committee. The five-member committee could include, in addition to Ngapho, the Panchen Lama, a brother of the Dalai Lama, a Chinese official, and a representative from Kham. Thus the "preparatory office" was a Preparatory Committee in microcosm, with only monastery representation lacking. The Panchen Lama and the Kham representative typified the division of Tibet into three zones, with the Dalai's brother as a sort of deputy in place of the Dalai Lama himself, representing the central zone.

The committee of five set up a broad organization by dividing the "preparatory work" into fourteen departments. A staff for each was selected. Heads of these departments often were taken from among Tibetan government officials, whose other jobs, while not abolished, simply ceased to exist because of the pressure of work demanded by the new posts. The Chinese cadres, who had been cooling their heels during the Dalai Lama's long meditations, now worked closely with Tibetan department heads.

In October 1955, a few weeks after the setting up of the "preparatory office," a Mimang-sponsored appeal was presented to the Dalai Lama in the name of the Tibetan people. Speaking from the "very deep valley of darkness and destruction," the appeal pointed out that "the Tibetan nation is facing as grave a danger as a candlelight in a severe storm." The paper cited Chinese breaches of the 17-Point Agreement and the "illegal organizations" through which the Communists had usurped powers of the Tibetan government. It appealed to the Dalai Lama to "stop the organization of the Patriotic Youth League, to close the Chinese schools, and to prevent the indoctrination of the Tibetan people in Communism." The paper stated that "we are resolved not to accept the establishment of the proposed Regional Autonomous Government because we already have the Tibetan Government of the Dalai Lama." It requested, also, that the Chinese Communist military representative in Tibet allow Mimang representatives to proceed to Peking to bring their appeal before the Chinese rulers. The appeal ended with a threat to "shed our blood and sacrifice our lives to oppose the Communists."

In order to present this appeal a group of three men from the secret section of the Mimang had come into the open. One of these men was Alo Chondze, a well-to-do trader; the others, whose names I have been unable to verify, included an educated white-collar worker in the employ of a Tibetan official and a subordinate lama who worked under a monk official. These men, along with a group of Mimang followers, had held meetings in various Lhasa houses during the time of drawing up and presenting the appeal.

A few days after the presentation the three leaders were called before the Kashag. They were forbidden to hold further meetings and were ordered to discontinue use of the name Mimang. The Kashag members said that they were acting on orders of the Dalai Lama. It was too late for representation now, the Kashag said, for "all matters were settled" when the Dalai Lama was in Peking.

The men were not apprehended, but the military authorities issued a notice to all houseowners in Lhasa, warning that house meetings were forbidden and that any houseowner who allowed such a meeting would invite arrest.

The Mimang, of course, expected this. The exposure of a few men had been necessary in order that a final attempt to influence the Chinese authorities could be made. Alo Chondze and the others, who knew they were under observation, stopped their political activity and did not contact Mimang associates. The underground organization carried on, knowing now that the threat of "blood and sacrifice," although perhaps futile, was the only course left to take.

CHAPTER XII

Open Rebellion

If there be an enemy to Buddha,
His followers must put on armor.

—TIBETAN PROVERB

THE decision of the Mimang underground to organize an armed uprising was made reluctantly. In fact it was made only when the demands of the Mimang constituents could be resisted no longer.

For several years Tibetans from every part of the country had been in the mood for militant resistance to the occupation force. Only the monastery representatives in the Mimang had been consistently against violence. They had counseled patience as long as they had hope that the Han could be persuaded to grant Tibet some reasonable autonomy. They knew that an uprising had little chance of success and, besides increasing the misery of the people, might well end in even greater repression.

To average Tibetans, however, patience was far more difficult than direct action. Thus, despite their respect for lama authority, they submitted to the policy of patience mainly because they knew that no uprising could be made without monastery leadership, money, and arms.

Even so, the impulse toward direct action became almost uncontrollable shortly after the Dalai Lama was taken to Peking. If the Chinese during this period had shown clearly a tendency to modify their demands for "reform," the lamas' counsel of patience might have prevailed. Also, if the Han had succeeded in subverting the Dalai Lama, they might have used him effectively to confuse and divide the people.

Instead the Chinese tried again to establish administrative control, this time through the Preparatory Committee, which every Tibetan knew would mean the death of Tibet as a nation and a culture. Moreover, despite indoctrination, the Dalai Lama was as stubborn as ever, and the effect of his statement in July 1955 was to sanction the people's resistance to the idea of the Preparatory Committee. At this point the Chinese had used unsuccessfully the last of their non-violent means for achieving the complete subjugation of Tibet. They could either give in, abide by the terms of their 17-Point Agreement and allow the Tibetans the autonomy that they had promised, or they could install their committee by force.

The Tibetans by now could see clearly behind the Communist mask, and they did not doubt that the Chinese would resort to force. Force could be answered only with force. The Mimang had no more arguments in favor of peace. And when the lamas faced the fact that the Preparatory Committee meant death to Tibet, they agreed that nothing could be lost and something might be gained by opposing the Han with violence.

Thus the lama Mimang representatives finally cast the deciding votes in favor of the uprising. They did not—as some outside observers mistakenly believed—instigate the revolt. Once they sided with the popular demand for direct action, however, they attempted to guide the uprising so as to make it as effective as possible, and they participated in it fully.

Outsiders often are confused by the seeming paradox that gentle Buddhist monks could participate in violence and killing. In lamaist Tibet, however, the important legends described the fierce battles between the holy ones who defended the religion against devils.

In the past Tibetan monks fought hard on occasions when their religion was threatened. In fact, a military order or caste among the monks was trained for combat with the enemies of religion and any lama, no matter how gentle and wise normally, was ready to battle ferociously in defense of the faith.

Moreover, when defending the faith the lamas were magnificent fighters. They were superbly disciplined. They could subsist on a meager diet, and the rigors of their duties gave them muscular strength and amazing stamina. A lama had no family ties or personal possessions which might soften the fanaticism of his zeal. He had no fear of death—on the contrary, in a battle against devils he welcomed death because he would be assured of a lofty rebirth. Finally, because of the communication between monasteries, the average lama had a clearer picture of the enemy's strength and deployment and was in a better position to plan effective tactics.

Under all these circumstances the fact that the lamas generally dominated the resistance movement was not surprising. They were mainly responsible for both the organization of the movement and for the over-all plan which the uprising was meant to achieve.

The plan called for simultaneous large-scale attacks on a number of the smaller but important Chinese posts. At the same time Chinese communications were to be systematically disrupted. Telegraph wires were to be cut, bridges destroyed, and above all the roads were to be rendered useless. The Tibetan underground knew that they could not hope to capture the heavily fortified Chinese main bases. By disrupting the enemy's communications, however, they expected to prevent reinforcements from relieving the attacks on the smaller posts. They also hoped to ambush and destroy Chinese relief columns sent from the main bases. If successful, the Tibetans expected that the Chinese would be weakened sufficiently so that the occupation force then could be kept off balance by continuous raids and sabotage. They did not expect to defeat the Chinese; they did not even think that they could maintain the resistance for long, but they thought that their efforts might attract attention—and help—from outside.

The Mimang leaders recognized that the vital factor in the plan was unity. Unless concerted action was made the plan had no chance of success. Many Tibetans now felt that their burden under the occupation was unbearable. These people might lose their restraint at any moment, strike out blindly on their own, and destroy all hope for the uprising.

Another difficult problem was communication. Couriers between the far-flung corners of Tibet were the only real means of sending messages. I have heard that some lamas, specialists in mysticism, communicated between monasteries by thought transference. I have also heard of lama couriers who, after years of training, could run for days at a time in a weird kind of hypnotic trance without food or sleep in the highest altitudes and through the worst blizzards. The more rational Tibetans—including lamas—however, laughed at such stories, and, in any case, the Chinese would have a distinct advantage with their modern communication system.

A final problem for the resistance leaders concerned the secret movement of their guerrilla fighters in large numbers. True, whole armies could be effectively hidden in that wild, trackless country, and much of the movement could be disguised in the form of caravans, pilgrimages, and work parties. Only one accidental slip-up, however, could warn the enemy who with their superior communications equipment would have time to prepare for the attack.

Nevertheless the Mimang went ahead with their plans. Throughout the country the people were organized into small fighting units. Much care was given to the choice of leaders for each unit; most Tibetans now realized that their traditional army system of untrained officials for officers was unworkable. The unit leaders were impressed constantly with the importance of restraining their men until the signal for the uprising was given.

Each leader also was assigned a specific task in the over-all plan of attack. Thus what training he gave his men could be limited to the functions expected of his unit. In addition he had the responsibility of seeing that his men were adequately equipped. If some of his troops possessed old-fashioned weapons, he could arrange, usually through a nearby monastery, for more modern guns and ammunition. Finally the unit leader saw that his men were adequately mounted and that each had cached a store of provisions so that the unit could move on a moment's notice.

The formation of these fighting units within Lhasa itself called for special meetings of the Mimang. The members finally decided not to have the Lhasans participate in the military aspects of the uprising. They feared that fighting might damage the Holy City and that the Chinese might retaliate by inflicting bodily harm on the Dalai Lama. The Lhasan members of the Mimang, therefore, seem to have concentrated on propaganda. The systematic organization of the uprising began during the middle of 1955, and at the same time Lhasans began a greatly increased output of their monastery-printed leaflets and posters. The purpose was to offset the now concentrated barrage of Chinese propaganda on the subject of the Preparatory Committee.

The Chinese meanwhile were making their preparations for the inauguration of the Preparatory Committee. The Preparatory Office finally submitted a detailed plan of the committee's administrative setup. The Kashag members tried to stall on its acceptance, but the Chinese now were openly threatening. The Kashag made a few face-saving changes and accepted it. After more delays the document was given the necessary signatures and seals were affixed to it. Tibet received the death blow to her independence.

Outwardly the Chinese reacted with jubilation. The Propaganda Department (now called the "Publicity Section" under the new administration) began to turn out plans for an elaborate celebration on inauguration day. Tibetans were told awesomely that Vice-Premier Marshal Chen Yi himself was to come to Tibet to officiate on the occasion. Lhasa took on an air of great activity. Hundreds of Tibetan laborers and Chinese troops worked frantically on the construction of an assembly hall for the inauguration. A few favored Tibetan officials were assigned staff cars—vehicles of the station-wagon type that had come in over the new roads in limited numbers. A hundred Tibetan youths who had finished their training in Peking returned to Tibet and after being assigned jobs under the new administration were feted with much publicity.

Underneath the festive exterior, however, the Chinese knew that trouble was brewing, and they began to prepare for it. More reinforcements were ordered. Patrols were increased. A strict ban on public meetings was enforced; even small groups of Tibetans, chatting in a bazaar street or teahouse, were closely watched by Chinese troops. Alo Chondze and his two co-workers were arrested on orders of the Chinese military. The inauguration was first planned for September 1955 but had to be postponed until the spring of 1956. A secret race was taking place between the Chinese authorities and the Mimang underground. The Chinese were trying to inaugurate the Preparatory Committee as quickly as possible, knowing that once it was formally established it could not be dislodged easily. The underground Tibetans were striving desperately to organize an attack that would take place before the inauguration and yet would be powerful enough to unbalance the occupation force so thoroughly that the inauguration would have to be put off indefinitely. During the first weeks of 1956 everyone in Tibet lived in dread of what might happen in the next moment.

What happened in February 1956 was the one possibility that the Mimang dreaded most: a large-scale unplanned local attack on the Chinese. Moreover, the attack came from the least expected quarter: the wild Golok tribes in the northeastern borderlands.

During all the years of the occupation the Chinese had made no real attempt to interfere with the fierce and independent Goloks. They expected, however, that eventually the millions of new Chinese settlers in the area would antagonize the Goloks. The Chinese military leaders therefore were given the task of disarming the border people before the new influx of settlers in the spring of 1956. A Chinese force of three thousand troops began by moving against a Tibetan settlement near Golok territory for the purpose of forcibly disarming the populace. The Tibetans put up violent resistance. The battle lasted two days. Hundreds were killed on both sides.

When news of this action reached the nearby Golok camp the leaders immediately gathered all the local tribes. A large expedition was organized. Nearly two thousand mounted men—including not only Goloks but Chinese Muslim guerrillas and a few Han army deserters—rode to the nearest Chinese garrison. They were armed mostly with swords and muzzle-loading rifles. In a pre-dawn attack they surprised the garrison and massacred most of its eight hundred troops. The Goloks' losses were small, and they captured an excellent supply of arms, but their victory was short-lived. The Chinese sent a punitive expedition into the area and inflicted several thousand casualties. Women and children, as well as the fighting men, were killed. The nomads' flocks were taken and their tent settlements were destroyed. The surviving Goloks, mostly the hardiest warriors, escaped to the hills with their weapons, and from that day on they lived only to kill Chinese.

The fuse was lit. Almost the whole of Tibet exploded into violence. The attacks against the occupying force, however, were small, unplanned, and generally ill-conceived. The Mimang underground leaders watched with dismay as the possibility for the only workable resistance plan vanished. They saw the Chinese, now fully alerted, were able to contain the Tibetan attacks.

A typical premature Tibetan uprising occurred in the southern district of Litang.

In this district, overlooking a broad, grassy tableland, the Litang village nestled into the hillside. On the hilltop were the huge white buildings of Litang Monastery, famous for having supplied two of the previous Incarnations of the Dalai Lama.

Litang district was slated for a Communist experiment in Tibetan land reform. Before attempting the reform the Communists had made every effort to strengthen their position: through gradual replacement most of the local government officials were well-paid Communist sympathizers; a certain amount of "public demand" had been built up through Communist-led meetings at

which the most downtrodden elements of the populace were encouraged not only to air their grievances verbally but to affix
signatures to protests. These signatures often were put down while
the signers were under the influence of free *chang* (Tibetan barley beer) at gala public meetings. Finally the road from the east
made quick military reinforcement possible if the people should
still resist "reform."

They did resist. Despite all the groundwork, when the time
came for a decision the people said that they did not want
"socialization" in their district. A month later two high Chinese
officers arrived and called a public meeting. The people of Litang
were told that they had no choice. The dark ways of old Tibet,
the officers said, were finished. Lhasa had decided that Litang
was to be shown the bright new ways of Chinese Communism.
The people were to follow the new way whether they wanted
to or not.

Two days later an ill-armed Tibetan mob attacked the local
Chinese garrison. The Tibetans inflicted heavy casualties and
made off with a sizable supply of arms and ammunition. The
following day a larger group attacked again and bottled up the
remaining Chinese forces in a warehouse. In the hope of securing
the warehouse stock the attacking Tibetans did not set fire to the
building. They maneuvered instead to cut off the water supply.
Then they waited, ready to pick off the Chinese who were forced
out by thirst. While the five-day siege of the warehouse was on,
the Tibetans destroyed the houses and offices of the local Communist officials and of Tibetans who were collaborating with the
occupation. The attacking forces also blocked the road to the east
and fought one engagement with a Chinese relief party, routing
the enemy and inflicting heavy casualties.

On the fifth day of the siege the planes came. Evidently the
Tibetans did not realize or had forgotten that the Chinese under
siege could still communicate by radio. The first wave of planes,
coming from the northeast, dropped about forty bombs. Casualties were light, but some damage was done to the monastery and
to several houses in the town below. The bombing brought out

the monks in a belligerent mood, and the Tibetan guerrillas were joined by a large party of well-armed lamas. The fighting at the warehouse went on for three more days. A few Chinese tried to make a dash from the warehouse into the hills. They were brought down as they ran or were pursued and chopped to pieces by Tibetan horsemen. The Tibetans felt that the siege was breaking, and their hopes were high. They were especially eager for the arms and ammunition in the storehouse. They planned that when the siege broke they would consolidate, replenish their arms, branch out, and help their neighbors.

The second wave of planes put a quick finish to their plans. The planes circled over the monastery-topped hill and dropped bombload after bombload. Wheeling back to the northeast, they returned again and again with more destruction. The ancient monastery with its priceless heirlooms, records, and treasures, was pounded into a mass of worthless rubble. The town of Litang was reduced to dust. More than four thousand Tibetans were killed in the bombing. The dead included most of the women and children and the aged, both laymen and monks, who were not participating in the siege. The half-crazed survivors now rushed to the warehouse. They captured it within only a few minutes, but they spent a much longer time killing the Chinese troops. They took the enemy weapons and fled back into the hills where, like the Goloks in the north, they organized themselves for the one purpose of killing every Chinese they could reach.

This, then, became the pattern of Tibetan resistance. After the first large uprisings in the spring of 1956 the Chinese moved to disarm all Tibetans by force. Whenever the attempt was made, the Tibetans resisted. Sometimes the resistance was successful temporarily. Generally the people were overcome and were forced to submit to house searches for weapons. In most cases, however, the people managed to cache a store of arms, and even when the Chinese used torture the Tibetans rarely revealed the hiding places. Invariably armed conflict between Chinese troops and a Tibetan community ended with the escape of many able-bodied men into the hills to join existing guerrilla bands or to form new ones.

At first the guerrillas fought in a kind of frenzy of hatred and revenge. Their forays, although demoralizing to the Chinese, had little strategic effect and often resulted in greater losses to themselves than to the enemy. Before long, however, the attacks showed more planning. The natural aptitude of the Tibetans for tactical surprise and their ability to use their terrain effectively began to count. Moreover, communication between the larger bands was established and the leadership improved. The guerrillas worked out elementary systems of supply; the monasteries and the Mimang underground helped with supplies and intelligence. The people remained loyal to the insurgents, who were rarely betrayed to the enemy and were aided by the non-fighters whenever possible. Finally the main guerrilla bands began to concentrate their attacks on enemy supply convoys that moved along the new roads. Within only a month or two after the real resistance began the Chinese were forced to move their supply trains in convoys of forty to fifty trucks. Each vehicle carried several heavily armed soldiers. The convoys moved slowly because around the next curve the drivers might find a yawning blown-out chasm, the rubble of a man-made landslide, or an ambush of desperate Tibetans thirsting for revenge.

The resistance stories that began to trickle out of Tibet concerned mainly the colorful exploits of the ferocious Goloks in the north and the Khambas in the east. At first one had the impression that the Khambas especially played the largest part in the resistance movement. This was mainly because the exploits of these nomads tended to be the most spectacular and were carried out in a large area that extended far beyond the borders of Tibet into China itself.

The fact was, however, that almost every part of Tibetan society contributed something to the resistance. Perhaps the lamas were the single segment that made the most effective contribution. Several large guerrilla bands composed entirely of monks were organized. They fought with great zeal, but they used much cunning as well.

Finally the full extent of the contribution made by Tibetan peasants is not generally realized. The peasants, traditionally used to complete subservience, rarely are considered as militant members of the resistance. Nevertheless many thousands of them joined the guerrilla bands and, when well led, proved to be excellent fighters. The most important function of the peasants, however, was to produce the food, fodder, and livestock without which the resistance could not last for a week. In addition, the peasants often provided shelter and protection for individual resistance fighters fleeing from the Chinese. Finally, many peasants learned to be invaluable sources of information concerning enemy troop movement and activities. Refugees coming to India have many stories to tell of the peasants' contribution to the resistance cause.

By the spring of 1956 tens of thousands of Tibetans in eastern Tibet alone were engaged full time in guerrilla fighting against the Han. In thousands of square miles of Tibetan territory, and even in the lands beyond the Yangtze under direct Chinese administration, no Han dared set foot. Only the strongest Chinese bases were safe from attack, and patrols more than a day's ride from these centers were almost sure to be ambushed. And, most important of all, traffic through the Kham region on the Chamdo-Lhasa road was becoming so hazardous that even the Chinese truck drivers, among themselves, called it the road of death.

In Lhasa the Tibetans who could not participate in the uprising awaited with resignation the arrival of Chen Yi and the inauguration of the Preparatory Committee. Yet they thrived on the stories of the fighting brought in from refugees. Their imagination was especially fired by the Khamba attacks on the Chamdo road, and many of the popular songs concerned the road of death.

> "The Motherland's dove of peace had no father
> (yet) Tibetans wait for the dove with small patience.
> Come to us quickly, Chen Yi—
> Over the road through Kham!"

Chen Yi and his huge motor caravan, however, took the long northern route via Sining. Reinforcements and supplies as well now came only by this route. Heavy reinforcements from Sining began moving into Lhasa before the arrival of the Chinese Vice-Premier. More than forty thousand troops were reported garrisoned in Lhasa alone. Strong guard units were posted on all houses of Chinese officers and cadres. The new building of the Preparatory Committee was under heavy day-and-night guard while workmen added the finishing touches.

Security forces were equally active. Lhasa houses were checked for Kham refugees. Any able-bodied refugee was subjected to long questioning, and many were placed under arrest. Chinese personnel was rechecked and weeded once more. Truckloads of possible dissidents were sent off by night, headed north by the long route—and now the only usable route—to China. Important Tibetan officials were closely watched and in many cases were refused permission to leave Lhasa. Anyone who visited the Indian Consulate was questioned. Suspicion and mistrust flourished. Tibetans found difficulty in speaking freely to each other, even in very small groups.

To add to the tension the Chinese sent a plane to circle over Lhasa on several occasions. No plane landed, for the airfield was still being completed; twenty-four-hour shifts were rushing the work on the landing field. But no Tibetan could hear or see a plane without recalling the stories of the bombings told by the refugees.

The Lhasans were finding the discipline of self-restraint inincreasingly difficult to bear. Only the knowledge that the great shrines of the Holy City and, above all, the person of the Precious One must not be jeopardized kept them from acts of violence directed at the center of the occupation authority. Judging from stories of Lhasans during this period, the lamas in the Holy City were particularly restive. They oiled the monastery guns and melted scrap metal to make pellets for the ancient muzzle-loaders. Among themselves they questioned how long an oppressed man could care for a gun without having a chance to fire it. Wandering in bands into the city at night, they spoke bitterly of the firearms locked away in the monastery storerooms. Chinese troop patrols followed the red-robed men and discouraged loose talk or large gatherings. Sometimes the monks turned on the patrols and fought them, sword against gun or hand to hand. After a few such incidents the Chinese authorities ordered all monks to be within their monastery walls by nightfall. The monastery authorities co-operated in seeing that this order was enforced; impetuous resistance, they knew, could only hurt the cause.

The Chinese authorities attempted to use this level-headed attitude of the monastery leaders as a weapon against the resistance in other parts of the country. They began with an appeal to the Dalai Lama to appoint a delegation of respected religious men to go to Kham and urge peace upon the population. The Dalai Lama agreed to give the matter thought, but he took no action. The Chinese then approached a high lama who was one of the Dalai's tutors. The lama humbly excused himself on the basis that he was a man of no influence in such worldly affairs as fighting. The next approach was to the heads of Lhasa's three large monasteries. The Chinese suggested that the monasteries appoint "peace" delegates from each of their institutions, preferably men of Kham origin or men of such stature that they would be known throughout Kham. The monastery leaders, however, flatly refused to co-operate in the scheme. Next the Chinese tried to "appoint" an official to lead a peace delegation. They chose Ragashar Shape, who was well known, liked, and respected in Kham. Ragashar told them candidly that he did not think such an approach would be effective and that he would not undertake what he considered a hopeless mission. Finally Ngapho was sent, along with a co-operative Red-tinged lama called Kamapa and a collaborating Kham chieftain. This committee of three went to Chamdo and "invited" Kham leaders to meet them there. A few chieftains answered the call, but they did not negotiate a peace. They simply repeated what unofficially had been made known; the Lhasa peace delegates were warned that they would not be granted safe conduct. "If the Chinese want peace in this area," resistance leaders said, "let them withdraw their armies and go home. Only then will there be peace in Tibet—the peace which was here before the Chinese came."

The Chinese authorities therefore fell back on their only means of winning control over the Tibetans: force. Even more troops were called in and the aggressive action against the resistance movement was stepped up. Air strikes were increased in number and size. In Szechwan, to the east of the trouble area, the authorities attempted to enlist local Tibetans for "Rebellion Suppression Work Units." In Sining troops were granted special funds for "mopping-up operations against bandits." The Lhasa garrison could not be cut down, and additional forces also were needed to guard the route to the north over which Chen Yi and his entourage soon would arrive. In the west, where resistance had spread to take the form of increased harassment of settlers and the sabotage of new construction projects, reinforcements had to be called in from Sinkiang.

Reinforcements were needed even in Shigatse. The Panchen had gone to Lhasa to join in the preparations for the inauguration of the Preparatory Committee. Dissension grew among his close followers and was reflected in a general restlessness of the people. A large party of more than a thousand Chinese forced laborers were working on Shigatse road and construction projects. The presence of these brutally treated and ill-fed examples of the "new China," coupled with reports of ever-increasing resistance from all parts of Tibet, gave the Panchen's people food for thought. They were apprehensive about the persistent rumors that "reforms" might come first of all to this area because of the Panchen's favored position with the Chinese.

Nevertheless, officially the Chinese refused to admit the existence of resistance. According to the news releases, all Tibet was agog with excitement over the honor of Chen Yi's visit. The Vice-Premier reached Lhasa in the middle of April 1956. His great cavalcade of nearly three hundred cars and trucks camped outside Lhasa the final night of the journey and entered the city the next morning in a triumphal parade. Accompanying him were high-ranking representatives from all parts of China, with special accent on "minority" peoples. Labor-group heroes were also included. Converts from the KMT, ex-capitalists who had seen the light of Communism, the secretary of China's Youth Association, and more than a hundred specially trained cadres who would stay to help Tibet on the road to "autonomy" swelled the entourage. Many entertainment groups came with the party—musicians, dancers, acrobats—who would increase the festivity of the occasion. Special cooks had been brought; they had fed the dignitaries along the way, and now they would prepare the banquets at which Chinese and Tibetan brothers—of an exalted level—would toast the new regime. And finally, of course, the party had its own heavily armed troop escort.

According to the official Chinese news releases, fifty thousand enthusiastic Tibetans lined the streets of Lhasa to welcome the party, which drove to the Potala under arches decorated with lanterns and golden-dragon emblems. According to Tibetan refugees who were there, however, the people greeted Chen Yi with a thunder of hand clapping. Hand clapping in Tibet is not applause but a sign of disapproval; it is used as a means of driving out devils. The people crowded close along the road, jockeying for positions from which they could spit on Chen Yi's shiny Russian-made car when it passed.

Chen Yi, replying to an address of welcome, said that he brought the "benevolent concern" of the Chinese Communist party and "a great deal of guidance."

A week later, on April 22, 1956, the inaugural ceremony of the Preparatory Committee began. It was held in the recently completed Great Lhasa Hall. Ngapho took charge only long enough to announce the purpose of the gathering. Then the Dalai Lama, who had been met outside the building by the forty highest officials and escorted into the already filled hall, reluctantly took over as chairman of the Preparatory Committee, as had been ordained by Peking more than a year before. The first vice-chairman was the Panchen Lama. The second vice-chairman was General Chang Kuo-hua, Chinese commander of the Tibet Military District. The secretary-general of the committee was the ubiquitous Ngapho. The three new, and still mainly theoretical, "regional" divisions of Tibet were represented on the committee by fifteen members from the Tibet Local Government (the central and Lhasan area, under the Dalai Lama), ten from the Panchen Lama Kanpo Lija, and ten from the People's Liberation Committee of Chamdo. Also included were five members from China's Central People's Government and eleven from the major Tibetan monasteries, religious sects, and people's organizations. By lumping together monastery representatives, Muslim representatives (as a religious sect), and representatives of "people's organizations," the Chinese were giving Tibet's priesthood due warning that its days of privilege were ended.

In all matters the Preparatory Committee was subordinate to China's State Council. All committee actions, including the appointment of senior officials, required Peking approval. Each of the three regional governments as well was *directly* subordinate to the State Council in Peking. The Chinese army was not under jurisdiction of the Preparatory Committee, but the committee was instructed to "assist the Tibetan Military Command in the consolidation of national defense and in the maintenance of local security." Under the Preparatory Committee were three subordinate committees: general, financial and economic, and religious affairs. The committee also had ten subordinate departments: civil affairs, finance, construction, culture and education, health, public security, agriculture and forestry, animal husbandry, industry and commerce, and communications.

Meetings of the officials went on for eleven days, with speeches by everyone of importance. Lhasa maintained an outwardly festive air. Groups of entertainers were scattered throughout the city, offering free shows in parks and pavilions. A plane flew over and dropped leaflets on the plane-wary public. Chinese and Tibetan flags flew from every public building. Over the loudspeakers came speech after speech.

Chen Yi, in his first speech at the inaugural meeting, stated that China's "greatest and most fundamental achievement" of the past few years had been that "we have been able to end the antagonisms between the Han and Tibetan nationalities . . ." The Chinese troops and workers, he claimed, "have won the all-out support of the Tibetan people." His words made strange listening for the Kham refugees whose husbands and brothers had died or were dying in the fight that raged to the east. To the Lhasans, of course, it was the same old story. They could look back with irony to the day when they had believed everything they heard on the radio because the sound had seemed like the magic voice of the gods. Now they believed nothing that came from the loud-speakers. Radio was another word for Chinese lies. Even so, they listened for the voice of the Precious One. His words would not be his own, but they would listen for the voice they loved.

The Dalai Lama also spoke of the new unity between Han and Tibetans. He said that "the masses of people and their leaders in Tibet have discarded their misgivings and gradually changed their attitude of mistrust, received from past history, toward the Han people . . ." He did not, however, credit the fine spirit of the Han soldiers and workers with bringing about this change. Rather he referred to the Tibetan delegations that had visited China and had "reported to monks and laymen on the might and strength of the motherland."

The Dalai Lama's speech contained a number of statements that hardly could have had Chinese approval; he may have inter-posed the statements into his "guided" text. Chang Kuo-hua, speaking of the road program, for instance, had accented the fact that it had given employment to "members of the priesthood and laity" and to "10,000 famine-stricken flood refugees." The Dalai Lama, however, observed that many people "sacrificed their valuable lives in the midst of road construction." He added, "I wish to express here my sincere condolences for these martyrs."

Again Chang Kuo-hua, in speaking of religious freedom, said: "Under the leadership of the Dalai Lama, the Panchen Lama, and the Tibetan Working Committee of the Chinese Communist Party, we must continue to respect and enforce the policy of freedom of religious belief and the protection of monasteries." The Dalai Lama agreed with this but added: "The basic problem

in the restoration and development of religion lies in whether
people are destroying religion or treasuring and protecting it as
their own life. It is an entirely different thing from political
reform."

And, on reform in general, the Dalai Lama did not hesitate
to disagree somewhat with Chen Yi's statement that "to eliminate
inherited backwardness and to make political, economic, and
cultural advances, a nationality will inevitably make necessary
reforms within itself." The Dalai Lama pointed out that news of
recent reforms in "neighboring provinces and municipalities" had
come to Tibetans and had "roused the suspicion and anxiety of
some people here." Perhaps he was giving his people a pledge
to do his best to delay "reforms" when he added, "It is unnecessary
to have fears and apprehensions for reform and to worry too
much about it."

Heartening as such words might be, however, the composition
of the Preparatory Committee afforded good reason for "fears and
apprehensions" about reform. Although the committee itself had
only five Central Government representatives in the total of fifty-
one members, Chinese were prominent in all of the subsidiary
departments where the real work would be done. The ratio here
ran about one Chinese to three Tibetans, and the Chinese were
in high posts; every department except the Culture and Education Office had a Han either as director or deputy director. And
many of the Tibetan posts were filled by the newly returned
Tibetan trainees who had been indoctrinated in China. Finally,
a part of the planning under discussion at the ten-day meetings
was the training program for two thousand new Tibetan cadres
within one year and ten thousand within four years. In short,
Chinese control over Tibet's government was greater than the
British control over the Indian government had been.

An equally serious threat existed in the three-zone division of
Tibet. Although each zone had its representation on the Preparatory Committee, the zones also remained separately under the
direct authority of China's State Council. If Lhasa was too dilatory
about accepting communization, the program could be presented

elsewhere without reference to the Preparatory Committee. Che Jigme, guiding influence of the Panchen, offered to set up a "prototype" committee in Shigatse and to be responsible for organizing "reforms" in that area.

After the meetings in Lhasa, Chen Yi and Chang Ching-wu went to Shigatse. They may have had Che Jigme's offer under consideration. Radio Peking and the Chinese press played up the Shigatse visit. Great crowds lined the way of approach, according to these reports, and threw ceremonial scarves and flowers into the delegation's open cars. "Thousands of peasants from areas nearby greeted the delegates with wheat gathered in last year's harvest. All the lamas of Tashi Lhunpo held a religious ceremony of welcome." The visiting dignitaries' speeches took on a different tone in Shigatse. They urged vigilance against "subversion" and warned Shigatse Tibetans to be on the lookout for "imperialists and reactionaries." They did not talk of unity; instead they accented local pride and the achievements to be made under the leadership of the favored Panchen. The people listened politely. Che Jigme's prototype committee, however, did not materialize, and incidents of violence marred the peace in Shigatse as elsewhere in Tibet. The garrison, which had been reinforced before Chen Yi's visit, remained at its reinforced strength.

No amount of reinforcements could have made Chamdo, headquarters of the eastern zone, a safe place for Chen Yi to visit. He did not attempt to go there, although on two occasions the Indian press reported that he had visited the eastern zone and that attempts had been made on his life. These reports may have been based on the existence of resistance plans to attack his party if he did enter the area. The fact was that Chen Yi did a minimum of sight-seeing in the Tibet Region of China. He did not even visit the three large monasteries. After his return from Shigatse he remained briefly in Lhasa and then was flown out in one of the two planes which landed at the new airfield near Lhasa in a pioneer flight.

It is possible that even the northern road was no longer considered a safe route for the Vice-Premier of the motherland. Although this road cut a northern curve between Sining and the Tsaidam Basin—purposely to avoid the dangers of Golok territory—the road had bred its own dangers. This was the area of the most concentrated settlement effort. The Western press in the summer of 1956 said that "already three million Chinese settlers are bringing the vast spaces in northeast Tibet under potatoes and wheat." This estimate was based both on information from Tibetan refugees and on China's own claims of success in the "reclamation of wastelands." The Tsaidam Mongols who had used the grasslands for seasonal herding had not been bothered at first by the settlements which sprang up along the road. Seeing the tents of a new colony, they simply moved off to some alternative but equally convenient grazing ground. When the settlements increased in number and grew in size, however, the nomadic Mongols, who are Lamaist like their Tibetan brothers, saw their way of life threatened. After the uprisings in the nearby Golok country and in areas to the south sporadic but violent outbursts of defiance broke out in this northern district as well. Guerrilla bands, which had harassed road-building work years before and had been scattered with brutal bombings, re-formed in the hills to make common cause with the raiding Goloks. Both Tsaidam Mongols and Tibetans of the area supported them with food, arms, and assistance in evading capture. The raiders' losses were heavy—for the road was a chain of garrisons—but they were able periodically to destroy a few culverts, delay and attack supply trucks, ravage settlers' crops, and run off the livestock.

In western Tibet the auspicious occasion of the opening of an all-weather motor road from Taklakot to Gartok was marked by more violence. The Chinese authorities planned a colorful ceremony for the opening of the road. The monks of the area's monasteries boycotted the event in a protest against the forced-labor policies which had built the road. The people of the area, following the monks' lead and also remembering the martyrs they had given to the road, went beyond the boycott; they turned out in large numbers to demonstrate against the road. They attacked the speakers' platform and the decorated archways with sticks, stones, and a few bullets. The ceremony was postponed, and army units were called to disperse the demonstrators. Many monks joined the people when they saw that repressive action would be taken. Among the dead, when order was restored, were monks and laymen and Chinese troops. Reinforcements were rushed in, and the area was cordoned off with troops to keep the violence from spreading.

Nevertheless, throughout Tibet the resistance continued to be less infectious than spontaneous. In the west and south, where heavy Chinese garrisons were stationed near the borders, trouble was common. It might come from any number of causes—resentment against the indoctrination of youth, the requisitioning of labor or supplies, new taxation, disrespect for religious practices, replacement of popular officials with Communist sympathizers.

An increasing number of stories found their way into the Indian press. Increasing numbers of refugees were leaving Tibet. Many were simply mute and miserable; they did not want to talk about their experiences. For now they asked only to get away and to find friends over the border. Others, however, talked freely. A few came for the purpose of talking—in the hope of arousing some awareness of the true situation in the Tibet Region of China.

A refugee monk official, for example, addressed an appeal, in behalf of "the millions of fellow Tibetans who are suffering so greatly today," to Prime Minister Nehru. He exposed in detail the policies of the Chinese Communists and called the "liberation" of Tibet "nothing but a newer form of brutal, ruthless colonialism to be more dreaded than the old because here the aim is not only exploitation but the complete absorption of a people—absorption or extermination are the only two alternatives offered to the people of Tibet by the Chinese." He cited the Communists' continuous violation of the 17-Point Agreement and asked Prime Minister Nehru to use his own influence, and to enlist the influence of other free Asian leaders, in requesting the Chinese to desist from their brutal policies and to withdraw the armies from Tibet.

Another high-ranking lama refugee, the abbot of Gyantse Monastery and former monk-governor of Gyantse, sent a letter of appeal to the Pakistan Prime Minister. Refugee lamas from Litang, who had personally witnessed the brutal bombings, talked to the press and tried to contact Indian officials who might be able to influence government policy. One of the Dalai Lama's older brothers, who had continued to reside in India despite Peking pressure, also helped refugee Tibetans in presenting appeals.

Meanwhile the Chinese were conspicuously silent on the subject of their Tibet region. In Kathmandu, where official emissaries from all parts of the world gathered for the coronation of King Mahendra of Nepal (an event which my father was privileged to attend as special U.S. ambassador), the Chinese envoys brusquely dismissed the news of revolt in Tibet as "all lies."

Early in August 1956, however, Liu Ke-ping, chairman of China's Committee of Nationalities Affairs and indoctrinator of the Dalai Lama during his Peking visit, broke the silence. In an interview with Italy's Peking correspondent for the Communist *L'Unita*, Liu Ke-ping said that a rebellion had broken out many months before, not in Tibet but in western Szechwan. It had been instigated by "remnant Kuomintang agents and a few feudal landlords." It had no support of the people who were, in fact, organized into self-defense squads to help the Chinese army units. Liu Ke-ping emphasized that the revolt had no "nationalist content" and said that the Lamaist church had neither taken part in it nor supported it. He also said that the highways had never ceased to be open to traffic. He assured the Italian newsman that the rebellion was now "mainly settled" and that its leaders were being treated leniently. The Italian correspondent's story of this interview was widely circulated by New China News Agency.

Quite apart from the mass of evidence presented by Tibetan refugees, Chinese sources themselves gave evidence that Liu Ke-ping's words were false. Radio Peking inadvertently supported Tibetan claims of having cut off and isolated certain Chinese forces; the Chinese broadcast referred to an air drop of supplies to their encircled army units in Tibet. The Chinese novelist Han Su-yin, coming to Hong Kong from Peking, told correspondents about talking to a Chinese air-force officer who told her of bombing missions in Tibet.

Chinese actions, more than their words, betrayed the true state of affairs in the mountain kingdom. In 1956, for example, the Indians invited the Dalai Lama to India to attend the observances for the 2500th year of Buddhism. They submitted their invitation through Peking, but the Chinese refused it without referring to the God-King. The invitation for the Dalai and Panchen Lamas to attend King Mahendra's coronation in Nepal was also refused. The Tibetan representative who did attend was not a Lhasa official but a member of the Bureau for Tibetan Affairs in Peking.

The Chinese made strong attempts to keep every influential Tibetan inside the borders during the uprising. The Communist authorities often must have regretted their previously made arrangement to allow Tibetan pilgrims to journey to India without exit permits during the holy year of Buddhism. A traveler had only to secure an entry permit from the Indian government. These permits were readily available to all Tibetan applicants at any Indian trade agency in Tibet. Thousands of pilgrims went throughout the year, and many of them did not intend to return as long as the Chinese Communists controlled their country.

One of the pilgrims was Alo Chondze, the Mimang leader who had been arrested in the spring of 1956. He and his two companions were held by the Tibetan police, who consistently opposed Chinese pressure to turn the men over to the military authorities. Mass agitation from among the people for the release of these men was almost constant. Eventually the heads of the three large monasteries demanded that the men be either tried or released. The Chinese understood well the risk of bringing these men to trial in the tense atmosphere of Lhasa during the summer of 1956. In the fall, therefore, the men were released upon an assurance of "good behavior" by the monastery heads. Before the release was effected one of the men died. The other two, when freed, managed to get to India. Like other refugees of standing, they talked to the free press and to Indian leaders, and they worked for the cause of national independence.

We know now that the Dalai Lama, in his position, could do little for the cause of national independence except keep up the spirit of his people. Nevertheless, we also know now that he wanted to make a more direct contribution to the nationalist effort.

The Tibetan people, looking to their God-King for some miraculous deliverance, understood his desire and felt that he was being tested beyond his strength. When the people gathered in assembly they prayed for their god to remain with them in his present Incarnation. As a living god who had returned by choice from his earned nirvana, he also had the power to will his own return to the blissful release from the Wheel. The people therefore entreated him to stay.

The Dalai Lama did not seek a new release. He sought only some solution to the seemingly hopeless problem of how he might save his people and their faith.

CHAPTER XIII

The Communist Threat to India

The moving glacier is not stopped by man-made boundaries.

—TIBETAN PROVERB

TIBET's neighbors to the south and west included India, Bhutan, Sikkim, Nepal, and Pakistan. The people of these countries living in the Tibet border area suffered economically as well as psychologically because of the Chinese occupation of the mountain kingdom. Their hardship increased the problems of the border nations whose governments were already taxed to the limit by the attempt to raise the living standards of four hundred million people.

Even more disturbing to the leaders of these governments was the picture of the new China revealed by the Communist action in Tibet. They traditionally had viewed China as a sprawling nation with a sophisticated culture and a peaceful, scholarly people who had suffered indignity and exploitation under the Western imperialists and brutality from the Japanese militarists. Thus the new picture of the Chinese with the brutality of the Japanese militarists and the arrogant aggressiveness of eighteenth-century European imperialists was difficult to accept. Moreover, acceptance of China in this new light would mean a complete reappraisal of the obstacles to progress. The worst obstacle would be the vast militarized Himalayan plateau used as a base for subversive action—and even aggression—against the subcontinent. Plans for coping with a brother Asian nation, grown suddenly and belligerently expansionist, had not been made in the border countries. Furthermore, such plans could be made only by abandoning all hope for a rapid rise in living standards, a fact that would not be well received by the impoverished and impatient millions. Governments would fall. Internal conflicts might become uncontrollable. The leaders in the border nations, therefore, could do little except hope against hope that their picture of the new China was somehow distorted and that they were misinterpreting China's activities in Tibet.

Nevertheless the Communist road-building program in Tibet could not be interpreted other than as an unfriendly gesture. When the roads connecting China and Tibet were completed, outsiders expected the pace of construction to slacken. Instead it was increased. Moreover, the new Chamdo-Lhasa road, instead of following the traditional and more direct caravan route, went south through even more difficult country to come within thirty miles of India's Assam border. After reaching Lhasa the road was pushed south again along the main trade route via Phari and Yatung right to the Indian border. In Shigatse, along the western trade route, a steel bridge was built across the Brahmaputra. The new road swung in a great arc along the Indian frontier in the southwest and west before going northward into Sinkiang.

The volume of Tibet's trade and commerce, even when the most optimistic dreams of "development" had been fulfilled, could not justify a fraction of this effort. Admittedly the Chinese meant eventually to exploit the natural resources that Tibet was thought to possess. But the Chinese expected to be fully occupied for the next two or three decades developing the easily accessible resources in their own country. As for possible increased trade with the border countries, the volume could not be raised until comparable roads were constructed across the borders; even then the volume could not be increased appreciably because the border countries themselves would be busy for decades with the problems of producing enough for their own people.

Thus the new roads in Tibet could not be for the purpose of trade, although the Chinese said that trade was their main reason for building them. The roads had to be for military purposes.

Other evidence indicated that Tibet's new highways were primarily for military purposes. The roads themselves, for example, were not the type that the local traffic of caravans and light vehicles would require; instead they were constructed to take the heaviest trucks which in that part of the world were available only to the armed forces.

Facing the fact that Tibet's roads were not intended for peaceful pursuits, the leaders in the border countries hoped that the military objectives of the Communists were solely the subjection of the Tibetans. This hope persisted despite Chinese propaganda to the effect that Tibetans welcomed the Chinese "liberators" peacefully and with great joy. Before long the fact that the Tibetans were far from happy under the Han occupation became obvious, but at the same time the number and deployment of the Han occupation troops indicated that the Chinese intended their forces for more than Tibet's internal security.

Even before the main highways were completed, for example, spur roads were built to strategic points on the border. Chinese army surveyors explored the valleys leading into Nepal and made plans for a more direct highway from Shigatse to Nepal. Also, as these branch roads were built, strong garrisons moved into border posts. Even larger contingents were stationed at Gyantse, Phari, and Yatung, the market centers for the Indo-Tibetan trade. In Tradum, at the head of an important pass into Nepal, new permanent barracks were built and filled with Han troops. Taklakot, a Tibetan village near the border where Nepal meets India's state of Uttar Pradesh, became a fortified city with more permanent barracks, heavy gun emplacements, and even a military airfield. From Gartok and Rudog, equally fortified Chinese army centers along the western frontier, mounted patrols searched India's border hills and the Ladakh region of Kashmir. In every village along the border at least a squad, and usually a platoon, of Chinese troops was stationed. These forces also patrolled constantly and often crossed the borders. The entire

Chinese force was linked efficiently by radiotelephone to the headquarters in Lhasa.

The Chinese military activity did not stop with troops. Powerful transmitters were installed in the border garrisons. A steady stream of propaganda was directed at the local population through loud-speakers. A completely different propaganda barrage was beamed to the people across the border.

The Chinese made personal contacts along the border as well. Workers from Nepal or India often crossed to take jobs on nearby construction. The workers were well treated and well paid; a Communist indoctrination course was included with the wages. Chinese troops crossed in the other direction. They went to buy firewood and timber and to cut logs for the construction of barracks and check-post hutments. They talked to all the border people they met. The people were reminded of their kinship to the Tibetans and told what great accomplishments were being made under the Chinese liberation. They were also told that the benefits now enjoyed by the Tibetans might soon be given to them.

The loud-speaker broadcasts to the Tibetans, of course, did not mention the benefits of the occupation; that would have been adding insult to injury. But they did repeat over and over that the Chinese were protecting the Tibetans from the "imperialist aggressors."

Just who these aggressors were, as Prime Minister Nehru said, was not clear. Judging from the almost frantic haste with which the Chinese were militarizing the Tibetan frontier, the expected aggression could come only from India, Pakistan, and/or the tiny border kingdoms. All together, these countries would have great difficulty in raising armies that totaled five hundred thousand men; the Chinese military forces were estimated at six million.

Moreover, any such action from the subcontinent against Tibet would require preliminary road-building projects through the mountains to the border. Everyone knew that the subcontinent nations did not use slave labor, and such road projects therefore would require an intense effort that would give the Chinese several years of warning.

Finally, the subcontinent countries were far from sufficiently allied to make the concerted effort necessary for any aggressive action against Tibet. India and Pakistan were in more or less constant disagreement. The co-operation between India and the small border kingdoms was at a minimum. All the subcontinent nations suffered internal conflicts and were devoting their full energies to the solution of grave social and economic problems. No one, therefore, could imagine that they were bent on imperialist aggression.

The Chinese usually prefaced the term "imperialist aggressors" with the word "Western." The accusation implied that the Chinese expected an attack on China through Tibet from India in conjunction with the Western nations. The implication, of course, was absurd, as anyone with an elementary knowledge of modern military tactics knew. The Chinese feared no such attack, but many Indians could not find any other explanation for the Chinese accusations against their country.

Moreover, the Chinese could point to evidence that indicated strong ties between India and what they called the Anglo-American bloc. India, for example, was a participating member of the British Commonwealth. Her constitution as well as her political forms and institutions were patterned after those of the Western democracies. She accepted economic aid from the Anglo-American bloc. English was her most important language for communicating with foreigners. Most of her students who studied abroad attended British or American universities.

Conversely India had no such real ties with Communist China or even with the other Asian nations. The Chinese used this fact effectively. By pointing with increasing frequency and asperity to India's Western ties they forced the Indian leaders to prove that India was not antagonistic to China. The proof was expressed by words and especially by deeds that increasingly benefited Chinese aims. Because of the obvious ties to the West the Indian leaders had no need to protest friendship with the Western nations; in fact, they felt that they could be sharply critical of these countries without causing a rift. The result was that the process of maintaining equal friendship with both the West and Communist China required a vastly superior Indian effort in behalf of the Chinese. European commentators who observed that India was "neutral on the side of the Communists" were not far wrong, although the Indian leaders meant only to keep a balance in their nonalignment.

Finally, the Chinese used their powerful military base in Tibet as a fist drawn back against India. The threat, together with the accusations that India was a tool of the Western imperialists, forced the Indian government to even greater co-operation with the Communists. India was distinctly in danger of becoming a "tool" of Communist China.

The Chinese would not have been able to enforce Indian co-operation by threats alone. They played on India's hopes as well as on her fears. India's hopes for peace were expressed in her nonalignment policy. The nature of this policy was the result of an ambivalence in the thinking among Indian leaders.

One aspect of the thinking accepted realistically that the West had had a strong impact on Indian culture. Most Indians not only agreed with the democratic ideals of the Europeans but also believed that Communism was antithetical to the principles of their religions. Among those whose thinking reflected this attitude was Sardar Vallabhbhai Patel who, in addition to Gandhiji and Jawaharlal Nehru, was one of India's top three nationalist leaders. He was firmly opposed to a soft policy on Communist expansionism. When the United Nations declared North Korea an aggressor, Patel advocated sending Indian troops to join the U.N. armies. And when the Chinese Communists attacked Tibet, he wanted to send a token Indian force in aid of the Tibetans. He knew that the force would be defeated, but his idea was to show the world that India was militantly opposed to aggression from any source. Patel, however, was mainly in charge of domestic problems while Nehru had responsibility for foreign affairs. Thus, although Patel nearly resigned in protest against the leniency shown to China, Nehru's policies predominated. Moreover, Patel did not live long enough to have a modifying influence on the other type of thinking which Nehru exemplified.

The other aspect of the thinking could be identified by deep suspicion of the West and by sentimentality on the subject to "Asianism." Many Indian leaders believed that the greatest evil in the world was European colonialism. Most of them had spent their lives fighting it and felt that eternal vigilance was necessary in order to prevent its resurrection. They could not imagine that Asians who had suffered the evil could ever be guilty of it. Once the Europeans were driven out, these leaders pictured a bright future in which all the Asian nations would co-operate peacefully to solve their common problem of uplift for their impoverished masses. Nonalignment was an attractive idea partly because of the understandable wish to avoid the distant ideological conflicts of the West and partly because of the opportunity it offered to develop a new ideology suitable to Asian problems.

Asian problems, of course, differed only in degree from those in the rest of the world. The sense of citizenship responsibility, for example, was not acquired automatically, and India's first experience with independence was violent internal disorder. Again the nationalist leaders were revolutionaries and politicians, but the problems of poverty, disease, and ignorance required the attention of economists, sociologists, administrators, and other such experts. The Indian leaders may have been dismayed by their discovery of the true size of their domestic problems, but they faced the facts honestly; because they were dedicated and sincere they made remarkable progress toward overcoming the obstacles.

They made less progress against the obstacles to international peace and co-operation. The Asians had felt a semblance of unity when they shared the common objective of driving out the European colonialists. Once the Europeans began to leave, however, the differences between the Asian nations, rather than the similarities, became apparent. Culturally the Asian nations were separated more than were the Western countries. The methods adopted by separate Asian leaders for solving similar domestic problems varied between all shades of ideological extremes. Several Asian countries pursued national objectives that were in conflict with the objectives of their Asian neighbors.

Nevertheless, many Indian leaders in particular and some of the leaders in the other uncommitted Asian countries would not give up the hope for a united and peacefully co-operating Asia. They believed that China was Asian first and Communist second.

The Chinese operating under Marxist principles, however, were far from sentimental about Asian relationships. Their attitude toward nonalignment was defined in 1952 by K. P. Karunakaran, a research associate in the Indian Council of World Affairs, who wrote, "Chinese Communists did not agree with the foreign policy of India. According to them, a foreign policy that was independent of the two blocs was irresolute and this was neither desirable or possible."

Mao Tse-tung made China's policy clear in a message he sent to India's Communist party on October 19, 1949. After pointing out that he considered the Indian government an "agent of the imperialists," he stated, "I firmly believe that relying on the brave Communist party of India and the unity and struggle of all Indian patriots, India will certainly not remain long under the yoke of imperialism and its collaborators. Like Free China, a free India will one day emerge in the Socialist and People's Democratic Family; that day will end the imperialist reactionary era in the history of mankind."

Nevertheless, in dealing directly with the Indian government and the governments of other uncommitted Asian countries, the Chinese gave assurances of great enthusiasm for Asian unity and of their intention to co-operate peacefully. The Indian leaders were only too anxious to accept the assurances as China's bona fides. The assurances, alternated with threats and accusations that India was a tool of the Western imperialists, succeeded in making India's nonalignment appear increasingly imbalanced in favor of China.

Many observers in India as well as in the West believed that the nonalignment imbalance had been tilted too far in China's direction when the Sino-Indian Agreement was signed early in 1954. The negotiations for the agreement began in late 1953. Indian representatives from the Ministry of External Affairs joined Ambassador Raghavan in Peking to reach a settlement with the Chinese concerning the Indo-Tibetan trade and pilgrim traffic. No representatives from the Ministry of Commerce and Industry were included in the negotiating group. Indian officials recognized that the significance of any agreement would be mainly political. Indian businessmen hoped that an agreement on a dependable pattern of trade with Tibet would be reached. All thinking Indians hoped that the conferences would indicate peaceful intentions on the part of the Chinese.

The Indians estimated that six weeks would be more than ample time for the negotiations. The talks went on for four months. In the Indian parliament during this period anxious questions were asked concerning the progress of the negotiations and the reasons for the delay. Government replies to these questions were reassuring but not specific.

Gradually the fact leaked out that the stumbling block to agreement was the Chinese insistence on matching trade agency for trade agency. India had inherited three trade agencies in Tibet; China now wanted to establish three trade agencies in India in addition to her embassy in New Delhi and consulates in Calcutta and Bombay. Suggested new locales for Chinese offices were Almora and Simla.

These two cities were both in the heart of the border hills. Indian newspapers spoke candidly of the proposed Chinese offices as centers of espionage and subversion. All but the Communist press supported government-of-India resistance to allowing such offices in the already disturbed hill territories. The opinion was expressed that India might be wiser, if pushed too far, to relinquish her own trade agencies in Tibet rather than to allow Chinese Communist infiltration in remote and vulnerable areas.

The agreement, however, was finally signed on April 29, 1954.

India kept her trade agencies at Gartok, Gyantse, and Yatung. In return China had the privilege of establishing agencies at Delhi, Calcutta, and Kalimpong. Because the Chinese already had representation in Delhi and Calcutta and a Chinese-controlled Tibetan trade agency at Kalimpong, the Chinese gain was rather more in face than in fact. The agreement, however, forced India to give up her inherited extraterritorial rights in Tibet, but this had been anticipated. Separate notes covering the time and method for withdrawal of the small Indian military escorts and the turning over of communications facilities and Indian-owned resthouses along the trade route were exchanged between the two governments. The agreement also set down the passes and routes to be used for pilgrim traffic and designated which of the traditional Tibetan market areas would be available for seasonal Indian trade.

The most significant aspect of the agreement, however, was the fact that it gave India's official recognition to China's control over Tibet. Immediately, in the Indian press and parliament, many voices questioned the wisdom of giving China "a kind of moral certificate in regard to her action in Tibet." Such recognition was hardly the way that nonalignment was meant to be practiced. One well-known Indian commentator, M. A. Venkata Rao, found it "uninspiring" that India should "yield to current Chinese imperialism" by blaming past British imperialism for the complicated status of Tibet. The most persistent question was: in the final signing away of Tibetan autonomy what had India gained?

Prime Minister Nehru answered by pointing to the preamble to the agreement, which contained his now famous Panch Shila. These "five points" bound the signatories of the agreement to respect each other's sovereignty and boundaries and not to interfere in each other's internal affairs.

Most of India's press accepted Panch Shila as a great diplomatic victory. Just as the Allies had abandoned Czechoslovakia to the Nazis to secure Hitler's promise for "peace in our time," Indian public opinion expressed the idea that Tibet's autonomy was a small price to pay for the good will solemnly promised between India and China. China was now bound over to good behavior, and India was making the first real test of "moral containment" as a practical instrument of foreign policy. Most Indians seemed especially pleased because the agreement appeared to indicate Chinese acceptance of the so-called "McMahon Line." This line had been the first and only formal demarcation of Tibet's boundaries. It had been fairly drawn and represented Anglo-Tibetan compromises and joint efforts. The agreement to accept the demarcation officially was proposed at the Simla Conference in 1914. The Tibetans agreed to the line, but the Chinese had ratified none of the treaty. After the fall of Nationalist China the Communists had referred to the McMahon Line as another example of Western imperialism, and every new Chinese map of the area seemed to show larger chunks of Indian territory included in Tibet. Indians believed that with the Sino-Indian Agreement on Tibet, India's view of the boundary had been accepted. They based their belief on the fact that the agreement had nothing whatever to say about the border question; this was interpreted as "tacit approval" of India's known stand—and Panch Shila promised China's respect for India's stand.

Not all Indians were so trusting, and Prime Minister Nehru's government faced considerable criticism because of the agreement. The Prime Minister defended it stoutly. He forbade any "mourning for Tibet's late autonomy." He was realistic. He called the agreement "a recognition of the existing situation in Tibet." But he was also idealistic. Answering criticism on Panch Shila and China's good faith, he wrote in a circular letter addressed to Congress party units, "Are we then to begin with enmity and suspicion and not give any other approach a chance? Surely it is better, with nations as with individuals, to hope for and expect the best, but at the same time to be prepared for any eventuality . . ."

Thus the Indian government saved face with its critics, but the government leaders were by no means naïve. They began at once to consider the preparations necessary for "any eventuality."

The first requirements concerned the economy of the border

people. For centuries these people had lived relatively undisturbed. On both sides of the border they had a kinship in appearance, language, and religion. The degree of kinship varied with the locale, but all the border people lived in harmony. Some important Hindu shrines were in Tibetan territory, and Lamaist monasteries existed in India. No insolent guards demanded to be shown papers. In fact, no one in the border area paid much attention to the border. The people carried on a brisk trade that had been the mainstay of the local economy for centuries. Tibetan caravans brought down wool, yak tails, salt, musk, borax, and furs. They carried back into Tibet cotton and wool cloth, metal tools and cooking utensils, sugar and other luxury foods, tobacco, dyes, and medicines. In many of the border areas the people were completely interdependent. In the frontier districts of Uttar Pradesh, Himachal Pradesh, and the Punjab, for example, more than 150,000 people of Indian citizenship were engaged in small border trade, the hire of transport animals and services, and the processing of local products of exchange. Wool from the western Tibet markets was woven into cloth in the Kulu and Kangra valleys of the Punjab. Western Tibetan herders exchanged their wool and surplus livestock for grain grown in the lower Indian valleys. The Bhotiyas, a caste of traders from Uttar Pradesh, spent six months a year peddling Tibetan trinkets in India's plains, where they bought stocks of Indian manufacture for sale in Tibet during the summer months.

When the Chinese came into the whole border area, they said that their troops and new roads were for the purpose of protecting the caravans from bandits and for encouraging more trade. True, bandits had always been a nuisance in the mountains. The mere hundred Indian troops in the Tibetan trading centers had not been able to prevent occasional raids. Now the Chinese moved in five thousand troops to the same centers. Even these troops, however, could not stop the raids altogether. A force many times larger would have been required to guard every mile of the many routes.

As for encouraging commerce, the trade at first was stimulated after the arrival of the Chinese. The trouble was that commodities demanded in exchange for Tibetan products were completely different. Tibetans now presumably wanted spades, pickaxes, boots, cement, construction steel, motors, batteries, explosives, drugs—and even fountain pens and wristwatches. They went so far as to want spare parts and tires for motor cars, even when there were no wheeled vehicles in Tibet at all. It seemed fairly obvious that the Chinese were using Tibetan commodities, not for the benefit of Tibetans, but to obtain goods needed in China. The worst examples of eighteenth-century European exploitation had been hardly so blatant.

India drew up no special regulations to govern this new aspect of the trade with Tibet. Instead India's existing priority controls were used to channel the Tibet trade away from strategic materials.

This was not always possible. Late in 1954, for example, it was announced in the Indian parliament that the government was selling 4,500 tons of rice to the Tibetans. The rice was needed in India, and the government knew that the shipment was intended for the Chinese armies along the border. Nevertheless, at the time the Indians dared not refuse trade in any commodity that Communist-controlled Tibet demanded to buy. They feared that such refusal might make the Chinese retaliate by disrupting the traditional border trade and thereby take away the livelihood of tens of thousands of Indian border people.

The Chinese were still insisting that their troops and roads were meant to stimulate border trade and to raise living standards throughout the area—anyone who did not believe that, according to Radio Peking, was a tool of the Western imperialist warmongers. Indians, moreover, tended to believe that the Sino-Indian Agreement guaranteed the continuance of Indo-Tibetan trade. The Chinese began their encouragement of border trade by stopping all Indians at the border. The Indian merchants were thoroughly searched and interrogated. Worst of all, they were disarmed. No one traveled in that wild part of the world without weapons for protection against bandits and savage beasts. The Chinese said that henceforth their troops would protect the caravans. Everyone knew that protection could not be guaranteed for every mile between the border and the Tibet centers of the Indian trade. Admittedly only a few unarmed caravans were raided by bandits and the Chinese were apologetic, but soon only the bravest Indian traders would take their caravans into the Tibetan passes.

Even the brave traders found before long that their business became less profitable. They no longer could deal with their old clients. Instead their business was with Chinese army officials or with the Chinese merchants who had taken over the Tibetans' trade. The prices now were fixed, and with every trip they were more to the advantage of the Chinese. Barter was no longer allowed, and the exchange controls made trade for the Indian merchants increasingly difficult.

Nevertheless, the trade continued, even if the living standards of the Indians began to fall alarmingly. Tibetan wool was needed desperately to keep employed the cottage weavers in the Punjab hill districts of Kangra and Kulu. Salt from the great lakes of the Tibetan plateau had always been used to supply the entire border area.

The Chinese then made wool and salt their own monopoly. Less and less of the vital commodities were allowed across the borders. Unemployment became widespread. In many Indian border villages the people were close to starvation.

If this were not bad enough, the Chinese with their propaganda media for the border areas tried to blame India's "capitalist imperialist government" for the suffering of the Indians. If an Indian village trader, for example, desperate for salt, approached the Chinese on the Tibetan side, he would be told flatly that no salt was available. He was even subjected to a harangue, the gist of which was that he could get no salt because his government was a tool of the Western imperialists who had contrived to deprive him of salt for their own profit. If the trader listened patiently to this, the Chinese might relent and out of Communist sympathy for the common man make a little salt available to the buyer. The price might be ridiculously high. It might be lower, however, if the buyer talked about his grievances and would listen to stories of progress in Tibet under the Chinese liberation. If the buyer was willing to talk about the Indian military forces and police on his side of the border, he might get the salt free.

The Indian government could hardly be blamed for trying to counteract such activity. They shipped their own salt into the area. In co-operation with their states' governments they inaugurated development schemes to rehabilitate the border people who had lost their livelihood. Educational and medical facilities in the area were increased. The Chinese propaganda now tried to blame the Indian government for destroying the border trade. Even worse, the propaganda concentrated on the ethnic relationship between the border Indians and Tibetans and accused the Indian government of depriving the border Indians of the chance for progress under Chinese liberation.

This was hardly the spirit with which the Indian leaders expected their Panch Shila agreement with China to be carried out. They responded by discouraging all unnecessary traffic in the area. Indian border posts were increased and manned by specially trained police.

At the same time Tibetan traders and pilgrims entering India were scrutinized more carefully. They were required to carry identification papers obtained through the Registration of Foreigners offices in India, where resident Tibetans also were required to report. The resident Tibetans were limited to a five-year stay in India unless they wished to become citizens. Many did choose Indian citizenship. Buddhist societies whose contacts enabled them to check on the identities of the residents gave invaluable help.

The Chinese, however, objected to Tibetans taking Indian citizenship and brought pressure on the Indian government to refuse it.

The pressure was part of the Chinese policy concerning Tibet's borders. The Indians who believed that the Chinese, when signing the Panch Shila agreement, had accepted the McMahon Line were wrong. The Chinese used Hitler's tactics as exemplified by Czechoslovakia's Sudetanland. The Chinese proclaimed that Tibetans were Chinese citizens. Anyone ethnically related to the Tibetans also became a Chinese citizen. And of course the land owned by a Chinese citizen was to be part of China.

Thus India began to face border incidents as soon as the Chinese troops arrived. In India's Almora district of Uttar Pradesh, for example, the Indian inhabitants had given Tibetan names to a few of their villages. The Chinese border guards used trickery in the attempt to register as Tibetan citizens some of the Indian Bhotiyas, a caste of Indian hill traders, from these villages. When the Bhotiyas were made to surrender their arms at the border they were told that they could keep their arms if they signed themselves as Tibetan citizens. To the simple Bhotiyas this seemed merely a matter of expediency. They would have registered if alert Indian border police had not intervened to explain to the Bhotiyas what the registration would mean. The Bhotiyas immediately withdrew to their own side of the border. The Chinese, angry at being caught in the trickery, crossed the border and tried to disarm the Bhotiyas. The Bhotiyas forcibly put the Chinese troops back across the border. No one was hurt, but the Chinese blamed the Indian police for creating a border incident.

The Indians had even more trouble with such incidents in Assam, just west of the area where Burma was having almost constant border trouble with the Chinese Communists. Chinese maps now showed their border cutting deep into Assamese territory. At Towang, where the Dalai Lama's escape party entered India in April 1959, the monastery had been traditionally controlled from Lhasa. The appointment of the head lama was made from Lhasa. After the occupation of Tibet the head lama of the Towang Monastery was changed twice. Chinese troops stationed just across the border came to Towang and engaged the villagers in conversation. Indian authorities then moved a small troop detachment into Towang. An Assamese official contacted the Tibetan ecclesiastical authorities and requested them, under the new circumstances, to allow the Towang Monastery to manage its affairs independently. Permission was granted, and Buddhist

scholars from Shantiniketan visited Towang to catalog the Towang collection of rare Tantric manuscripts. The Indians allowed
the scholars to remain in Towang to translate the manuscripts
so that the knowledge would be available to Buddhists everywhere, but they did not permit more Chinese troops to enter
India.

Nevertheless, Indians had to be constantly on the alert to prevent the infiltration of Chinese agents. In the Assam hills area,
adjacent to the disturbed hill region of Burma, Naga tribesmen,
agitating for independence, had been carrying on near warfare
with the Indian authorities for several years. Chinese Communist agitators with funds and arms had to be kept away from the
insurgent Nagas.

The Indians had a similar problem in Ladakh, which is part
of Kashmir and has two hundred miles of common frontier with
western Tibet. A thousand years ago Ladakh was a part of Tibet. Subsequently, however, Ladakh became a separate kingdom
and even controlled a part of Tibetan territory. In the seventeenth
century Tibet regained this lost territory, and the relations between the two countries have been amicable ever since.

The Ladakhis are ethnically similar to Tibetans and have the
same religion. Ladakh monasteries, both the Red and Yellow Hat
sects, are closely connected to Tibetan monasteries and their
lamas go to Lhasa for higher training. Finally, the two countries
are economically interdependent, and as a result the Ladakhis
feel closer to Tibetans than to Kashmiris.

At present the greatest fear of the Ladakhis is that they will be
dominated by Pakistani Muslims whose secular government is
based on religious law of the Koran. Both India and Pakistan
claim Kashmir State, of which Ladakh is the far eastern district,
and the dispute has unsettled the state. The local government
under India has not interfered with the Ladakh Monastery authority, although land reform in the case of large private estates was
instituted. Nevertheless, the Ladakhis have been impoverished
to the point of desperation by the loss of trade with Tibet and
Sinkiang since the Communist occupation. Moreover, because

of the political complications in Kashmir and because most of the Ladakh territory is bleak and rocky, the Indian government has been unable to give the people adequate help.

The Ladakhis, therefore, are discontent. Fearing Muslim domination and believing that the Indians are too weak to stand up to the Chinese Communists, they are an easy target for the Chinese propaganda.

And the Chinese have been working on the Ladakhis openly and to the full extent of their media facilities. The kinship between Tibetans and Ladakhis is played up. The Ladakhi fear of Muslim rule is kept constantly stimulated. The few Communist-controlled Tibetan lamas try to influence Ladakh monasteries. Ladakh leaders are invited for carefully controlled tours in Tibet and given lavish hospitality. The Indian government is derided for not providing adequate livelihood for the Ladakh people, and promises of great prosperity under Chinese liberation are made.

The Indian leaders could hardly pretend that such acts were friendly. The preparations for Prime Minister Nehru's "any eventuality" became more serious. Roads from the Indian plains to the Tibet border were widened, improved, and extended. Several new roads were built. A network of airfields from Ladakh to Assam was constructed. More troops were stationed in the area and given special training and equipment. And, finally, more of the border areas were sealed off. One should realize that the cost of such preparations cut seriously into the Indian government's appropriations for national economic improvement and was incurred reluctantly.

Regardless of cost, the preparations were necessary for reasons other than counteracting Chinese propaganda. Indian officials also needed to prevent the smuggling into Tibet of strategic materials, for which the Chinese were now paying high prices. In addition, the move was meant to eliminate contacts between Indian Communists and the Chinese Communists.

Despite the controls, some Indian Communist party workers did manage to penetrate the border areas. In the summer of 1953

India's top Communist member of parliament, using the immunity to which his position entitled him, had toured the whole Himalayan region. Shortly thereafter a new party office was opened in Rampur, an isolated hill town roughly fifty miles from the Tibet border on the road from Simla. From this office the Indian Communists presumably made frequent contact with the Chinese Communists; in any event, they consistently spread the propaganda line devised by the Chinese for the Indian border people. The Indian government curtailed these activities sharply, however, when it began to take precautions against the whole Chinese military build-up in Tibet.

Although the Indian precautionary measures were taken only after the Chinese began to militarize the Tibet border, and although the precautions were dwarfed by the immense Communist effort, the Chinese reacted as though India were preparing open aggression on the People's Republic. Nevertheless, it was the Chinese patrols that constantly probed the Indian defenses. The Chinese troops became openly hostile to Indian traders and officials. The Indian trade agents in Tibet were subjected to many indignities and were constantly frustrated in their job of helping Indian merchants in the Tibet trade. When the Indian agent at Gartok lodged a protest against anti-Indian activities he was told rudely to go back to his office and not to interfere. Later the agent was reported to have been arrested by the Chinese. Ultimately this was denied, but the fact that he had been deprived of his wireless transmitter and was not allowed out of his compound was confirmed.

One could understand why the Chinese wanted no Indians in Tibet. The Chinese propaganda now aimed at the Tibetans was distinctly anti-Indian. India was described as an imperialist power bent on military aggression and destruction. The Chinese said that the Indians intended to use the new border airfields for bases from which to bomb all Tibet and to exterminate the Tibetan people. It is difficult to see what the Chinese intended to gain by this propaganda line. It fooled none of the Tibetans whose attitude toward India now was conditioned by a contempt for her weakness rather than fear of her strength. The propaganda, however, did worry the Indians and force them to further efforts to prove their friendliness.

The Indian government was even more worried by the Chinese activities against the semi-independent states which occupied about half of the 1800-mile border between India and Tibet. In these states the Indians did not have the authority to take precautions against Chinese encroachment without permission of the states' rulers. Moreover, some of the most important passes from Tibet into India went through these states.

In Sikkim, for example, the Natu La was the main thoroughfare between Tibet and India. Sikkim was ruled by a maharaja who had signed with India a treaty that put the state's defense and foreign relations into Indian hands. Also, the maharaja ruled with the advice of Indian officials. Thus the state, for all practical purposes, was part of India. Nevertheless, most of the ruling family were Tibetans. The Sikkimese were ethnically close to the Tibetans and they were Buddhists; many were Lamaists and looked to Lhasa as the peak of spiritual authority. The Dalai Lama's treasure was reportedly stored in Sikkim, having been brought there for safekeeping during his retreat in Yatung at the beginning of the Chinese invasion.

Despite—or perhaps because of—Sikkim's close ties with Tibet, the Sikkimese were not fooled by the Chinese "liberation" of Tibet. They therefore looked to India for help, and so far the people have been little affected by Chinese propaganda.

The people in the neighboring state of Bhutan, however, did show signs of having been affected by the Han propaganda. The Bhutan maharaja also signed a treaty with the Indian government, but he opposed any sizable Indian penetration of the country. This made India's responsibility for the country's defense more than a little difficult. The Bhutanese terrain added to the difficulties. The two easiest passes along the entire frontier led from Bhutan valleys into Yatung and Phari in Tibet. Bhutanese traveling to India usually went through either of the Tibetan towns and then entered India through the Natu La in Sikkim.

The Bhutanese soon began to show signs of doubt about the Chinese "liberation." Bhutanese traders reported the effects of inflation in Tibet. Rumors of the Tibetan hatred of the Chinese impressed the Bhutanese.

The result was that the Bhutanese turned more to India. Indian engineers were allowed to enter the state to work on a flood-control project. India began other development projects designed to raise Bhutanese living standards.

CHAPTER XIV

Nepal—the Strategic Kingdom

Death comes later,
Today's happiness is profit.
—TIBETAN PROVERB

THE largest and perhaps weakest link in India's frontier defense network is Nepal. It has a population of eight and one-half million and fronts Tibet for five hundred miles. Several easy passes lead from Tibet into Nepal. Access from Nepal into India, however, has always been difficult, mainly because of a wide belt of almost impenetrable malarial jungles that divides the Indian plains from the Nepalese valleys. These jungles, together with the world's loftiest mountains—Mount Everest is in Nepal—have made the country a magnificent barrier to the north.

Nepal, although occasionally under Chinese influence in ancient times, has been independent for many centuries. A British resident was stationed at Kathmandu after 1814, but the Nepalese-British relationship gradually took the form of an alliance. Nepal was an effective northern barrier to the Indian plains and supplied the famous Gurkha soldiers who served as British mercenaries. The pay of the soldiers, who made regular remittances to their families in Nepal, was an important part of the country's economy. Britain was accused of keeping Nepal a backward country in order to retain her "Gurkha factory." Whatever her motivation, Britain interfered little with the internal policies of the state. Britain recognized Nepal's independence by treaty in 1923; the U.S. documented her recognition of that status for Nepal in 1947,

France in 1949, and independent India in 1950. Nepal became a member of the United Nations in December of 1955.

Nepal's Gurkha troops invaded Tibet on two occasions—first in 1790 and again in 1854. After prolonged fighting the Tibetans and Nepalese ended the war by the treaty which continued to govern their relationships up to, and even a few years after, the time of the Chinese Communist occupation of Tibet. Under this treaty Tibet paid an annual tribute of Rs.10,000 to Nepal, and Nepalese businessmen enjoyed certain extraterritorial rights in Tibet. Nepalese offenders in Tibet could be tried only under a court of three judges, two of whom had to be Nepalese. A Nepalese representative was stationed at Lhasa, and trade agents resided at Shigatse and Gyantse. Gurkha bodyguards were attached to these offices. A number of Nepalese businessmen lived in Lhasa, and many seasonal traders traveled between the two countries.

China now claims, as in the case of Tibet, that Nepal has been traditionally a part of the great motherhood. Chinese maps show Nepal within China's borders. When the 1856 treaty was signed between Tibet and Nepal, the Chinese amban in Lhasa served as mediator and the preamble of the treaty made reference to the Emperor of China. Considerable argument has arisen about the proper translation of this preamble—which states that Nepal and Tibet are "respecters" of the Emperor. The Chinese consider that a "respecter" is a subject, but the Nepalese rulers have consistently maintained that "respecter" means only that and no more.

When Communist China began her threats to "liberate" Tibet, all the Himalayan people felt that Nepal might be a similar target. Early in 1950 the Prime Minister of Nepal went to New Delhi for talks with Prime Minister Nehru and two agreements were drafted and signed. One was a treaty of friendship and the other a trade treaty. At the same time, as Nehru later revealed, the Indian leader advised the Nepalese Prime Minister to institute popularly demanded reforms in Nepal and to unify his people. The country, although nominally ruled by King Trib-huvana, had been under the actual rule of the powerful Rana family for almost a hundred years. Nehru urged the Rana Prime Minister to broaden the government and to give a voice to the people through elected representatives.

In the spring of 1950, some six months before the invasion of Tibet, Prime Minister Nehru reassured the Indian parliament on Nepalese-Indian relations. He pointed out that Nepal, although independent, was "geographically part of India" and that the interests of Nepal and India "so far as present developments in Asia are concerned" were identical. "For instance," he added, "it is not possible for any Indian government to tolerate any invasion of Nepal from anywhere."

Only a few days after the Chinese Communist troops invaded Tibet insurrection broke out in Nepal. King Tribhuvana asked for asylum in India and, once he had reached safety, the anti-Rana forces fought, in the King's name, for the overthrow of the Rana regime. India worked to bring about not only a peace but a settlement which would assure stability for Nepal and popular support for the government.

Rana leaders, who had not taken the Indian Prime Minister's advice in time, now agreed to most of his proposals. A cease-fire was brought about in January 1951, and an agreement was negotiated in New Delhi with Prime Minister Nehru as mediator. The King returned to Kathmandu, proclaimed the end of Rana rule, formed an interim cabinet which included insurgent elements, and granted amnesty to all rebels who laid down their arms within a specified period.

One insurgent leader, Dr. K. I. Singh, refused to be a party to the peace and continued to lead his fighting men until Indian troops, at the request of Nepal's government, apprehended and jailed him. He escaped, was rejailed, escaped again to enjoy a twelve-hour control of Kathmandu, and then fled when reinforcements of Indian troops arrived. With a small band of his followers he made his way into Tibet. By this time he had become a popular idol to many Nepalese and, from Tibet, a threat to the newly reformed government of Nepal. The Chinese Communists refused to extradite Dr. Singh. They had granted him, they said, "political asylum."

The reports concerning Singh's activities in Tibet, and later in Peking, were conflicting. Many assumed that he was being groomed to lead a "liberation army." The Indian press carried reports in 1952 that he was "enlisting volunteers among Tibet's Nepalese residents." Others disavowed his Communist leanings and felt that he was a prisoner of the Chinese. Prime Minister Nehru, in calling Dr. Singh "no Communist," said that he was merely a freebooter whose effort had failed. Singh called himself a Nepali Congressman (the Nepal Congress was an offshoot of the Indian Congress party and had been started by a group of Nepalese in India) who was in revolt against the Congress leadership.

In any event, his popularity in Nepal was considerable. He returned to Nepal from China in the summer of 1955 and was given a hero's welcome. He was wooed by various political factions and, so he said, was offered the prime ministership by several groups who sought association with him. Only two Nepalese parties, of which one was the Communist, expressed no interest in him. In the case of the Communists this, of course, might have been a blind. Singh himself, when questioned on his experiences in Tibet and China, maintained that he had "passed as a peaceful political refugee." When he returned, after "repeated requests," the Chinese government escorted him to the border "with full security precautions." He said that the Chinese always suspected that certain imperialist powers were planning to assassinate him in order to strain Sino-Indian and Sino-Nepalese relations. Singh's band of followers, who returned with him, were reported to be in bad physical condition, a fact which again might be analyzed as a blind.

Dr. Singh turned a deaf ear to the existing political parties in Nepal and started a new one. He toured Nepal, visited India, and increased his already large following. His party platform called for representative government with the King as a constitutional head; land reform and development of all Nepal's resources for the good of the people; nonalignment with either power bloc, and the acceptance of all outside aid offered without strings. He became Prime Minister in 1957, but his power was short-lived; he was ousted in early 1958 for yet another return to direct rule by the King and a group of advisers. During his brief rule Singh loaded the government with his close associates and worked at consolidating his power.

His ultimate aims still remain a question. Nepal is too vulnerable to take the risk of allowing him to demonstrate his answer.

Meanwhile Nepal's new government floundered repeatedly and the country was far from the "peace and stability" which Prime Minister Nehru had said were vital to India's security. Half a dozen political factions which had little in common once they had overthrown the Rana regime fought among themselves. Cabinets were formed and dissolved; periods of direct rule under King Tribhuvana and, after his death, King Mahendra spanned the long gaps between cabinet crises. Because all ruling elements had come from the Rana family Nepal had a dearth of trained or experienced administrators. The country, therefore, was forced to lean on Indian help and guidance; yet Indian "interference" was always a popular line for any Nepalese political agitator to take. Certain irresponsible Nepalese politicians, in a naïve effort to increase the country's independence from India, intrigued with the Chinese in order to play off India and China against each other.

Nevertheless, Nepal is utterly dependent on India economically. The country has been called bankrupt, and its two main sources of income are the customs duties which India collects for Nepal and the wages and pensions of the Gurkha soldiers who served in both the Indian and the British armies. Sixty thousand Gurkha pensioners now live in Nepal. The very subsistence of the Nepalese people depends to a large extent on India. Thus India, if only for her own protection, is forced to work out co-operative development plans which will raise the standard of living for the long-suffering and increasingly discontented populace.

During the early years of the Chinese Communist occupation

of Tibet traditional Tibetan-Nepalese relations were left undisturbed. Tibet continued to send the annual tribute of Rs.10,000 to Kathmandu; Nepalese trade agents retained their customary prerogatives in Tibet. Early in 1954, however, while the Sino-Indian Agreement was being negotiated in Peking, Nepal began to feel a little pressure from her new northern neighbor. Chinese authorities warned the Nepalese representative in Lhasa that he should plan soon to withdraw his Gurkha bodyguard. Nepalese traders in Lhasa were urged to invest more capital in Tibet and to consider the question of becoming permanent residents. The Rs.10,000 tribute was not sent at the customary time.

In April of 1954, although the tribute had not arrived, Nepal's Prime Minister M. P. Koirala told a press conference that the century-old Nepal-Tibet treaty was still operative regardless of the "so-called occupation of Tibet." When the treaty needed to be revised, he said, the Nepalese government would approach the Dalai Lama and not Peking, for the Dalai Lama was still the sovereign ruler of sovereign Tibet. These rather daring statements came as a surprise to the Indian press, whose correspondents had taken it for granted that Sino-Nepalese relations would be "regularized" after the Sino-Indian Agreement was concluded.

The press was right, and the theme of "sovereign Tibet" was not heard again from Nepal. After the Sino-Indian Agreement was concluded, Nepal's Foreign Minister made a statement welcoming the agreement and said that the government of Nepal would take up the question of their own relationship with Tibet "very soon." He said the Nepalese government had not yet been approached on this subject by the Chinese, but "if they approach us formally we will do the right thing at the right moment." A few months later the Chinese Communists suggested to the Nepal government that the old treaty should be revised in the light of "Tibet's new status in the People's Republic of China."

Negotiations were begun in the summer of 1956. The resulting agreement provided for the withdrawal of Nepalese bodyguards from Tibet and for the opening of a Chinese Consulate in Kathmandu. The existing Nepalese office in Lhasa now became a consulate accredited to China. The agreement also provided for trade agencies in both countries. Prior to the signing of the agreement commentators in India and Nepal speculated about whether the document would cover delineation of the borders. The Nepalese Prime Minister was reported to have said that a "clear demarcation" of the frontier would be included. Other reports, however, said that a Nepalese Foreign Office spokesman denied this statement and added that Nepal was "not in urgent need of demanding demarcation . . . and was not likely to press such a demand." The agreement, when published, said nothing about the borders.

Nepalese traders in Lhasa, who had hoped that the agreement would carry some assurance for the maintenance of their special position, were temporarily disappointed. Later, however, a separate note was negotiated which did assure the traders of foreign-exchange facilities in Lhasa and seemed to protect their position. Also, the Chinese changed their attitude toward the Nepalese of Lhasa. Several of the traders were granted large orders to be executed in India and were allowed a high profit margin— exactly as the Tibetan traders had been wooed a few years earlier. Nepalese subjects of mixed blood in Tibet were given a choice of retaining their Nepalese nationality or declaring themselves Tibetan. If they chose to take Tibetan citizenship they were eligible for free medical care and could enter their children in Chinese schools.

Nepal's Prime Minister (then Tanka Prasad Acharya) went to Peking shortly after the agreement was signed for a "social visit" at Chou En-lai's invitation. Passing through Hong Kong, Prime Minister Acharya spoke of Nepal's long frontier with Tibet. He said that Nepal *must* have good relations with China.

When Prime Minister Acharya returned from Peking he apparently brought with him some hope of a brief reprieve for his country. He quoted Chou En-lai as saying, in effect, "You needn't worry about us. We have plenty on our hands for at least twenty-five years."

Chou En-lai could afford to be candid about China's long-range plans. Obviously Nepal was a tempting spot for "liberation." As Prime Minister Nehru repeatedly pointed out, India's Himalayan barrier lay on the other side of Nepal. Nepal's southern slopes joined India's plains, and with the aid of modern drugs the jungle barrier was no longer a great obstacle. Moreover, the troops of the "Gurkha factory" could fit well into the plans of Asia's new imperialist power. Already evidence was accumulating that the Chinese Communists were working to indoctrinate the trained and seasoned Gurkha pensioners (many of whom retired very young) through agents from the border training schools.

The Chinese, according to Nepalese friends of my father, have two such schools in Tibet. Both are near the Indian and Nepalese borders. Some of the instructors are Indian Communists, working under Chinese specialists trained in Peking. The students are mostly young people from Sikkim and Nepal. They are trained in propaganda, party organization, espionage, sabotage, and the use of firearms.

They also learn that India is an imperialist, expansionist power who imposes hardship on the border people out of greed. From kerosene-lantern slides the students see that the Tibetans under the Chinese liberation are joyful with incredible new prosperity. On the other hand, India's development projects, which represent some of the most remarkable engineering and social achievements in history, are either lies or evidence of encroachment and evil intention. The U.N. technical aid and the U. S. Point Four aid in India and Nepal are "capitalist-imperialist bribery."

When these trained subversives return to their own countries, the authorities usually are able to keep a careful check on their activities. Nevertheless, these authorities and the efficient Indian police cannot control all the border areas, and the trouble is growing from month to month.

Border troubles inevitably spring up near Chinese installations. A particularly troublesome place is the area where Tibet's border meets the junction of Nepalese and Indian borders. Here, on the Tibet side, the Chinese Communists have built an impressive base at Taklakot. Early infiltration across the borders was explained by the custom of Tibetans to cross into Nepal or India for timber. But normal Tibetan needs are small; new Chinese installations require great quantities of timber, and increasing numbers of Chinese overseers and laborers cross the border. Inevitably disputes arise.

One Tibetan local official, undoubtedly under the "advice and guidance" of his Chinese military overlord, went many miles inside Indian territory and carried on a ceremony to install his "successor" in an area which included the Hindu holy place of Badrinath and also Gangotry, source of the Ganges and a holy shrine. He supported his claim to jurisdiction in this area by citing the fact that the Badrinath temple traditionally sent annual gifts to the Tibetan monastery of Toling across the border. These gifts were conveniently interpreted as tribute, although actually they were simply seasonal good-will offerings to smooth the way for the many pilgrims who visit Hindu shrines in Tibet and who travel through Toling territory en route to the holy places.

The pilgrim routes needed smoothing, for despite the provisions for safe passage of pilgrims set down in the Sino-Indian Agreement the Chinese authorities in Tibet were anything but hospitable. Pilgrim traffic was discouraged in many ways. All pilgrims were searched at border posts and were relieved of any arms, cameras, binoculars, compasses, books, and papers. Even the Finance Minister of an important Indian state, on pilgrimage to Manasarowar, was subjected to the indignities of a complete search. The Indian army adopted an unwritten policy not to allow any of its officers or men, while on leave, to make pilgrimages to the traditional holy spots. The army did not want to risk antagonizing the Chinese authorities and making the situation worse for all Indian pilgrims.

Another border incident which began in 1956 still remains a subject of high-level negotiation between Peking and New Delhi. It started when some Indian troops went hunting at a place called Bara Hoti, a small plateau at sixteen-thousand-feet altitude on the

Indian side of the border. Chinese troops on the Tibet side heard the shooting and apparently took it to be hostile gunfire. They returned fire and also took up positions in the area—on the Indian side of the border. When the Indian press reported that Chinese troops were occupying a disputed border area, New Delhi's Ministry of External Affairs contradicted the report and said that the matter could be "easily verified" at a suitable time. How easily, however, was indicated by the fact that two announcements of talks on the subject were made during 1957 but no talks took place. Another announcement in the spring of 1958 shifted the scene of the discussions from Gartok in Tibet to New Delhi. This negated the local nature of the incident. Later six Chinese representatives arrived in Delhi from Lhasa and indicated that they would wait to be joined by another party of negotiators from Peking. And yet both Chinese and Indian maps showed that the disputed territory was on the Indian side of the border. Despite the fact that Chinese troops had illegally crossed the border, Chinese authorities had demanded that the area be "neutralized" until the dispute was settled. In parliament Prime Minister Nehru said, "I don't know what this means; there is no war . . ."

In all the Tibetan border areas Chinese Communist policy upholds and repeats all the Chinese expansionist claims which history has recorded and adds a few new ones. Despite protests from India, Nepal, and Pakistan, new Chinese maps ignore the borders which have been set by tradition, by factual control, and in some cases even by recorded treaty. In their early days of power the Chinese Communists simply blamed the Nationalist maps and said they had not had time to prepare new ones. When the Communists brought out their own maps in 1951, however, they announced that their maps "agreed" with the Nationalist maps. They no longer bothered to justify themselves. Late in 1958, for example, the widely circulated magazine *China Pictorial* carried a double-page color map which advanced the Chinese borders deep into Indian territory. *China Pictorial* is distributed in both Hindi and English editions. Thus the publication supplied a clear answer to India's wishful interpretation of the Sino-Indian Agreement as "tacit approval" of the McMahon Line.

Demands of the "development" of Tibet ignored the borders. The new road from Gartok in northwest Tibet to Yehcheng in Sinkiang, for example, makes use of passes which take the road across nearly a hundred miles of Kashmir territory. Tibetan traders' reports that such a road was under construction were confirmed by Radio Peking in the fall of 1957 with an announcement that a convoy of twenty trucks from the Sinkiang city had reached Gartok.

Secure as the Chinese Communists may be in their strength, they do show some consciousness of the doubtful status of their border claims. The Indian press in 1954 reported that the Chinese authorities in Tibet had made repeated efforts to "borrow" certain historical documents from the Tibetan government and take them to Peking for display. These documents dealt with the historic border and some were used to support Tibet's claims that became the basis for the McMahon Line demarcated at the Simla Conference in 1914. The Tibetan government strongly resisted Chinese efforts to remove the documents, knowing that they would disappear in Peking. Eventually, of course, the Tibetans were forced to yield to Chinese pressure, and the documents vanished.

Chinese officials miss no opportunity to refer to China's "historical claim" on the various border territories. In addition, Russian Soviet publications and broadcasts build up the fiction of China's historical sovereignty over Nepal, Bhutan, Sikkim, and eastern Kashmir.

In India the historian K. M. Pannikar, writing on the subject of the Himalayan barrier, said, "Why it has so far not been penetrated for the purpose of attack on the Indian plains is not because there are no passes which open out to India, but because the Tibetan plateau was never in the past organized as a military state."

The Chinese Communists organized Tibet into a military state and the passes to the Indian subcontinent were now open to them.

India was making a show of resistance, but she was weak; thus, when the Chinese used their combination of threat and blandishment against her, the Indian officials felt that they could only compromise.

CHAPTER XV

Mission to India

A hornless yak can expect the frayed line rope,
A helpless person can expect closed doors.

—TIBETAN PROVERB

A STROKE of good fortune aided the Tibetans. The year 1956 marked the 2500th anniversary of Buddhism. The religion had originated in India. Although few in India now practiced the faith, the hospitable Indians staged a great celebration as a benevolent gesture to Buddhists throughout the world. The ancient shrines were refurbished and arrangements were made to receive thousands of devout guests. The Indian government as well as the Buddhist societies invited the Dalai Lama to participate in the observances. Who had a more legitimate right to accept such an invitation? The Dalai Lama was perhaps the most important single Buddhist alive and the acknowledged leader of an important branch of the religion.

The Indian invitation was sent properly through Peking. This time, however, the Indian approach was slightly different. The government of India advised the Peking government that the Indian representative in Lhasa would seek audience with the Dalai Lama in order to receive and communicate the God-King's reply.

The Chinese authorities in Tibet made it clear, upon orders from Peking, that the Dalai Lama was to refuse the invitation. A personal cable from Chou En-lai to the Dalai Lama backed up these instructions. The Peking communications to the Dalai maintained a polite tone, taking the approach that "it is your decision, *but . . ."* The Dalai Lama was to receive the Indian envoy with polite words of thanks and a polite refusal of the invitation.

The God-King, however, took counsel with all his advisers. He talked to his tutors, the Kashag members, and the monastery heads. Their opinion was unanimous that he should accept the invitation and honor the Buddhist observances with his presence.

The Indian representative in due time asked for audience and was received. The Dalai Lama expressed polite words of thanks to the government of India and India's Buddhist societies for the invitation. He added polite words of acceptance. Only later did he notify the Chinese authorities of his action.

Perhaps this invitation was the miracle for which the Tibetan people prayed. Perhaps in free India, on the anniversary of the Buddha, their beloved Dalai Lama would find the help without which Tibet could not survive.

As a truly devout Buddhist the Dalai Lama was thrilled with the idea of visiting the original shrines of his religion. As a twenty-two-year-old young man he was excited at the prospect of seeing more of the world about which he knew so little. And as a patriotic Tibetan he hoped that the trip to a neutral country would provide some opportunity for him to help his suffering countrymen. A thrill of hope stirred all Tibetans.

In the afternoon of November 24, 1956, hundreds of people collected in the valley below Natu La, the pass into Tibet from the Indian border state of Sikkim. Most of the people were Buddhists; they ignored the sleet and icy wind as they turned prayer wheels or whispered the 108 prayers on Buddhist rosaries. Among the crowd were many Tibetan refugees who had escaped Communist persecution. Others were Tibetans who lived on the Indian side of the border. Also present were many Sikkimese who ethnically were similar to their northern neighbors. Nearby the Maharaj Kumar (crown prince) of Sikkim talked quietly to an officer of the military honor guard, to an Indian government official, and to a few Indian journalists.

Suddenly, as if by magic, the mists cleared and watery sun-

light illuminated the pass above. A caravan of 150 horsemen was
seen winding down the snow-covered trail. Their faces were
covered with wired-leather masks against the biting wind, but
they wore rich furs or silk brocades in stunning colors. Despite
the lavish costumes the Dalai Lama could be identified immediately; he was wrapped in a magnificent robe, heavy with glittering
gold. His quilted silk headdress was also in gold, embellished with
the blue and pink of turquoises and coral.

The honor guard snapped to attention. A brass band struck up
the Indian national anthem. The Buddhists in the crowd pressed
forward eagerly; to them this was a moment that could happen
only to a fortunate few once in a lifetime: the sight of the Living
God, the Precious Protector, the Reincarnation of the Merciful
One, the High Lama Vast in Virtue as the Ocean. They surged
around him, and neither the police nor the soldiers could hold
them back. Finally the young Dalai Lama was able to calm them.
He then received their adulation and gave his blessings.

The flowery welcoming speeches began. In reply the young
God-King spoke with utter simplicity; he said that he was happy
to participate in the Buddha Jayanti observances and that he
appreciated the honor of India's invitation. The mists closed in
again. More sleet began to fall. The party moved down to
Chenghu, eight miles below the Natu La, where a resthouse had
been made ready for the visiting dignitaries. Here the Dalai and
his party waited to be joined by another almost as colorful party:
the entourage of the Panchen Lama.

In India, however, Tibetans did not need to fear the Chinese
troops. Moreover, many of the Tibetans who had come to see the
Dalai were refugees from Communist persecution in their own
country and they hated the Chinese. Thus when the false
Panchen's caravan arrived at the Chenghu resthouse an angry
murmur went through the crowd waiting in the snow outside.
The crowd had been growing steadily larger and now numbered
several thousand people. Evidently their emotions were mixed;
the presence of the Dalai Lama gave them great joy, but the
knowledge that their god was being forced to share the same

house with the false Panchen angered them. Nevertheless, except for the singing of a few ribald songs meant to insult the false Panchen, the crowd took no action. In any case, a heavy guard of Indian troops and police was deployed around the house in battle position and was kept on the alert throughout the night.

The next morning the caravans of the two lamas, now swelled by the camp followers to almost two thousand horsemen, moved further down the steep, winding trail in a stream of glittering color. They proceeded to Karponang, which was at the comparatively low altitude of ninety-five hundred feet and which marked the point where a road, usable by vehicles with four-wheel drive, began. A subtle change now came over the greeting ceremonies. Among the officials waiting to receive the lamas was Pan Tzu-li, the ambassador from Communist China to India; he unobtrusively took charge. When Indian journalists asked to interview the Dalai, they were told that the weather was too cold and that the two great lamas would be taken at once to Gangtok, the Sikkimese capital. The ceremony was cut short. The entire group of officials crowded into hundreds of light trucks, jeeps, and Land Rovers (the British equivalent of a jeep). The other thousands of spectators ran alongside the vehicles which rumbled down the steep hill road.

In Gangtok the lamas were taken to the monastery of the maharaja's palace. By now the spectators who crowded onto the lawn of the monastery numbered an estimated ten thousand. More troops were called in, and loud-speakers exhorted the people to remain quiet.

The lamas were taken from the palace at two o'clock the next morning to begin the drive to Baghdogra in India, where planes at the local airport would fly them to Delhi. The crowd of spectators was now even larger, and they blocked the road. At the town of Tarkhola people threatened to throw themselves in front of the vehicles unless the Dalai Lama stopped and showed himself to them. The procession was halted for ten minutes while the God-King gave blessings.

According to an Indian journalist who witnessed the entire

greeting ceremonies in Sikkim and later described them to my father, the crowd was in an undetermined mood, sometimes joyful and sometimes sullen. The people were becoming increasingly sullen as the Chinese officials gave more evidence of being in control of the celebration.

The Indian journalists were already annoyed by the Chinese control. In the first place, the Chinese were preventing them from interviewing the lamas. Moreover, the Chinese ambassador had sent instructions to the newsmen that, in writing their copy, they were to refer to the mountain kingdom not merely as "Tibet" but as the "Tibet Region of China." Finally the newsmen were told that they were to give equal publicity to the Panchen Lama. The Indian journalists were not used to being told by governmnet officials how they should write their stories, and they considered the Chinese attitude tactless and arrogant.

At Baghdogra airport the Chinese officials went too far in their tactlessness. For the ceremonies here two ornate thrones had been erected under a huge gaily decorated awning. In accordance with protocol the Dalai Lama's throne was elevated higher and was more ornate. Two hundred yards of hand-painted cloth stretched from a scarlet welcoming arch to the audience tent and served as a carpet on which only the two lamas could walk. The sun was shining; a band was playing, and the huge crowd seemed happy and festive.

Shortly before the two honored guests were to arrive the Chinese discovered that the printed welcoming speeches contained no mention of the Panchen. Further, they decided that the Panchen's throne was to be on the same level and as ornate as the Dalai's. The local Tibetans who had been in charge of the decorations had little affection for the "false" Panchen, and although they obeyed, they went about the tasks so slowly that finally the Chinese officials themselves had to do the work. The news that the Chinese were raising the Panchen's throne flashed through the crowd, and the air of festivity vanished.

A few moments later the lamas arrived and entered the welcoming arch. The crowd immediately became unruly. The people broke through the barriers and rushed toward the lamas, shouting angrily. Immediately in the presence of the Dalai Lama, however, their mood changed again, and those near him fell to their knees and tried to touch his feet. With great effort troops managed to get the lamas and the maharaja out through the back of the tent.

The mob then surged around the Dalai Lama's throne to kneel before it and touch it. The entire ceremony had to be abandoned. A similar mob threatened the safety of the planes that drew up to take the lamas on board. Police were forced to escort the lamas into the airport restaurant and to barricade the room. The departure was delayed for more than an hour.

In New Delhi the plane carrying the Dalai Lama, his closest advisers, and the top Chinese officials landed first. Prime Minister Nehru, Vice-President Radhakrishnan, and several hundred Indian officials and foreign diplomats greeted the God-King. A contingent of superbly smart Indian troops was drawn up for review. Next a delegation of Buddhist priests from many countries held burning incense sticks and waited to touch the feet of His Holiness when the official ceremony was finished. A huge throng of the devout and the curious strained from behind a barrier for a glimpse of the young god.

He was taken to Hyderabad House, the erstwhile New Delhi residence of His Exalted Highness, the Nizam, and now used by the Indian government to accommodate exalted visitors. Only after the Dalai Lama left Palam airfield did the other two planes land. The Panchen Lama was received politely but with less ceremony. The Maharaja of Sikkim was given a royal salute of fifteen guns.

After the Dalai Lama had been in Hyderabad House for twenty-four hours and was still unable to hold a press interview the Chinese strategy became more clear. Although forced reluctantly to permit the Dalai Lama's visit, they obviously intended that he should have as little contact as possible with the insidious influences of the free world.

In fact, the newsmen soon learned, through brief contacts with others among the Dalai Lama's party, that the Chinese had warned the whole Tibetan delegation especially about the free press. The newsmen in capitalist countries, the Chinese said, were notorious for their impertinence and disrespect. The Chinese therefore requested the Indian officials that His Holiness should not be "bothered" by the press. The Tibetan delegates themselves were instructed that, if cornered by a free-press correspondent, they were to say only, "We Tibetans and Chinese are a people of great solidarity."

While the Dalai Lama was being shielded in Hyderabad House from contaminating contacts, the announced visit to India of Chou En-lai took on added meaning. Peking obviously considered that the Dalai Lama's presence in Delhi was dangerous enough to warrant on-the-spot presence of the Chinese Communist Premier himself. It was also clear that the Chinese Communist leaders hoped to make political profit from the Dalai Lama's visit. Chou En-lai, appearing in the role of an affectionate uncle to the gentle religious leader, would gain not only personal prestige in the eyes of Asian Buddhists but would also exemplify to all Indians the benign tolerance of Chinese Communism.

Meanwhile, in the hope of getting some news of the forbidden land, the press turned its attention to other members of the Dalai Lama's entourage. Besides his personal attendants, the Dalai Lama brought with him representatives of Lhasa's three great monasteries, several noted scholars, and seven interpreters for English and the Indian languages. In addition, his mother, sisters, and brothers were in the party; later two more brothers who had taken refuge outside Tibet joined the group at Hyderabad House.

Finally the group included three cabinet members who have the title of Shape. Next to His Holiness, the press was most curious about these Tibetan politicians. All three had collaborated with the Chinese occupation authorities. Were these men Chinese stooges assigned to prevent any independent action from the young God-King? Or were they secret patriots, waiting for the right opportunity to rise against the aggressor?

Ngapho Shape seemed to be the favorite of the Chinese Communists. Although a Kashag member, he had been administering

Tibet's eastern province of Kham when the Chinese attacked. He surrendered to the aggressors almost at once and urged the Lhasa government to negotiate a peace. It was he who had signed for Tibet the 17-Point Agreement which "liberated" the country. Since then he had held some position of authority in every Communist-sponsored department or committee under the reorganized Tibetan government.

Ragashar Shape had been the Defense Minister at the time of the invasion. After the surrender he accepted the post of "vice-commander" of the Tibet Military District under a Chinese general. Ragashar also acted as liaison officer for foreign affairs between the Tibetan Autonomous Government and Peking.

Surkhang Shape was the son of Tibet's former Foreign Minister. In Lhasa society he was considered rather an opportunist with a not very strong character. Since the occupation he had been associated closely, both socially and officially, with the Chinese. He was regarded as modern and liberal-minded; at the time of the invasion, for example, he had been educating his children in India.

Thus all three of the Shapes seemed to be Quislings at the worst or collaborators at the least. Nevertheless, only Ngapho was considered inextricably enmeshed in the Chinese Communist regime in Tibet. Ragashar was thought to be the least influenced by the invaders. He was a mild-mannered man in his early fifties. He had served loyally under the previous Dalai Lama and was still popular with the Tibetan people.

The press was able to have some small contact with the Shapes, but the interviews only served to deepen the mystery of whether they were for or against the invaders.

During this time the Dalai Lama was being kept so busy that his failure to hold press conferences did not seem unreasonable. Every morning, however, he gave audiences at a simple pavilion in the gardens of Hyderabad House. Thousands passed by the pavilion for his blessing. For a day or two the people who lined the street leading to Hyderabad House were mainly Buddhists, but gradually the audiences attracted a wider group. Many Hindu families came to stand in line; bearded Sikhs and even a few

Muslims waited patiently for the auspicious blessing. A scattering of Western Christians came and found that they, too, were welcome. Each person who passed dropped a coin below the dais; the money was gathered into a basket each day and taken to the office of India's Buddhist society to augment a building fund. The blessings from His Holiness were given for only an hour and a half each morning. Afterward the Dalai Lama delivered a simple sermon to the assembled people. His talks, however, were always on religious subjects and told nothing of the conditions in his country or of the problems of his people.

Inevitably the Dalai Lama had private interviews with Prime Minister Nehru. Despite pressure from the Chinese Embassy, Mr. Nehru insisted upon having his own interpreter. What precisely took place during the two long talks was never officially revealed. Through officials in India's Ministry of External Affairs, however, certain journalists were able to confirm, if not publish, the fact that the Dalai Lama had described the plight of his country and had asked the Indian Prime Minister for help in freeing Tibet from the Chinese invaders.

The Indian Prime Minister must have been placed in an awkward position. Largely through his sincere efforts India had been proclaimed as emphatically dedicated, in international affairs, to "enlarging the area of peace" and to supporting "the aspirations of all colonial peoples to national independence." Logically, therefore, the Dalai Lama turned to Mr. Nehru when the peace in his country was shattered by aggressors who intended to colonize Tibet so thoroughly that not only would her "aspirations to national independence" become hopeless but the very existence of her people would be threatened.

Admittedly, in dedicating India to enlarging peace and reducing colonialism, Mr. Nehru, in common with most Indians, had assumed that the worst threat to peace came from the distant conflict between the U.S.S.R. and the United States and that colonialism was an evil of the European nations. Mr. Nehru, however, could hardly point to this assumption in answering the plea from the leader of the suffering Tibetans.

To make matters worse for Mr. Nehru, the Chinese Communist Premier was about to arrive in Delhi. The Indian government, attempting to pacify the new China, had been making only the friendliest overtures to Peking ever since the Communist regime was established there in 1949. On the rare occasions when India had questioned China's actions—the intervention in Korea and the attack on Tibet, for example—the Chinese had been decidedly waspish in telling the Indians to stay out of China's affairs. Thus, quite aside from offering aid to the Tibetans, if Mr. Nehru gave only sympathy to them—if he even acknowledged that the Tibetans had a legal right to appeal against the aggression and colonial domination from which they were suffering—he could expect the Chinese to consider that the Indian government had been guilty of an unfriendly act.

Meanwhile the Indian officials were preparing an elaborate reception that would discourage any hostility in Premier Chou En-lai. The Indian government opened all the stops of its hospitality. Along the highway from Palam airport into the city the Buddhist symbols in honor of the Dalai Lama were removed; they were replaced by the five-star flag of Communist China, which flew side by side with the Indian flag from poles along the route. Inhabitants of all the towns near Delhi were told where to congregate for free truck rides to the airport to join the welcoming masses. Schoolgirls practiced a drill to perform for Chou En-lai. Flower vendors worked overtime, stringing thousands of garlands. And special slogans to be chanted by the welcoming masses were composed.

The Dalai and Panchen Lamas joined the dignitaries who met Premier Chou En-lai at the airport. They stood toward the back of the small platform behind Prime Minister Nehru. After Mr. Nehru and Chou had exchanged greetings, Chou turned to the lamas and greeted them briefly but with well-practiced charm. The lamas stood quietly by while Chou was garlanded and re-garlanded by lesser Indian officials and while he reviewed the guard of honor. The great throng that had collected at the airport seemed delirious with joy. The chanting chorus from thousands of throats was deafening. "*Hindi-Chini, bhai-bhai!*" Indians and Chinese are brothers.

Friends of ours who were in Delhi at the time wondered whether these frenzied people could be the same ones who had stood reverently with folded hands for His Holiness the week before. Foreign correspondents in Delhi asked whether the gentle devotion of the previous week was insincere or whether the insincerity was present now in the hoarse voices cheering for the man who threatened the freedoms India had newly won. Perhaps the tireless chant expressed a hope rather than a fact. Perhaps what the Indians really meant was, "Indians and Chinese *must* be brothers; your armies stand at our frontiers, and we lack the strength to oppose you as an enemy."

In any event, with Chou's arrival the three main actors in the drama of Tibet were now on the stage together. Prime Minister Nehru played the pivotal role. He was the elder statesman, unquestionably one of the ablest in the world community. He was every inch an aristocrat. He was experienced and he possessed a brilliant mind. Although he sometimes reacted to petty annoyances with a flash of impatience, he always stood up well in a crisis. His one deficiency, so it seemed, was that he was more at ease with theory than with practice. Typical of such a person, he could write well but when forced to speak or converse extemporaneously he often expressed himself awkwardly and his ideas were not easy to follow. In dealing with the Chinese Premier and the Tibetan Dalai, he was faced with a choice between the security of his country and the moral principles for which his country stood.

Such a choice would never confront the young Dalai. He believed firmly that one did not compromise with morality. To him a people who forgot their principles in favor of security would lose far more than they could possibly gain. He played the most pathetic role in the drama. He was armed only with righteousness, a useless weapon against the cynicism and amorality of the Communists. The weapon presumably wounded Mr. Nehru but did not overcome him. It was said that the Indian Prime Minister was exasperated by the Dalai's naïveté but touched by the boy's idealism.

Although we do not know what Chou En-lai thought personally of the Dalai, we can safely assume that he regarded the Tibetan leader merely as a pawn to be manipulated to China's advantage. Nevertheless, Chou's chief characteristic was charm. Even Americans who met him socially found him affable and amusing. He had a stocky peasant's figure and heavy features that broke frequently into a broad grin. He was deft with a compliment. He told jokes well and, moreover, his humor, although a bit heavy for our taste, appealed more to Westerners than to most Asians.

Those who knew him better, however, and had to deal with him said that he was a fanatic, devoted wholly to the cause of Chinese Communism. Like many Communist leaders, he was motivated less by a logical belief in his ideology than by an intense hatred for those who opposed it. Thus his charm was a cultivated weapon that he used to weaken his enemies; he discarded the weapon quickly when the enemy was subjugated or when he found that it was not effective.

Evidently the Premier's charm had little effect on Prime Minister Nehru. A high Indian official who was closely associated with the talks between the leaders of the two largest Asian nations described the scene to my father. He said that outwardly the two men seemed to get along well. The Indian Prime Minister played the gracious host, Chou the appreciative guest. "Chou was the overfriendly sort, however, a type that seems to bring out the haughty aristocrat in Jawaharlal [Nehru]," he said. Chou could talk convincingly about peace—to those who desperately wanted peace—but a few deft questions from Nehru made Chou "lose both his charm and his temper." Prime Minister Nehru in forty years of leadership had coped with a number of dubious politicians, and he was difficult to shock, but even he was "appalled" by the cynicism of the Chinese Premier. Here was Chou in Delhi, "praising Panch Shila and suggesting that the Western imperialists should follow its principles; in public he was radiating friendship, speaking of brotherhood, and promising peace." This was only a week after Mr. Nehru had listened to complaints of the Chinese tactics in Tibet from the Dalai Lama himself.

In Chou's talks with Prime Minister Nehru, however, the Indian government was told bluntly not to interfere in Tibet. The Dalai Lama was to be treated as a religious figure only. Moreover, the Dalai's tour of India was to be limited henceforth to the arranged schedule, and he was to be sent back to Tibet the moment the tour was finished. The Indian Prime Minister evidently listened with stony silence and did not commit himself on whether or not the Indian government would obey.

The only publicity given in India on the nature of these talks appeared in the *Times of India* on January 4, 1957. Speaking to a session of the Congress Working Committee, the news item reported, Prime Minister Nehru revealed that Chou had complained to him about the use of Kalimpong in India "as an international base by the United States and others to undermine Chinese influence in Tibet." Mr. Nehru had replied that "India's attitude is one of willingness to help if specific instances of subversive activity are pointed out."

On January 14, 1957, Shridharani of the *Amrita Bazar Patrika* wrote, "There is no doubt in Delhi's mind that there are some spies of foreign countries there (Kalimpong). And yet Delhi has not quite relished the complaint of Chou En-lai. Was it the polite Chinese way of suggesting that Peking is aware of even Indian activities there?"

Meanwhile, two days after speaking bluntly to Mr. Nehru, the Chinese Premier was given the unusual honor of addressing the Indian parliament. While Chou was praising Panch Shila to the M.P.'s, the Dalai Lama was making a sad little speech to a gathering of Buddhist scholars. He predicted that "someday the exploitation of man by man and the ways and deeds of violence" would end. He also expressed his "appreciation of the efforts which many peace-loving great countries make day and night toward the freedom of small countries and toward the elimination of aggression and war."

The few newsmen who had not given up on Tibet coverage

interpreted the Dalai Lama's comments to mean that Prime Minister Nehru had given him no hope. The Dalai Lama was now casting about, in an inconspicuous manner, for other support.

Thereafter he had little chance of openly seeking support for Tibet. Chou En-lai kept a watchful eye on the young God-King. Outwardly it was a benign eye. The Dalai Lama attended official receptions held by the Indian government. He was entertained by the representatives of such Buddhist countries as Ceylon, Bhutan, Sikkim, and Nepal. He was officially entertained by the Russian Embassy and was a frequent guest at the Chinese Embassy. And, of course, he took part in the meetings of the Fourth World Buddhist Conference. Either Chou En-lai or the Chinese ambassador to India—or both—were always in the background, smiling and affable, but making sure that His Holiness spoke no more than a few words to any one person.

When the Dalai Lama began his tour of the Buddhist shrines, the Chinese presumably felt that in the hinterlands he needed less supervision. Prime Minister Nehru left for the United States, and Chou En-lai now continued his good-will tour of Southeast Asia. His talks invariably emphasized culture and religion. Chou spoke feelingly of the ancient cultural ties between India and China, although the actual number of Hindi-Chini "brothers" during the long histories of the two countries numbered less than a dozen.

Inevitably conflict arose between the Chinese and the Tibetan God-King. A Buddhist Conference was also meeting in Nepal. Chou wished to include a Nepalese visit in his good-will tour and he ordered the Dalai Lama to accompany him. Chou's motive was clear; the Dalai Lama and his advisers, however, were opposed to the God-King's being used to enhance the prestige of the Chinese Communist Premier. Also, the Dalai Lama feared that, once so close to Tibet, the Chinese might send him back to Lhasa without his having the chance to talk to Prime Minister Nehru again. Thus the Dalai Lama refused to go to Nepal. Chou En-lai insisted, and the God-King was forced to include the Nepal trip in his planned schedule.

Nevertheless, late in December the Nepal trip was suddenly canceled and the Dalai Lama was called back to New Delhi by the Chinese. Trouble had broken out in Tibet, and Chou En-lai was returning to Peking. News from Tibet, coming through Nepal, told of more uprisings. New action was raging to the west of the Communist stronghold at Chamdo and even in Lhasa itself. The Chinese bombed a village and eighty-three Tibetans were killed or injured. Chou wanted the Dalai Lama to return to Tibet at once. Moreover, he wanted the young ruler to go directly to Lhasa and not via Kalimpong and Darjeeling where many exiled Tibetans, including alleged resistance leaders, were living. Chou En-lai also brought up these points to Prime Minister Nehru. He intimated that the government of India would be held responsible for the Dalai's early return and for "safeguarding" the Tibetan ruler from the many Tibetans now in India.

Even before the Dalai Lama had arrived thousands of Tibetan pilgrims had straggled over the passes into India. Many of them had covered most of the journey on foot and had arrived in Delhi in ragged robes and torn boots. They settled down to wait for their Precious Protector in camps on the outskirts of Delhi. Newsmen turned to these people when they could no longer hope for interviews with the Dalai Lama or members of his party. Among the pilgrims were refugees who had escaped Communist persecution and did not intend to return to Tibet. But pilgrims or refugees, they were interested only in their God-King. It was they who queried the journalists, and their question was always the same. "Will the Dalai Lama be forced to go back to Lhasa?" When questioned themselves, the Tibetans invariably expressed the hope that their ruler would find some way to stay on in India where he could seek the free-world help that Tibetans needed in order to drive out their invaders.

In the Tibetan camps around Delhi excitement grew when Chou En-lai left India and returned to Peking. This was the climax to the Tibetans' last hope for outside help.

Meanwhile, according to those who were with him at the time, the Dalai Lama was concentrating on the problem of whether he should return to Lhasa or try to remain in India. He understood that in Tibet he was partly a hostage for the Chinese. His people loved him so deeply that they would submit to the invader rather than risk reprisal against him. For this reason the Tibetan uprising against the oppressors could never reach full scale unless he was safely out of the country.

On the other hand, the Dalai Lama feared that even if he did stay outside and allow the resistance to develop fully the Chinese still might succeed in subjugating Tibet. In that case the people's suffering would have been wasted and Tibetans would find themselves in more hopeless circumstances than they were now.

As before, the Dalai Lama refused to act without first knowing the opinions of as many of his people as possible. He therefore sought advice from the scholars, high lamas, and the officials who accompanied him. Again the reply was unanimous: Stay in India! Even the three Shapes who were thought to be collaborators gave this advice. And the pilgrims believed, one and all, that he could serve his country best in India.

The Dalai Lama listened and then retired for several days to meditate and to seek divine inspiration in making his decision.

Tibet was now at a crossroad in its history.

CHAPTER XVI

The Hard Way

India will be destroyed by false scruples;
Tibet by false hopes.

—TIBETAN PROVERB

At the end of January 1957 the Dalai and Panchen Lamas ended their tour in Calcutta. The Panchen, always obedient to the Chinese, announced that he would leave India within a few days. The Dalai and his group, however, flew to Baghdogra on January 22, 1957, and proceeded to India's Darjeeling-Kalimpong district. In this area most of the Tibetan exiles and refugees were settled. The Panchen, of course, obeyed Chinese instructions to avoid the area, and indeed his life probably would have been in jeopardy if he had entered it. The Dalai, therefore, was acting boldly in defiance of the Chinese wishes. In Kalimpong he moved into Bhutan House where the Thirteenth Incarnation had resided in exile after the Chinese invasion of 1910. The Fourteenth now listened to the advice of his countrymen who were the most bitterly opposed to the Chinese occupation of Tibet and, in free India, could speak without fear.

Meanwhile, on January 24, 1957, Chou En-lai returned to New Delhi for his third visit within two months. He had an immediate conference with Prime Minister Nehru. The details of the discussion were not released officially to the press. Nevertheless, press representatives learned that the talks concerned mainly the Middle East crisis. During the discussion, however, Chou En-lai instructed Prime Minister Nehru to see that the Dalai Lama was sent back to Tibet without further delay.

Thereafter Indian officials politely informed members of the Dalai Lama's group that, while His Holiness was always welcome, his continued presence in India might cause conflict between Peking and New Delhi.

The time had come for the Dalai to make a vital decision. According to members of his entourage, he knew now that the only course of "direct action" open to him was to go into self-imposed exile. The decision on whether or not he should take this course would define the future of his country.

The arguments for his not returning to Tibet were strong. Such an act from the undisputed leader of all Tibetans would be an immediate formal announcement that the entire mountain kingdom was opposed to the Chinese occupation. All the Chinese propaganda broadcasts and news releases to the effect that Tibetans welcomed the Han "liberators" and were joyous over the Communist "reforms" would be proven false.

Moreover, with the Dalai safely in exile, the Tibetans would no longer feel the necessity for restraint. The entire nation could rise up in a final united effort to throw off the oppressors. Away from Chinese control over his words and deeds, and committed wholly to the policy of resistance, the God-King could fire his people into a frenzy against the invaders. Finally, his prestige should enable him to obtain moral support at least, and perhaps material aid as well, from the world's free countries. Eventually, through his efforts the United Nations might be persuaded to act on the problem of Tibet as they had on the problem of Korea. In short, the only hope of success for the Tibetan resistance groups seemed to be in the possibility of the Dalai Lama's exile.

The God-King's advisers, without exception, asked him not to return to Tibet. The Kashag members, led by Ragashar, had protested to Chou En-lai in Delhi about the Chinese actions in Tibet and had demanded the withdrawal of Chinese forces. Even Ngapho had supported the demand. Chou En-lai was said to have been quite pleasant and reasonable during these discussions. He had suggested that the Shapes, on their return, continue the talks with Chinese representatives in Lhasa. The Shapes realized that they would have a much stronger bargaining point during such talks if the Dalai Lama remained outside Tibetan territory. They therefore argued unanimously in favor of exile.

While the Dalai Lama meditated, considering the advice, delegates from the Mimang arrived. They brought a message saying that their constituents were unanimously of the opinion that His Holiness should remain in India so that the resistance could attain its maximum effort. Only a few days later a similar delegation from the monasteries brought a petition saying that the entire priesthood favored their leader's exile. Tibetan public opinion in every segment that counted, therefore, was in favor of the Dalai Lama's remaining in India.

India at the moment seemed the biggest obstacle to the Dalai Lama's self-imposed exile. Indian public opinion then was concerned mainly with the Kashmir issue. Moreover, Marshal Zhukov from the U.S.S.R. was at the time a state guest in India. He was making himself popular by praising India's achievements and policies. Both he and Chou En-lai lost no opportunity to point out how much better off the world would be if the Western imperialists would abide by Panch Shila. Chou En-lai told Indian officials that if the Dalai Lama were allowed to remain in India the Chinese would regard it as an unfriendly act.

This faced the Indian government with an embarrassing dilemma. The Indian leaders had committed the government to a policy of trying to win China's friendship. They therefore risked failure of their policy if they gave official recognition to the Tibetans' pleas. In effect, the Tibetans were asking the Indian leaders to face the reality of a new and terrible menace on the Himalayan frontier.

Both Russia and China, despite their new and presumably progressive ideology, retained the same expansionist aims that the British had frustrated in the Czars and Manchus. In these countries not even the methods for achieving the aims had changed. The Chinese in Tibet, for example, were copying the divide-and-rule technique perfected by the eighteenth-century British. Just as the early European imperialists had said that they were bringing the benefits of Western civilization to the unfortunate Eastern people, the Chinese now claimed that their "liberation" would benefit the Tibetans.

These "benefits" included the complete loss of independence for Tibetans, the exploitation of their natural resources for use by the Chinese, the destruction of Tibetan culture, and finally the obliteration of the Tibetans themselves through inundation by Chinese colonists. Moreover, the Tibetans were being given these "benefits" because their country made a useful military base from which the Chinese could extend their "liberation" over much wider and richer territories.

The common denominator in these "liberation benefits" was the fact that they benefited only China. Communism supplied little more than rationalization and slogans. To Tibetans the difference between their subjugation in the name of Communism or in the name of a Manchu Emperor was indiscernible.

As for the Chinese actions inside Tibet since the signing of the Sino-Indian Agreement, Prime Minister Nehru heard the story directly from the Dalai Lama. The Communists, the God-King said, now broke the 17-Point Agreement continually. The first easygoing generosity had been replaced by repression; the traditional government was becoming a shell with the real powers held by the Chinese military. All classes of Tibetans had lost their economic security, and the people faced starvation while they labored to feed the occupying troops. The three-zonal system was meant to destroy Tibetan unity. The monasteries were being threatened both by direct assault on their powers and by weaning away the youth from the traditional ways. Worst of all, the Tibetan people as a whole were in the process of being obliterated by the inundation of Chinese settlers. Thus the Tibetans, with no outside support, either moral or material, and even with no real leadership, had risen spontaneously to fight off their oppressors. Under these circumstances, and in the name of human decency, the Dalai Lama appealed to the Prime Minister for help.

India, of course, was helpless. Those who were close to the Prime Minister at the time said they had never seen him so discouraged. The Dalai's words drove home the fact that India's policy toward China had little chance of success. The Chinese seemed to be exploiting India's friendliness as an Indian weakness. In world affairs the Chinese were demanding morality from others, but they themselves discarded it when it stood in the way of their national aims. The Indian government had long since lost its chance to reverse its policy; India now was committed to the futility of using moral persuasion against an amoral neighbor.

Nevertheless, the Dalai Lama told his advisers that Prime Minister Nehru showed genuine sympathy for Tibetans' freedom aspirations. At the same time he could give the Dalai Lama little cause for hope. He did not believe that the Tibetans would achieve independence through peaceful means. Moreover, he added that if the Tibetans tried increased violent action they would succeed only in bringing on more repressive measures from the Han. He could advise the Dalai Lama only to work for as large an area of autonomy as possible and to keep up peaceful pressure on the Chinese for strict adherence to the 17-Point Agreement. Finally he warned the young God-King not to rely on outside sources for help. Other countries, the Prime Minister said, would help Tibet only when and to the extent that such help would fit in with their own self-interest.

Thus, in trying to decide whether he should remain in India or return to Tibet, the Dalai Lama knew that officially he could expect no co-operation from India. The Dalai Lama, however, was much wiser since he had left Lhasa in November of the previous year. He knew now that India's self-interest would require that she support any peaceful effort that would delay the day when the roof of the world was no more than a base for further Chinese aggression. If the Dalai Lama did request political asylum in India, international law would require that the request be granted. Moreover, the very fact of the request from the leader of the Tibetan people would force India's official recognition of the true state of affairs in the mountain kingdom. India then might still maintain her nonalignment policy toward China as a Communist nation, but her policy of friendship and moral containment thereafter would be based on a more realistic appraisal of Chinese deeds and intentions. A minority but vocal opinion in India believed already that the government should make such a reappraisal with regard to the Chinese in Tibet. The Dalai Lama was being advised by Indian officials that he should leave India, but he knew that if he chose to stay he would not be refused.

Thus India's position, awkward though it was, presented no real obstacle to his decision and no argument against exile.

In fact, only one argument against his exile had been raised. The simple people of Tibet—the peasants and laborers, those to whom privation was normal existence and who had little understanding of political complications—wanted him to return. They felt lost and helpless without the Precious Protector. Merely knowing that he was in the Potala gave them hope and the courage to endure their lot. Such people sent him a number of tear-stained petitions, crudely composed but sincerely written, pleading with him to come back to them. The government and monastery officals, the educated landowners, and the Mimang patriots felt that they knew what was best for the country and they tended to belittle these petitions.

The Dalai Lama, however, had been taught that the Tibetan people were his only possession; their need was his very reason for existing. He took the pleas of his people seriously.

Early in February 1957, after several days of meditation, the Dalai Lama called in his highest officials. He had made his decision. To the officials' distress their God-King announced that he would return to the Holy City. The officials, believing that the Dalai Lama had given up the struggle and now considered their country doomed, began to weep. One younger lama, momentarily forgetting the status of his god, cried out, "You are mad—it is like throwing yourself on a fire." The Holy One, however, calmed his advisers and tried to explain the reasons for his decision.

Unquestionably the fact that the poor people of Tibet needed his presence in the country had an effect on his decision. Neverthe-

less his experiences in India had taught him a great deal. He had
seen that in a free country the individual was allowed to choose
his own values and seek his own salvation. At the same time even
the material accomplishments in India were more impressive than
those he had seen in China. And finally he knew now that the
Indians were not and never could be "imperialist aggressors," as
the Han described them. As a Buddhist he could not recognize
that people in themselves were evil; only ideas accepted by people
could be right or wrong. Thus the Dalai Lama believed now that
his people's conflict with the Chinese was not on a person-to-
person basis. Instead the Chinese were obsessed with ideas that,
for Tibet at least, were wrong. The problem was to convince the
Chinese of this fact, and such an effort required his presence and
leadership in his own country.

From now on, therefore, Tibetans united under his leadership
would oppose the Chinese openly. In the coming struggle they
could depend only on their own resources, mainly spiritual rather
than material. Finally His Holiness agreed that if the Han could
not be made to perceive the truth, and if no other choice were
available, he would condone the violence of a physical struggle
against the oppressors.

When the officials understood the Dalai Lama's reasoning they
believed that his decision had come from the inner wisdom of the
Incarnate God. They felt uplifted and drawn closer together. The
God-King put them to work on drawing up a list of minimum
demands which they would present to the Chinese Communists.

The final list followed the points which Ragashar and the other
Kashag members had discussed with Chou En-lai in Delhi. The
demands were: (1) that Chinese troops would be evacuated
from Tibet; (2) that the status quo as under the Thirteenth Dalai
Lama be restored; (3) that the two former Tibetan Prime Ministers be reinstated, and (4) that all the Communist "reforms" be
abandoned.

On February 15, 1957, the Dalai Lama and his entourage left
Gangtok. He did not fly to Lhasa, although previously a plane
had been made available to him. In a formal ceremony of fare-

well two hundred Indian and Sikkimese troops formed a guard of honor; the Maharaja of Sikkim, an Indian official, and the Chinese ambassador spoke their final words. A few members of the press stood by. Thousands of the loyal hill people waited stoically in their woolen robes to follow the line of jeeps which bore the party to the end of the motor road. After leaving the motor road and changing to animal transport the party climbed slowly toward Natu La.

The procession had little of the color and magnificence of the Dalai Lama's arrival three months before. Now the travelers were wrapped in fur-lined robes and masked against the bitter February winds. They rode slowly and in silence. Except for the wind the only sound was the occasional rattle of stones released by the horses' hoofs to roll briskly down the steep path. As the travelers climbed higher they entered mist and occasionally felt the sting of wind-driven sleet.

The way was hard. But the God-King had chosen for them the hard way.

CHAPTER XVII

Defense of a Religion

Anger is the greatest sin; patience the greatest virtue.
If I find no one to anger me,
How can I be inspired to meditate on patience?
—TIBETAN PROVERB

WHEN the Dalai Lama and his party entered the Tibetan border town of Yatung they found that pilgrims from Bhutan and from all parts of the Chumbi Valley had converged to greet the Holy One. Also, according to the Chinese publicity, the God-King was greeted here by the Deputy Political Commissar of the Tibet Military District and the Director of the Rural Work Department of the Tibet Party Work Committee. These two officials, of course, were Chinese. The rest of the long, slow journey was the same. Pompously titled Chinese officials were on hand to extend formal greetings and to remind the Dalai Lama that he had returned to the Tibet region of China. Nevertheless, reports that came into India a month later said that the Dalai Lama had made many severely anti-Communist statements during his many talks and sermons on the return journey. News of these speeches went ahead of the Dalai's entourage; Lhasa was reported to be waiting tensely in the expectation of new developments when he arrived.

The traveling party spent the Tibetan New Year in Gyantse, where the Dalai avoided Chinese official celebrations and devoted himself to monastery observances. The party then moved on to Shigatse, seat of the Panchen.

In Shigatse, the part of Tibet in which the occupation force felt the most secure, the Han struck a vicious blow in retaliation for the Dalai Lama's anti-Communist speeches. Outwardly everyone was cordial. Protocol was observed meticulously. The Panchen even came out further from the town than custom decreed in order to meet his superior lama. The customary conferences between the various grades of lay and monastery officials were held. On the night before the Dalai's party was to set off again a large farewell banquet, attended by both Chinese and Tibetans, was held. The usual speeches and flowery compliments were made.

In the morning Ragashar was dead. He had been poisoned. The Chinese news release said that he had died of "bad circulation," which the Western press presumed to mean heart failure. But he was only fifty-four, and he had been in perfect health when he left India. Tibetans who took care of the body claim to have discovered traces of poison. In India neutral newsmen referred to his death as "unexpected and unexplained" and recalled that Ragashar was the Kashag member who had presented Tibetan demands to Chou En-lai and reportedly had received a personal promise from the Chinese Premier that the demands would be given consideration. Ragashar was the one Kashag member who had cleverly blocked so many of the Chinese demands in Lhasa, and his loss was a serious blow to the new unity and purpose which the God-King had inspired.

The Dalai Lama's party, therefore, was still grief-stricken when it arrived in Lhasa in early April 1957. Again the populace turned out in great joy to welcome back their Precious Protector. As usual, the Chinese press concentrated on the Chinese general, "The Political Commissar of the People's Liberation Army in Tibet." He was shown presenting *kadak* to the Dalai Lama and accompanying the young ruler in inspecting a guard of honor.

For a few weeks following the Dalai Lama's return the Indian press carried stories to the effect that attempts had been made on the God-King's life. He had been fired on while moving to the summer palace; a bomb had been sent to him; he had been poisoned. The reports evidently indicated the nervous expectations of Indians and exiled Tibetans.

Actually, however, the Dalai Lama's policy of frank and firm resistance began to have immediate effect. Although Ragashar's death undoubtedly weakened the ranks of his supporters, the Dalai Lama himself held to his resolve. On April 11, hardly a week after the Dalai Lama's return, the first hints of a revised Tibet policy came out of Peking.

On that date Bando Yanbe, the Tibetan official who headed the Department of Industry and Commerce under the Preparatory Committee, speaking in Peking, said that "reform in Tibet must be carried out step by step and when conditions are ready for it." He admitted failure of attempted reform "in some areas" and resultant fear and panic on the part of Tibetans. "But Chairman Mao," he said, "has now directed that reform in Tibet shall not be introduced during the period of the Second Five-Year Plan and that its introduction or otherwise during the period of the Third Five-Year Plan must depend upon the wishes of the people. He has also directed that work in Tibet shall be carried out in accordance with the Seventeen Articles."

Later reports were received in India that Lhasa was in confusion because of many sudden changes that had taken place since the Dalai Lama's return. Several of the highest Chinese officials had made a quick trip by plane to Peking. Large-scale troop withdrawals from Lhasa were begun, with most of the withdrawn troops being sent to the Chamdo area or to the Nepalese border. Many Chinese construction projects were stopped and the majority of Chinese laborers were returned to China. Some Chinese schools in Tibet were closed, and from other such schools the Tibetan students were dismissed. All public propaganda rallies had ceased, and group-study meetings were canceled.

On April 22, 1957, the first anniversary of the establishment of the Preparatory Committee, the Dalai Lama spoke bluntly about the committee's shortcomings. It had failed to reduce and stabilize prices; its new training schools had enrolled more cadres than could be trained, and friction existed between Han and Tibetan cadres; Han cadres had made mistakes "due to the lack of understanding the practical circumstances of Tibet." The Dalai Lama's words hinted at delaying tactics that had been successful. For instance, "Some Tibetan cadres working in local governments refused to work in the Tibetan Autonomous Region Preparatory Committee on the pretext that they had some work in the local governments. On the other hand, they also loafed in their jobs in the local governments on the pretext of having work in the Tibetan Autonomous Region Preparatory Committee." Perhaps excusing this attitude, he said, "But different people look on the committee in different ways." Although he promised "action to rectify the shortcomings and mistakes," the whole tone of his speech showed little concern for the welfare of the Preparatory Committee.

General Chang Kuo-hua, speaking on the same occasion, said that the committee's work in one year had been "fruitful," and he listed some of its accomplishments. At the same time he admitted the committee's mistakes and said that "the preparatory work for democratic reform started too early and the scope of work extended too far in some areas due to the lack of sufficient and general analysis as regards the subjective and objective situation in Tibet." He said that the conditions for reform "do not completely obtain" in Tibet and reiterated the Central Government's decision that reform should not be carried out in the Second Five-Year Plan. "Whether it shall be carried out in the Third Five-Year Plan or not shall be decided through joint negotiations by leaders, delegates, and the people of Tibet in the light of circumstances then," he said, and added: "This will increase the possibility of peaceful reform in the future." Because reform would not be carried out "within the next six years," General Chang said, "it is certainly necessary to cut down the organs which have been expanded for democratic reform. At the same time, some of the Han staff members who came to Tibet to prepare for democratic reform also should be transferred to other areas to take part in the socialist construction for the homeland. Precisely because of this we are now retrenching and transferring a number of staff to China proper." He ended his speech with an exhortation to "unite together under the banner of anti-imperialism and patriotism" and to "sincerely carry out the Agreement on Measures for the Peaceful Liberation of Tibet and all tasks of the Preparatory Committee." He also added a warning against subversive activity and "the treacherous activity of separatists."

The withdrawal of cadres and laborers began almost immediately. A five-year moratorium on new construction was implemented and truckloads of the laborers began to move out along the northern route. Many offices were closed and others were scaled down. Houses of New Lhasa, which had been occupied by Chinese cadres and their families, were vacated. A few of the houses in Lhasa which had been rented or requisitioned from Tibetans were turned back to their owners. *Tibet Jih-Pao*, the news sheet published in both Chinese and Tibetan in Lhasa and intended primarily for the cadres, carried its last local news in the June 18, 1957, issue. This issue reported on the plenary session of the Tibet Party Work Committee and "concurred" with the plan to withdraw cadres, who "will be transferred to jobs in China, where they are badly needed for national construction." The Party Committee had decided, the report said, to concentrate now on "promoting racial solidarity in Tibet" and on "forming a united front to combat imperialism and promote patriotism."

During June 1957 the Dalai Lama instituted a program of public sermons and prayers. He addressed his assembled subjects daily, and tens of thousands of Tibetans converged on the city to hear his words. The Dalai Lama spoke only on religious subjects, but the Chinese showed a mounting nervousness about the mass gatherings. While their own people were moving out by truck and jeep, Tibetans on foot and horseback seemed to be taking over the city. More than thirty thousand Kham refugees were reported in Lhasa at that time, and the sermons attracted more than sixty thousand Tibetan pilgrims. All around the city huge camps spread out. The ever-present food problem was aggravated. Chinese mingled among Tibetans at the sermons, straining their limited Tibetan vocabularies to reassure themselves that the God-King's words were truly words of religion. And, reassured today, they could not know what the calm-countenanced youth might say to his people tomorrow.

The Chinese authorities, using the food shortage as an excuse, suggested that the program of sermons might be curtailed. They were told, however, that this was impossible because the sermons were being conducted according to a traditional pattern of auspicious omen.

The Chinese then instituted an ominous program of their own. Each evening the Chinese garrisons encircling Lhasa engaged in machine-gun practice. Tibetans, gathering around their campfires, talked against a background of rapid gunfire. No pilgrim, however, was frightened away from Lhasa. Every day more people came from greater distances to hear their God-King and to show him their loyalty and love. Only on the final day of his talks did the Dalai Lama depart from his religious theme. On this occasion he concluded his sermon with a plea for unity and co-operation among all Tibetans. It was a simple and unadorned request; he did not need to tell his people what they were to co-operate for or against. All Tibetans knew that their government's program now was to press the four demands.

Meanwhile the Kashag had been equally active. Despite the warning implicit in Ragashar's death, the Kashag members stood together to back the demands which they had drawn up in India. Their unity was perhaps aided by the absence of Ngapho, who was touring Mongolia en route to Peking. Thousands of leaflets, setting down the demands, were circulated in Tibet. Pilgrims who came to hear the sermons received, through Mimang contacts, little bundles of the leaflets which they could conceal in their robes and carry home to the less fortunate who had not been able to hear the Precious Protector's words.

Finally, however, the Chinese forced the Kashag to publish a retraction of the demands and to state that the Chinese had not made any previous promises concerning the demands at any time or place. In the forced Kashag retraction the Tibetan people were told not to believe leaflets which were being circulated in Tibet, for these had been sent by "imperialist-dominated" Tibetans in Kalimpong. The Kashag statement, when released, bore only the Kashag seal. To the people this was a sign that it was forced. If it were a true document it would also bear the seal of the Dalai Lama. Tibetans merely hid their leaflets carefully and treasured them more.

In this same auspicious month of June 1957, flushed by a few signs of victory, the Tibetan government issued new currency for the first time in many years. Chinese currency had never been accepted by the Tibetans. The Chinese, rather than allow the Tibetans to have their own money, had continued to pour silver into the country. Now they did not openly oppose the new currency.

The Chinese were in no position to make unpopular moves at this time. The Dalai Lama's prestige in the border countries was at its height after his Indian tour. Tibetan refugees were gaining a hearing and press coverage in many countries of the free world. Moreover, inside Tibet the rebellion continued. Large areas of Kham remained under Tibetan control. The Lhasa-Chamdo road still was impassable. Thus, while the Han laborers and cadres moved out on the northern route, the Communists now began to bring in still more troops over the same route. Reform had been postponed, but military domination, the Tibetans were warned, would remain.

Before long Tibetans received strong indications that military action against the resistance would be increased. In August of 1957 the Preparatory Committee's director for the Chamdo region announced an end to government "leniency" in dealing with the Kham rebels. He referred to "repeated" promises of amnesty for rebel leaders during the preceding year and warned that the Chamdo area government must maintain "social peace" in this region or there would be "greater disasters for the people."

Similar disasters were hinted in a new propaganda line of the Tibet Working Committee of the Communist party. This committee published, also in August 1957, an outline of the new policy of "postponement of reforms." One feature of the policy was that no one should take the postponement as a "basis for interfering with the democratic reforms of the areas of Tibetan nationalities in Szechwan." The propaganda program also called on the Tibetan people to "protect highways essential to national defense." At the same time, Tibetans were reminded that the Chinese "constitution and laws do not provide the slightest facility to those elements who engage in counterrevolutionary activities under the cloak of religion." Thus the Chinese refuted three claims which they had been repeating for more than a year: that the Szechwan trouble was "mainly settled"; that the Kham road was not closed; and that the clergy was not participating in or supporting the rebellion in Tibet.

Despite the veiled threats, the over-all tone of Chinese Communist propaganda was conciliatory. Nevertheless, we know now that the Han were secretly preparing for massive reprisals. They were tightening their security network throughout Tibet. House-to-house searches for weapons and resistance fighters became frequent. Every bridge was given a strong guard of Chinese troops. The truck convoys were protected so well that even supplies over the road from Chamdo began to come through again. The detachments at the numerous check posts were enlarged; they interrogated Tibetans more closely and clamped down on all but essential travel. The use of terrorism and torture for extracting information from the people became widespread. For the first time a concerted effort to confiscate the funds and arms hidden in the monasteries was made. Several monasteries, suspected of offering considerable help to the resistance, were suddenly attacked, ransacked, and damaged. Invariably, numbers of monks were killed. And of course the Communists began to use their steadily increasing military force in a co-ordinated nationwide attack against the freedom fighters.

Against the Dalai Lama they increased the pressure for his collaboration. While outwardly deferential, they now ordered more and more of his signatures on documents and pro-Communist prepared statements. They used threats, not against him, but against the Tibetans. Increasingly, the Dalai Lama had to make decisions either in favor of his people's immediate welfare or of their country's future.

Occasionally these decisions were easy to make. In October 1958 for example, the Chinese told the young ruler, in effect, "Either you will raise a militia and see that the resistance is cleaned out, or we will bring in sufficient troops to do the job thoroughly ourselves." Tibetans showed enthusiasm for such a militia. Before long, however, the Chinese realized that the Tibetans wanted the arms for use against the occupation force. The fact was that no able-bodied Tibetan could be trusted as a collaborator.

The result of the increased Chinese pressure against the Dalai Lama, however, was to make him feel more cut off from his own people and from the outside world as well. Nevertheless, he still attempted to reach the outside with the story of his country's plight. He had invited India's Prime Minister Nehru to come to Lhasa in the fall of 1958, and the invitation had been accepted. Although Chinese Premier Chou En-lai announced his intention of going to Lhasa at the same time, the Dalai Lama and his advisers hoped for another chance to convince India's leader of their country's true state of affairs under Chinese Communist domination. Shortly before the visit, however, the Chinese officials suddenly rescinded the Dalai Lama's invitation to Prime Minister Nehru. Their excuse was that Tibetan refugees in India had stirred up the people in Tibet to such an extent that Nehru might not be safe in the mountain kingdom. India's Prime Minister did go to Bhutan and on the way he crossed Tibet's Chumbi Valley. Several hundred resistance fighters tried to contact him to present him with a petition for help, but the Chinese military guards saw to it that Nehru made only official contacts. Speaking in Yatung, the Indian Prime Minister, with a touch of sarcasm, referred to his presence in Tibet as "rather accidental," and added, "Nevertheless, I am glad to have been given this opportunity, for a brief time, to set foot in this land."

To the Dalai Lama and his advisers, the Chinese cancellation of Nehru's trip was a blow and further proof that the Communists regarded the 17-Article Agreement as worthless. The Dalai Lama, whose "established status, functions, and powers" had been guaranteed by the agreement, could not even invite a guest to Lhasa where, traditionally, his word was law.

Meanwhile the whole of Tibet knew of their God-King's humiliation. This, plus the fact of the Chinese attacks on the monasteries and the increased brutality of the occupation force, increased rapidly the anger of the Tibetans. Whenever the Chinese now held a parade or public celebration, Tibetan spectators came only to jeer and shout anti-Communist slogans. The few Tibetan collaborators could no longer appear in public without large Chinese bodyguards, and even then the sight of the collaborators usually caused riots among the people.

"Mao's Panchen" was the most hated of these collaborators. He was sent anonymous letters of abuse and threats. He rarely appeared in public. The Chinese were even forced to prevent pilgrims from entering his monastery for fear that he would be assassinated.

At the same time, the resistance grew more intense and effective. The guerrilla-held territory extended until most of the south and southwest were free of the occupation force. As many as fifty forts in the Brahmaputra basin were said to be in Mimang hands. Strong Khamba bands penetrated as far west as Shigatse. Both Chinese military roads were closed often by sabotage. Guerrillas managed to destroy bridges; they raided supply dumps and occasionally even ambushed the powerful supply convoys. They learned to use a war of nerves against the Chinese; rumors would be circulated that a guerrilla attack would be made against a certain Chinese outpost. The attack, then, if it was made at all, would be directed at another post, or perhaps against the Chinese reinforcements rushed to the expected trouble spot. By late 1958, although the Chinese continued to build up their force, they were forced to abandon most of their smaller patrol posts and to reinforce the large centers. Reports reaching Hong Kong from the Chinese mainland told of the evacuation by air of thousands of wounded and "badly mutilated" Chinese soldiers from Tibet.

The rising fury of the resistance was an indication that the Tibetans' hatred of the invader was becoming greater than their fear of his power. Nevertheless, one fear remained and, in fact, grew. When the Chinese began to attack the monasteries and practice their brutality on the monks, the Tibetans realized that the enemy would have no hesitation about harming the Dalai Lama. Thus even the simple and uneducated people who had pleaded for his return from India early in 1957 began to fear for his life. They, as well as the more knowledgeable segments of Tibetan society, now believed that he would serve his country best by being safely outside. This meant that the Dalai Lama's final attempt to negotiate and compromise with the Communists had proven useless. Resistance, futile as it might seem, was the only course left. The God-King no longer had a reason for remaining in Lhasa.

CHAPTER XVIII

Escape of the Dalai Lama

Without weapons, only Buddha can defeat an enemy.
—TIBETAN PROVERB

EVENTS moved swiftly to a climax. In February 1959 huge crowds of Tibetan laymen and monks converged on Lhasa for the festival heralding the Year of the Earth Pig. Tension reached a record height. Early in March elements of an entire new Chinese army division began to arrive in the capital. Suddenly a rumor flashed through Lhasa that the Chinese intended to take the Dalai Lama to Peking again. Probably they were planning to have him attend the Second National People's Conference scheduled to convene on April 17, 1959. In any case, the rumor touched on the fear that now seemed to grip all Tibetans. A wave of spontaneous riots spread throughout the city.

Early in March 1959 more than thirty thousand Tibetans staged a demonstration. The people tore anti-Western posters from the walls and put up anti-Communist posters instead. The crowd converged on the Indian Consulate General, shouting appeals for help. The Chinese opened fire on the crowd and many Tibetans were killed. Thereafter the funerals for these martyrs sparked new riots.

The next incident was created by another rumor. The Chinese had released a statement that the Dalai Lama had agreed to attend a cultural show. The date suddenly was fixed for March 10. Evidently the Chinese had specified that the Dalai Lama was to be unattended by any of the traditional Kham guards. The people took this to mean that the Chinese intended to kidnap the Dalai Lama. A crowd of ten thousand surrounded the Norbulingka and physically prevented the Dalai Lama from attending the function. The people then raised a bodyguard among themselves for the Dalai Lama.

Crowds of Tibetans were now in the streets almost constantly. They were fired upon frequently. Women in large numbers had joined the demonstrations and many were killed or wounded.

On March 12, during one demonstration, Tibetan officials told the crowd that the 1951 treaty with China, the 17-Article Agreement, should be repudiated. This was the treaty in which Tibet was promised autonomy while the Chinese would have control over defense and external affairs. Hereafter complete independence was demanded.

Later the Chinese would contend that a few "upper-strata reactionaries" in the Tibetan government, bribed by "Western imperialists," had "torn up the 17-Article Agreement for the Peaceful Liberation of Tibet" and had demanded instead "so-called independence." The inference was that a few "upper-strata evil persons," with a few ignorant and misguided followers, had formally renounced the treaty in favor of "so-called independence," whereas the mass of Tibetan people welcomed Chinese liberation. None of this was true. No formal or official repudiation was made, but the Tibetan people themselves denounced the "liberation" agreement in no uncertain terms.

At the same time, the Lhasans were using passive resistance against the invaders. Tibetan servants were persuaded to walk out on their Chinese masters. Chinese schools and hospitals were boycotted. And everywhere posters appeared, denouncing the occupying powers as "Chinese dogs" and warning them not to invite the Dalai Lama anywhere.

Meanwhile Chinese troops were pouring into Lhasa. On March 17, 1959, the force evidently made some kind of attempt to remove the Dalai Lama from the palace to take him to the military headquarters. Immediately the Norbulingka was surrounded by a huge throng of Tibetans. Two of the mortar shells fired by the Chinese fell into the palace courtyard.

Neither of the shells did any real damage, but they provided the final argument for the most important decision the Dalai Lama had ever made. Resistance was now the only hope for his country and his people. Henceforth, he must do what he could to help the freedom fighters.

His first duty was to escape from the Chinese. Plans were made immediately. By nightfall, members of the Dalai Lama's family, household servants and bodyguard, two of his tutors, and three patriotic Kashag members slipped out of the palace one at a time by a secret route. The Dalai Lama removed his glasses and disguised himself as a member of his bodyguard. In the company of other guards he started on a routine tour of inspection, then mingled with the crowds that still surrounded the palace. A dust storm came up and made the Chinese patrols less vigilant. The God-King successfully eluded them. Outside the city the Dalai Lama, who had brought his official seal, met the other members of his party, who were carrying stocks of food, money in the form of gold bars, and a few personal religious relics. The party made its way toward the banks of the Kyichu. Here, because of more Chinese patrols, the party had to separate again and proceed in groups of two or three, but all of them crossed the river on the ferry without being detected. Again the party reassembled. The group was joined by other escapees, important Tibetan officials and ecclesiastics. Now the entire party pushed forward rapidly through some of the earth's most difficult terrain. They made for the seventeen-thousand-foot Che Pass across which lay the region of the Tsangpo (Brahmaputra) River.

Meanwhile a large contingent of fierce Khamba resistance fighters had converged on Lhasa and were engaging the Chinese garrison in a bloody battle. Both the fighting and the demonstrations of March 17 were part of a resistance plan to permit the Dalai Lama and his party to escape from Lhasa. Because of the ruse, the Chinese did not find out about the escape until March 19. In anger they shelled the Norbulingka, damaging it severely.

They lost no time, however, in organizing a full-scale pursuit.

The Chinese had about seventy-five thousand men and the latest military equipment. Strong detachments, mounted on swift horses, patrolled every possible route to the border. The bamboo-and-rope bridges and ferryboats were destroyed or removed. Planes searched from the skies, reporting any movement on the ground to troops who moved in at once to investigate. Paratroops stood by to be dropped near concentrations of resistance fighters. Finally the Chinese used the utmost brutality against the local Tibetans in the effort to extract information concerning the escape route.

No real plans had been made for the escape route; perhaps for that reason the secret could be kept. The party had swollen to almost two hundred people. The people crossed the wide Tsangpo and were met by a contingent of Khamba fighters who took over the job of protecting and guiding the Dalai Lama.

At first the decision was to proceed along main routes to Bhutan. The Dalai Lama and his companions soon found that the destroyed bridges and constant enemy patrols made this route impossible. The party turned eastward, therefore, making their goal the Indian border. They traveled extensively by day, keeping to the shelter of trees and the huge rock formations in that wild country. They had to use small boats made of yak hides to cross rivers and streams. Occasionally the sound of planes forced the people to disperse and hide. Nevertheless, they openly entered villages, where they were greeted with great joy and excitement. When they stopped for rest, the Dalai Lama and his party stayed in peasant huts.

Once south of the Tsangpo, the escape party made for Minden-Ling, a resistance stronghold thirty miles away. Next they rode twenty-five miles east to Tsetang, capital of Lhoka Province and another resistance center. From here they cut southward into the mountains for forty miles via the Trigu valley to Trigu Lake; this spot was in Tibet's Nyem area and contained one of the country's largest concentrations of freedom fighters. The party rested here for the next and most strenuous fifty-mile lap south, through more violent mountains, to Tsona Dzong. Once the people had reached this village, the rest of the way was comparatively easy. The Indian border was only ten miles down along the Towang Chu River.

The party made a final trek of twenty-six miles down the valley to Towang, subdivision headquarters of the Kameng Division of India's N.E.F.A. (Northeast Frontier Agency). They reached the famous monastery here on April 5, 1959, and only now did they feel they were safe. They had traveled more than two hundred miles. The journey had taken over two weeks, which, considering the terrain, was fast and indicated that they had traveled hard.

Meanwhile, back in Tibet, the whole country seemed to be in revolt. Five days were required by the powerful Chinese force to put down the rebel attack in Lhasa. Hundreds, and perhaps thousands, were killed. Lhasa suffered much damage and the two nearby monasteries of Sera and Drepung were in flames. On March 23 a Military Control Committee was set up in the capital. A dusk-to-dawn curfew was imposed. The Chinese communiqué announcing the Control Committee belittled the whole uprising and stated that as soon as order had been restored the local administrative bodies would resume the functions of autonomy. In typical Communist double talk the communiqué added, "At present, Tibetan autonomy and military control by the Chinese People's Liberation Army are simultaneously in force."

On March 28, however, Communist China's Chou En-lai issued an order which implied more of the true extent of the uprising. After announcing that the Peking government had ordered the dissolution of Tibet's local government, he stated, "Most of the Kaloons of the Tibet local government and the upper-strata reactionary clique colluded with imperialism, assembled rebellious bandits, carried out rebellion, ravaged the people, put the Dalai Lama under duress, tore up the 17-Article Agreement on Measures for the Peaceful Liberation of Tibet and, on the night of March 19, directed the Tibetan local army and rebellious elements to launch a general offensive against the People's Liberation Army garrison in Lhasa . . . During the time when the Dalai Lama, chairman of the Preparatory Committee for the Tibet Autonomous Region, is under duress by the rebels, the Panchen Lama, vice-chairman of the Preparatory Committee, will act as chairman . . ."

Thereafter the Communist propaganda took the line that the mass of Tibetan people loved the Chinese and welcomed Chinese "autonomy," but that a few Tibetan upper-class reactionaries, along with some bandits, abetted by "Western imperialists" and aided by "Chiang Kai-shek gangsters" and "Indian expansionists," demanded "so-called independence" for Tibet, committed the crime of rebellion against Communist China, and abducted the Dalai Lama. And anyone who disagreed with this was either a dupe of the Western imperialists, a capitalist warmonger, or an American.

Nevertheless, the free world, which had been electrified by the exciting escape, finally had a chance to hear the other side of the story. On April 9 the Tibetan freedom fighters formed a pro-visional government. In their new manifesto they accused the Chinese of violating the 17-Article Agreement. They stated also that the Chinese had tried to break up the country into decen-tralized regions. They had vilified Buddhism and Buddhists and had tried to undermine the religion. They had taken thousands of Tibetans to China for forced indoctrination. They had executed many more thousands. They were guilty of "colonialism" in that they had settled 5,800,000 Chinese in northeastern Tibet and that four million more would be settled elsewhere in the country. They had used forced labor to build military roads. And, "in the name of progress," they had brought in vast amounts of military equip-ment and troops to suppress Tibetan nationalism.

Nine days after this manifesto, the Dalai Lama reached Tezpur in India's plains and made his first formal statement to the free world. He repudiated the Communist claim that he had been abducted by rebels. He also accused the Chinese of violating the 17-Point Agreement and of other crimes. He accented freedom for his country rather than mere "autonomy" under Chinese domination.

The Chinese reacted sharply to the statement. The puppet

Panchen, speaking of it, said, "The people of Tibet and I express great wrath and firm opposition" to the statement "issued in the name of the Dalai Lama." The Chinese Communist news agency commented: "The so-called 'statement of the Dalai Lama' issued through an Indian diplomatic official . . . is a crude document, lame in reasoning, full of lies and loopholes . . . So-called independence for Tibet has always been a scheme of the British imperialists for carrying out aggression against China and first of all against Tibet."

Even India was accused of having aggressive designs on Tibet and China. The Indian government was sharply criticized for having the temerity to discuss Tibet in the parliament; according to the Chinese, the matter was purely an internal problem that did not concern the Indians.

The Indians, however, felt that the matter did concern them. The entire press, with the exception of the Communist section, was vehemently pro-Tibetan. In parliament, all the opposition members, except again the Communists, repudiated the government's policy of appeasement. Prime Minister Nehru's government, although committed to recognition of China's suzerainty over Tibet and to the hope of winning Communist friendship and co-operation, nevertheless granted the Dalai Lama asylum. The Chinese accusations were answered with dignity and restraint. And while the Indian officials still attempted to find some formula for a peaceful settlement of the Tibet problem, they refused to accept the Chinese lies and they gave their official sympathy to the suffering Tibetan people.

The suffering of the Tibetans had never been so great. The Communists now did not try to hide the fact that they meant to crush the people once and for all. More troops were air-lifted in a steady stream. Armored vehicles were brought in. A well-planned and co-ordinated attack against the entire resistance movement was begun.

Whole villages have been wiped out. In many others the head men were sent to concentration camps and every able-bodied man put to forced labor. Many of the monasteries, together with their valuable relics and libraries, have been utterly destroyed, the monks either killed or scattered. The border has been sealed in the attempt to stop all traffic to or from the outside, and all radios in Tibet have been confiscated to prevent any semblance of the truth from reaching the people. Food supplies have been controlled in an effort to starve the Tibetans into submission.

The fact that the Tibetans refuse to submit offers little basis for optimism about their country's future. They face extermination —genocide—in an all-out resistance to the Communists. But the alternative is absorption and extinction, the Chinese long-range weapons, which would seem to be even more powerful. Already the number of Chinese colonists who have been forcibly settled in Tibet is larger than the entire Tibetan population. The pace of settlement is not being slowed even now. Within a generation or two Tibetans will have a Chinese complexion, and their way of life will be forgotten.

Long before that, indoctrinated Tibetan youth will hold the reins of local government. As early as March 1958 the Standing Committee of the Preparatory Committee in Lhasa passed a resolution, the main point of which was that 90 per cent of the personnel in Committee Departments would be Tibetans. The fact that they will be "re-educated" Tibetans is implicit in the very existence of the resolution. Within only a few more years, adults from among the thousands of Tibetan children taken to China early in this decade and brought up there will be returned to administer the country according to Peking's wishes.

Even in the monasteries that may escape utter destruction in the Chinese reprisals, the seeds of decay have been sewn. The highest spiritual leaders have been forced into temporal positions and bedecked with Chinese Communist titles. The young monks who have reached adulthood since the occupation cannot be expected to retain all of the traditional aloofness from worldly affairs or intensity of reverence and faith. Fewer children have entered the monasteries to train for the future leadership which now is so much in doubt.

Some of the Tibetan officials also have unavoidable doubts about the future. Quite apart from the few collaborators, the older officials especially have difficulty in sacrificing for today's struggle when they see tomorrow's leaders being educated in Peking. The officials who allowed their children to remain in Indian schools do not delude themselves that their sons can ever return to the "Tibet Region of China." Some defeatism, therefore, is inevitable.

Thus the outlook is dark. It is not, however, unrelieved by hopeful glimpses of light. Aside from the resistance movement, the Tibetans continue to harass the Chinese colonists to the point that conditions often are made too difficult for the "grafted ones" to remain. Every Tibetan family tries to protect its children from indoctrination. Few of the Tibetan youth who have had "re-education" in China can yet be trusted to collaborate. The monasteries, despite attacks, maintain their communications network and in fact continue to improve it; the monks, finally dedicated wholly to the resistance, provide the leadership and moral support necessary for the people in their final struggle.

The resistance struggle, of course, continues to dominate the scene on the Tibetan stage. With the Dalai Lama and his most important advisers safely settled in Mussoorie in India, the battle becomes more violent every day. The odds may be on the superior weight of the Chinese force. The fact remains, however, that the Chinese Communists, with many times the number of troops necessary to capture Tibet in 1950, now face an enemy many times more ferocious, cunning, and experienced; the invaders have less control over the country today than they did then. The freedom fighters have learned unity and the advantages of concerted action. They have adjusted to the new targets of modern civilization. Men who offered fodder and water to the first truck they saw now know how to cripple an engine effectively. Many fighters were killed by the first dynamite they captured; now not a stick of the precious explosive is wasted when portioned out for bridge and block-house targets. Fighting monks, whose backs had become bent from long hours over holy books, salvaged manuals and instruction sheets from captured enemy supply dumps and learned how to work the heavy equipment they captured.

Thus the Tibetans can make their resistance long and costly for the enemy. To mount the necessary all-out attack against the Tibet resistance, the Chinese will require a huge percentage of Communist China's total available truck transport and motor fuel. Both are in short supply, and the entire amount is required for the minimum industrial programs promised within China itself. Soviet Russia, China's supplier of arms, motor transport, and fuel, will undoubtedly have to render much more assistance.

The Chinese military itself has suffered much discredit, not only throughout Asia, but within China itself. Touted as irresistible, the People's Liberation Army, which numbers twice as many men under arms as the entire Tibetan population, still has been unable to subdue the untrained and ill-armed Tibetans. Evidently stung by this evidence of inherent weakness, the Communist propaganda is shrill in blaming the Tibetan resistance on "K.M.T. bandits, Western imperialists, and Indian expansionists." Anyone, however, who has seen the Tibet border region—some of the most difficult and inaccessible terrain on earth—knows that the problem of trying to send supplies to the freedom fighters in any appreciable quantity is impossible. Moreover, the Chinese, with their military roads on their side of the border and with their constant use of strong patrols, can prevent all but a barest minimum of contact between the resistance and the outside. Finally, anyone who has seen how sincerely the Indians have maintained their neutrality and how pathetically the Tibetan refugees have asked for even the most elementary supplies to help their resistance fighters, knows that the Chinese are only deluding themselves with their propaganda.

Leaders throughout the uncommitted Asian countries can no longer delude themselves about the aggressive imperialism of Chinese Communism. The Tibetan resistance has unmasked the rulers in Peking, and never again will the neutral Asians feel quite so trusting about their sprawling northern neighbor. We can expect that, for some time to come, the Communist leaders will have to speak softly and grant many concessions before they win back even a portion of the authority they previously commanded in Asian affairs.

Nevertheless, the most important aspect of the Tibetan cause is less in the fact of the violent resistance than in the extraordinary *nature* of it. The struggle against the aggressors is a great deal more than a rebellion. The fighters wage their war with no hope of victory as the term is understood in a military sense; in fact, they fight to die. They resist and go on resisting until they are killed. They die because they cannot live the life that the Communists are trying to impose on them. When one fighter falls, another always takes his place. Moreover, this strange and terrible conflict, part suicide and part holy war, still keeps spreading. The hysterical note in much of the Communist propaganda about Tibet shows the increasing bewilderment of the Chinese concerning the problem.

The Chinese Communists made one serious error in dealing with the Tibetans, an error that may prove fatal to their whole regime. They credited the Tibetans with the same values by which they themselves were motivated. In trying to enforce land reforms, for example, they assumed that the Tibetan peasants could be made to react as had many of the Chinese agricultural workers. They thought that the Tibetans could be easily inspired to hate their landlords and welcome the division of the owners' lands. The Communists were invariably dumfounded to find that the peasant sincerely did not want the land redistributed. He may have hated his landlord. Like anyone else, he wanted an easier and better life, and he certainly would not have objected to owning land. The trouble was that he did not consider such matters as important as his opportunity to work for a better and higher rebirth in another life. What he really objected to, therefore, was the Communist threat to his religion, and he expressed his resentment by resisting the reforms which he sensed ultimately would destroy it.

To the Communists, this attitude represents superstition and ignorance. Unquestionably, superstition and ignorance are a part of Tibetan peasant life, but they are not a part of the religion.

Buddhism represents an idea which, for several millenniums, a large percentage of the human race has found to be valuable. In all of history no one has succeeded in destroying such an idea with brute force. On the contrary, force invariably has had the effect of giving the idea fresh vitality. The Buddhist idea is the essential core of Tibet.

The Chinese Communists have little chance of destroying this essential core. They will impose changes, and their impact on Tibetan culture will be great. Change in itself, however, was unavoidable. Even if Tibet had remained free, the modern world would have imposed itself sooner or later on the mountain kingdom in one form or another and from one direction or another. The issue in Tibet, therefore, is not so much what particular changes the country must undergo, but how the "idea" that represents the real meaning of Tibet will adapt itself to the change.

This is the real problem that faces the Dalai Lama. In 1959 he was twenty-five years old. During the ten years since I photographed him, the Tibetan God-King faced trials that would have broken a much more mature and experienced leader. To his followers, his success in making his little kingdom a unique exception to the now-familiar picture of Communist puppet states is not hard to explain. Their Precious Protector is a god who draws on the wisdom of eternities of self-willed lifetimes back to the misty emergence of Chenrezi from the nirvana he had earned. We who are too bound by the pragmatisms of the modern world to accept this explanation can only be humble in the acknowledgment of a strength which we do not understand. The Dalai Lama has retained his spirituality under unprecedented attack. He has served his people selflessly and wisely from the days of his childhood. Today, leading his few million people in a desperate and unaided struggle against the doctrines which have enslaved so much of the world, the Dalai Lama proceeds calmly, with the "small heart" of caution, and with utter confidence in the final triumph of truth. He brings his people the gift of hope.

Perhaps this is "the jewel in the heart of the lotus."